MARITAL COUNSELING

A Biblical, Behavioral, Cognitive Approach

H. Norman Wright

1817

Harper & Row, Publishers, San Francisco
Cambridge, Hagerstown, New York, Philadelphia,
London, Mexico City, São Paulo, Sydney

Scripture quotations in this publication are from the following versions:

NASB: New American Standard Bible. © The Lockman Foundation 1960, 1962, 1963, 1968, 1971, 1973, 1975. Used by permission.

AMP: The Amplified Bible. Copyright © 1962, 1964, 1965 by Zondervan Publishing House. Used by permission.

TLB: The Living Bible. Copyright © 1971 by Tyndale House Publishers, Wheaton, Illinois. Used by permission.

RSV: Revised Standard Version of the Bible, copyrighted 1946 and 1952 by the Division of Christian Education of the NCCC, U.S.A., and used by permission.

KJV: The Authorized King James Version.

First Harper & Row edition published 1983

Library of Congress Cataloging in Publication Data

Wright, H. Norman
  MARITAL COUNSELING.

  Includes bibliographical references.
  1. Marriage counseling.   2. Pastoral counseling.
I. Title.
[HQ10.W72 1983]   362.8'286   83-47738
ISBN 0-06-069694-X (pbk.)

---

86 87 10 9 8 7 6 5 4 3

TABLE OF CONTENTS

OTHER BOOKS BY H. NORMAN WRIGHT

Adults—How to Help Them Learn
After You Say "I Do"
An Answer to Building Your Self-Image
An Answer to Depression
An Answer to Discipline
An Answer to Divorce
An Answer to Family Communication
An Answer to Frustration and Anger
An Answer to In-laws
An Answer to Loneliness
An Answer to Parent-Teen Relationships
An Answer to Submission and Decision Making
An Answer to the Fulfilled Marriage
An Answer to Worry and Anxiety
Before You Say "I Do"
Building Positive Parent-Teen Relationships
Celebrate Your Marriage
Characteristics of a Caring Home
The Christian Faces Emotions, Marriage and Family Relationships
Christian Marriage and Family Relationships
The Christian Use of Emotional Power
Communication and Conflict Resolution in Marriage
Communication—Key to Your Marriage
Communication—Key to Your Teens
The Family That Listens
A Guidebook for Dating, Waiting and Choosing a Mate
Healing of Fears
Help, I'm a Camp Counselor
How to Be a Better Than Average In-law
Into the High Country
Living Beyond Worry and Anger
The Living Marriage
Living with Your Emotions, Self-Image & Depression
Marriage and Family Enrichment Resource Manual
A Marriage for All Seasons
Pillars of Marriage
Pre-Marital Counseling
Preparing for Parenthood
Preparing Youth for Dating, Courtship and Marriage
Seasons of a Marriage
Training Christians to Counsel

Chapter 1

What Happens to Marriages?

Many marriages today are like the house built upon sand. They have been built upon a weak foundation of dreams. Because in dreams the mind does not have to distinguish between reality and fantasy, one is able to create without restraint. Often, therefore, dreams are the starting point for successful endeavors; however, dreams not followed by adequate planning usually do not come true.

Marriages built on dreams are risky because dreams do not consider the disappointments that are inevitable in every marriage. When the rains of reality and the winds of stress burst against such marriages, the relationship that holds them together crumbles. Much more is involved in fulfilling dreams than merely expecting them to come true.

Expectations Are Not Fulfilled

Someone has suggested that there are two basic causes for trouble in marriage: not finding in marriage what one expected to find, and not expecting what one actually finds.

As most couples marry, they expect stability, security, and predictability in their marriages.

Stability is freedom from change. The word stability

actually means resistance to change. It is the property that causes something when disturbed to restore itself to the original condition. We do not generally like change and usually resist it.

Security is freedom from want. We want our needs to be fulfilled, especially by our marriage partner.

Predictability is being able to know in advance and therefore avoid surprises. Having the ability to forecast the future, at least in a general way, gives us a feeling of control.

There are periods of time in the lives of most couples in which one or even all three of these expectations are not fulfilled.

One reason for unfulfilled expectations is that they may have been unrealistic from the beginning. Some common unrealistic expectations are:

1. My wife will always want to be a homemaker.

2. My husband will take care of the yard and keep the car running just like my father did.

3. I will decide where to take our vacations.

4. We will spend our vacation time with our parents.

5. My husband/wife will always want to have sex when I am in the mood for it.

6. My husband/wife will want to spend all of his/her free time with me.

Many individuals have emotional difficulties that remain undetected by others. Some of these people are drawn together into marriage because the personality of one is abundantly full of a trait lacking in the other. Thus they marry and are satisfied by fulfilling each other's neurotic needs. They unrealistically expect these needs to remain the same forever.

In such a relationship, one person derives satisfaction

from having the other be dependent and lean upon him, while his partner has a tremendous need to be weak and dependent. Some want to control and dominate; others want to be controlled and dominated. In time, however, partners in these marriages tire of their position and want to assume the other's role of dominating or being dependent.

Another reason for unfulfilled expectations is unexpected circumstances. Many of life's events can be planned for in advance, like having a baby, and many bring security and satisfaction. Some events, however, come as a surprise and bring tension, pain, and unexpected circumstances. Loss of a job, illness, birth of a child with a defect, and sudden death in the family are crises for which one cannot plan.

According to family service experts: Any sudden change becomes a threat to whatever marital balance has been achieved. It tends to reawaken personal insecurities that the marriage has successfully overcome or held in check. You've noticed how sick people tend to fall back into childish ways—they become terribly dependent, demanding, unreasonable. Similarly some people regress in other kinds of emotional crises. Long-conquered patterns of behavior reassert themselves, at least until the first impact of the shock has been absorbed.[1]

Even minor changes may become crises:

— A spouse no longer wants to go to the other's favorite restaurant for dinner.

— A spouse wants to change a family tradition that includes the other's parents.

— A spouse announces that a new business opportunity has opened in another state and wants to move.

— A spouse stops preparing a favorite dinner.

— A spouse gets rid of a favorite piece of furniture. When unexpected circumstances occur, many couples are able to adapt to the new and put aside the old. Others do not cope with the new circumstances and need marital counseling.

The normalcy and potential of change is a message which couples need to hear even before they marry. The turmoil and disruption of many relationships would be non-existent if this were to occur. The marital journey has been well described by Dr. Mark Lee.

Anyone who has ridden in an old New York subway car will recall his sensation of pitching and rolling as the train raced along worn tracks or slowed to a stop in a station. Standing passengers move as one body back and forth with the car's sway and changing velocity. All that prevents a pile-up of bodies on a turn or quick stop is the overhead strap. Almost oblivious to what is happening, passengers grip a strap, automatically tightening and loosening their holds to meet changing situations. In their free hands they hold books, or newspapers, which they avidly read.

The experience may be made an analogy to marriages. A marriage changes pace, speeds along, even stops. Tracking is sometimes smooth, sometimes irregular. Tunnels and open spaces alternate. Those who take the ride sometimes relax, and sometimes hold on for dear life.[2]

A husband discussed this process of change as he responded to the question if the love in his marital relationship had changed after twenty one years of marriage. He said:

I still feel passion and excitement with my wife. But all of life moves in patterns and cycles, and I think marriages go the same way. A marriage has its dry moments and hot moments, its ups and downs. Most marriages today don't make it. I think the ones that do, survive by going through these changes. As long as you're allowing something to happen within your marriage, then I think there's some chance for its survival. The secret of a good marriage is change. It's gotta move. If it stops, it's dead.[3]

Unsatisfactory Marital Behavior Patterns Develop

When marital relationships begin to crumble, couples complain about various aspects of their marriage. Bernard Greene reported a study of 750 couples complaining of marital problems and derived the following list of common complaints:

Lack of communication

Constant arguments

Unfulfilled emotional needs

Sexual dissatisfaction

Financial disagreements

In-law trouble

Infidelity

Conflicts about children

Domineering spouse

Suspicious spouse

Alcoholism

Physical attack

Greene found the following problems, in order of frequency, present among couples experiencing conflict in their marriages:

1. *Narcissistic spouse* — whose orientation is self-centered and not on the marriage.

2. *Indifference* — an actual negative approach toward the partner's feelings, needs, and wishes; or even a lack of respect for him, leading to a lack of concern.

3. *Inability* — an incapability to reinforce and support the partner; what Bern refers to as "stroking."

4. *Inflexibility* — a rigid set of attitudes and values which do not permit the individual to deviate from a fixed pattern or code.

5. *Inexperience* — a lack of experience in positive, meaningful, relationships.

6. *Crossed transactions* — digital (calculating) and analogic (using analogies) modes of communicating in which areas of verbal and nonverbal communications have little in common.

7. *Avoidance maneuvers* — where one partner avoids communication by withdrawing (however, since in a marriage one cannot **not** communicate, the partner still gets the message of rejection).

8. *Distortion* — messages are received, but not as sent.[4]

In counseling one often sees these problems in one of several common unsatisfactory marital behavior patterns.

One such pattern has been called the *half-marriage*.[5] In this pattern one spouse (for example, the husband) appears retiring, inexpressive, and nonverbal. He withdraws from confrontation, yet he is angry about the pain he feels from the relationship. The other spouse (the wife in this case) appears outgoing, expressive, and verbal. She moves ahead in a strong, even attacking manner, which is her way of expressing the anger she feels about the pain from the relationship.

Outwardly they appear to be different, but inwardly such a couple is much the same; they simply manifest their needs differently. They each want to be taken care of by the other, yet they have learned to cover this desire cleverly. They each want the other person to be strong so they can lean upon the other, yet neither wants the other to lean on him. Each has built a protective cocoon around himself to hide his inner feelings and thereby appear to be strong.

Often we hear a Christian wife say that she wants her husband to become "the spiritual leader of the home" and take charge of the family affairs. At the same time she becomes involved in a number of community or church activities in order to withdraw from him and show that she is strong and doesn't need him. In spite of all the activity outside her home, she is still lonely. She becomes angry with her husband and uses her anger to cover up her feelings of inadequacy and to convince herself and others that he is the cause of her unhappiness.

As the years go by, each partner intensifies his pattern of behavior. In so doing they suffer in most areas of their marriage. He probably retreats sexually, which angers her even more. Sexual dysfunction in both spouses is common —he becomes impotent and she nonorgasmic. Quarrels and even separation are common.

Other couples you will see will appear outwardly *"well put together."* The husband is reserved and cold, and the wife is quite pleasant. An aura of success in their life is evident. Inwardly, however, both partners are overly sensitive and hurt.

Despite the outward appearance of self-sufficiency, they both want to be taken care of by another person. This dependency need shows up in their struggle for intimacy. Often the wife pushes for emotional closeness as if she were trying to ignite a fire under her husband. She wants assurance from him that she is loved and accepted. The harder she pushes, the more he retreats into his protective shell.

The husband's withdrawal does not stop the wife, for she sees it as a challenge. She maneuvers and coaxes him to win his love but to no avail. Then she decides he should love her regardless of what she does, so she explodes with anger. He withdraws even further.

The dating and courtship behavior of an outwardly well-put-together couple can assist you in analyzing their relationship. The wife was probably a very fun-loving, vivacious, and independent person, which made her husband comfortable as they dated. In essence, she provided the effort and entertainment. She felt that he was the type of person who could take care of her because he was a strong, silent, and dependable male. The person with the attaching personality (in this instance the wife) usually is more responsible for making the relationship permanent.

Some couples are best classified as *married singles*. You will see them in your congregation and in your office. They are legally married, but their relationship is not intimate. The two who were supposed to become one never became one. Some of these couples married out of obligation (pregnancy, for example) or for some convenient reason. They may be deeply involved in a career or profession, and marriage may be only an addendum. The real marriage is to someone or something outside of the supposed marriage.

Another couple you will see act like *married children*. Both spouses are dependent and seek a parent in the other. They throw temper tantrums, they are physically violent, and they seek instant self-gratification. Both are takers; neither is a giver. They are lonely and want affection but never have learned how to give to one another. Often the tie to their own parents has not been broken, and interference from the parents is common.

If you were to observe them for awhile, you would find both of them spending most of their time outside the home with friends of their own sex. Each expects the other to stay home and take care of the house. They become jealous over the outside interests and try to interfere with each other's outside life. When conflicts arise, they withdraw or go to others for support. If they do disagree and face an issue, they behave like children—fighting, hitting, and throwing. They seek help from the police or a counselor.

In the *sadomasochistic marriage* you will often see a passive wife and an angry or aggressive husband. He attacks and belittles her. She accepts his attacks as though she deserves them. Each year of marriage this unsatisfactory marital behavior pattern intensifies. He attacks and she gives in; and the more she gives in, the more he attacks. He blames her for their marital problems, and she accepts the blame. The pattern continues until her masochistic receptacle overflows and then she hysterically explodes.

Even though their behavior is markedly different (yet complementary), their inward life is very similar. They are both dependent, want to be taken care of by the other, and have low self-esteem.

Marital Satisfaction Fluctuates During the Family Life Cycle

Another phenomenon frequently observed in counseling is the fluctuation of a couple's level of marital satisfaction at the various stages of their family life cycle. Numerous studies have been conducted in an attempt to determine changes during the cycle. Figure 1, which is based upon several research studies, indicates changes in satisfaction at seven nuclear family stages among typical middle-class couples. Many couples will reflect this trend while others will vary considerably. The allowance for variation is important since projecting this pattern onto all couples would be invalid. Considering the potential adjustments which occur at each stage is one means of identifying the stress and disruption of a marital relationship.

Jane Aldous, in her excellent book **Family Careers — Developmental Change in Families,** described the fluctuation that occurs in marital satisfaction:

Marriages may be made in heaven, as the popular saying goes, but their maintenance occurs in an earthly setting. The emotional euphoria with which most marriages start is eroded over time by establishing daily routines, by growing irritations from constant association, by competing attractions of jobs and children, and by coping with the multitudinous problems, both large and small, that family life in an industrialized society entails. Fortunate couples develop an intimate understanding unique to the relationship that replaces the raptures of the first period of the marital career.[6]

There are many predictable changes that occur as couples proceed through the various stages of the family life cycle. Some of these changes become cripplers of marriage in the process.

Figure 1
Husbands' and Wives' Marital Satisfaction over the Family Career

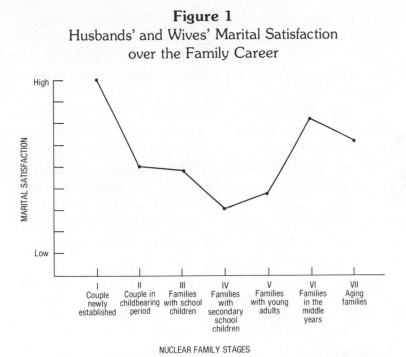

Source: Jane Aldous, **Family Careers—Developmental Change in Families** (New York: John Wiley, 1978), p. 202.

After The Honeymoon

Philip Yancey, in his excellent book **After the Wedding,** described one of the reasons for a sudden drop in marital satisfaction after the honeymoon: adjustments to married life.

Why can't couples predict adjustments before they get married? We've already seen that their romantic perspectives often blind them. Also, there are adjustments

about habits they would not know about before marriage
(he tosses and turns at night; she hangs pantyhose in the
bathroom; he throws tools into messy, disorganized
drawers). These can usually be worked out by compromise.

The really tough problems of adjustment come when
partners have different expectations about marriage.
What if a wife is used to big birthday celebrations and
elaborate Christmas decorations and the husband isn't?
What about a husband who expects a seductive, affectionate wife who will hang on him publicly—what if he
finds she's physically aloof? Though hints of these
differences appear in courtship, often the huge gulf does
not yawn open until after marriage, when the two are
thrust together for sixteen hours a day, not just when
they want to be together.

Does the husband expect the wife to forfeit a career to
be housewife and mother? Does the wife expect the
husband to be a career climber? Does the wife expect the
husband to keep a well-running, clean car? Who should
clean the garage? Who is to take the initiative in sex?

If your expectations differ, conflict will result.[7]

Other adjustments couples must make include need
fulfillment, adjusting to differentness, establishing goals,
expressing emotions, communication styles, decision
making, power structure, roles, adjusting to family background, and in-laws, just to mention a few.

As couples begin the family life cycle, several factors help
create problems:

1. Lack of preparation for marriage. David Mace, a
pioneer in the field of marriage enrichment, described this
lack of preparation:

... When I try to reconstruct, in counseling with couples,

their concepts of the making of a marriage, I find that it adds up to a most confused hodge-podge of starry-eyed romanticism, superstition, superficial concepts, and *laissez-faire*. Seldom do I find any real understanding of the complexity of the task of bringing two separate individuals into a delicately balanced coordination of each other's thoughts, feelings, wishes, beliefs, and habit-patterns.[8]

Mace goes on to say that neither partner is able to recognize his/her own need to make radical change in thoughts and behavior in order to maintain a close relationship. Instead, they seem to believe that their closeness will be continuous because of sexual attraction. He also suggests:

> There is rarely any clear realization that disagreement is inherent in a partnership as intimate as that undertaken by two people in marriage today; with the result that, instead of recognizing conflict as the raw material out of which the marriage must be fashioned, they flee from it as from some alien element that threatens to destroy their love. I find that they have generally entered marriage with little readiness for its demands, having spent the pre-marital period in a round of pleasure-making activities that bears little relationship, and even less resemblance to the realities with which married life now confronts them.[9]

2. Inability to handle disappointment, hurt, and suffering.

3. Unawareness of the effects of the various stages of the family life cycle.

4. Imbalance or lack of understanding concerning an individual's striving for identity and intimacy. What is identity? It is the sense of "who I am." What is intimacy?

Intimacy is a relationship of closeness, total honesty, and trust.

A man builds his identity through his occupation or profession. Many men pursue goals of making a good living and finding a good life, which prove to them they are adequate and of worth. (This typically male process is undergoing some change, however, as many women are now pursuing careers and professions.) Because their identities are built in this manner, men devote their time and energy to their work. The marital relationship often takes a secondary position. When couples marry, the timing is such that most men are just at the point of establishing themselves in their line of work. Their main task at this time is establishing identity *through* their work. At the onset of marriage a wife is seeking to build an intimate relationship with her husband. This is where frustration may occur. It can be described as *identity versus intimacy.*

Underlying part of many wives' strong emphasis upon intimacy is their own striving for building their sense of identity. Often they build an identity through their husband or family. (This typically female process is undergoing some change, too, as many women are now being employed outside of the home and some marital roles are changing.)

Many wives become discouraged after a few years of marriage because the intimate relationship with their husband does not develop as expected. Thus, in time a wife may turn her efforts for intimacy toward the children. Perhaps this accounts for why many mothers find it so difficult to let go of the children when they are old enough to leave the nest.

If this situation continues—the husband building identity through work and the wife building intimacy and identity through the children—a crisis will eventually occur. Many husbands in their forties realize they have reached the end of the line for upward progress in their work. There is nowhere else to go, so their goals begin to change. They may now turn back to their wives with a desire to build intimacy. They could be in for a shock, because many wives, after the children leave home, begin to consider how their own identities have developed. They may now decide either to complete their own education or to pursue a career. Their desire for an intimate relationship with their husbands is not very intense after so many years of no reciprocation on his part. The issues of the meaning of achievement and values in relationships need attention during marital counseling because often they are the underlying cause of the symptomatic problems couples bring to counseling.

Childrearing

Notice the drop in marital satisfaction on the chart during the childbearing years. Why does the presence of children affect marital satisfaction so much?

Becoming parents may be a normal stage in the family life cycle, but the limited learning couples bring to their new roles creates worries that in extreme cases affect infant care. (This, in turn, affects the marital relationship.) There is often a lack of formal or informal training for performing parental roles. The implicit socialization for such roles that the child experiences in taking the roles of his father and mother while interacting with them is absent when he or she is an infant.[10]

The pregnancy period itself is used by relatively few couples as a time to prepare for parental roles. Unless the

couple already has children, the couple's preparation
generally consists of obtaining the clothing and equipment
the coming baby needs. Reading, seeking counsel from
friends, discussing the situation with other couples, or all
three constitute the usual sources of information on infants.
Since there is usually no actual experience with infant care,
the information sought may be inappropriate or irrelevant.
Even couples active in prenatal courses such as the Lamaze
training classes for natural childbirth feel unprepared for
performing parental roles after the child's arrival.

The pregnancy period differs in this respect from the
period prior to marriage when the couple is committed to
each other. At that time, husband and wife can try out
interaction patterns and, in developing their marital role,
explore attitudes and expectations concerning those roles
and other family issues. They can also discover issues on
which they disagree and how to handle conflict.

The suddenness of the arrival of parental responsibilities
accentuates the problems of lack of learning. There is no
equivalent to the honeymoon period in which parents and
infant can become gradually acquainted. A demanding and
helpless baby allows for no respite regardless of how
unpleasant the care is or how inadequately parents give it.[11]

There have been a number of studies testing E. E.
LeMaster's thesis that, though normal and expected, the
transitions to parenthood constitute a "crisis" for the
marital relationship.[12] Particularly among middle-class
couples who tend to be concerned about the quality of
marital careers, the parent-child relationship can compete
with the husband-wife relationship for time, nurturance,
and affection. The husband-wife companionship that has
developed through the courtship and early-married days is
disrupted by the baby, forcing a reorganization of the

relationship to include a third person.[13]

Couples who make the transition successfully have also had time to work out mutually satisfactory marital arrangements, since they had been married for some time, at least three years. Husband or wife have also taken a preparation for marriage course.[14]

These results indicate that the accomplishment of the family development task of morale maintenance in the beginning stage of marriage is linked to how threatening parenthood is to the marital relation. If couples have a communication structure characterized by a way of conversing that results in agreement and the smoothing over of conflict, they are more apt to be effective family planners and to be more satisfied with their marriage.[15]

In general, most research findings tend to support the parenthood studies just discussed. Couples who had entered the parental career were less satisfied with marriage than they were before the child was born. This decline was not universal, however; so let us examine the varying marital arrangements of new parents who did and did not become less happy with their marital relationship. Couples whose marital satisfaction went up with the arrival of the first child were those characterized by a segregated marital role organization.

These couples talked with each other less, turned less often for help, and were less emotional toward the spouse in times of conflict than were new parents who were less satisfied with marriage. The former couples appeared to be less dependent upon each other for satisfaction of affectional needs. The type of marital role organization they possessed is consistent with such an interpretation. Their traditional beliefs that husbands should not perform household tasks supported a segregated type of conjugal organization. The wives also seemed to view motherhood as the fruition of their family careers. They placed high value on such material role behaviors as preference for breast feeding, concern about the child's crying, and "being child-centered in plans for feeding." The marital career being of lesser importance, therefore, would compete less with the parental career.[16]

The Middle Years

A number of cross-sectional studies have shown a decrease in marital adjustment over time, whether recently married couples and couples in their middle years of marriage are compared, or whether the same couples are compared in their early and middle periods of marriage. There is some evidence that middle-class couples shift from shared interests and household concerns to segregated activities. Occupational and parental demands appear to account for the shift.[17]

Working-class couples, however, do not experience joint marital role organization to such an extent. From the beginning, their marriages have been more often characterized by a segregated task organization in which roles are assigned according to traditional male-female roles. It is among middle-class women, who are more apt to expect interaction with husbands in many areas, that one finds resentment at competing responsibilities. Thus, middle-class wives with organizational roles outside the home maintained higher levels of marital adjustment. They chose to engage in outside employment in order to share more of the concerns of their occupationally-committed husbands. But national surveys show marital strain when women are employed outside the home through economic necessity which is more often the case with working-class couples.[18]

To summarize, the decline in marital satisfaction associated with a change from joint to segregated marital arrangements occurs among person-oriented couples who have initially, at least, experimented with role making. Such couples are disproportionately found among the more educated segment of the middle class. The declines in marital adjustment that working-class couples also appear to experience over the child-present years, therefore, do not stem from a loss of shared activities, since rarely were they there in the first place to lose. The coming of children for this group serves as a common interest rather than a divisive force, but the additional expenses and responsibilities children bring can also create conflict, particularly in couples hard-pressed for funds. In addition, new expectations coming from the current emphasis in the broader society on greater sexual freedom and women's rights exacerbate differences in families of all classes.[19]

This crisis time is also the time for what was described by Ken Kesey in his novel **Sometimes a Great Notion** as the "go-away-closer disease." The husband or wife may be starving for contact with the spouse but avoids contact like poison when it is offered. He or she may long for human relatedness but ends up sabotaging any chance for it to happen. Barriers are erected to keep anyone from getting too close, too intimate, too involved—yet the person is unhappy and restless in isolation.

How does one catch this strange go-away-closer disease? It seems to come in varying degrees with the middlescent malaise. The anger or frustration or disappointment we feel about the world and what it has done to us (or prevented us from doing) is directed at the person with whom we live in closest proximity. It is another form of kicking the cat. We may sense that things have gone awry, but for some reason we find it impossible to talk about the situation with our spouse. The next step is to stop ourselves from caring about, or feeling for, or doing as much for the other person because our own problems require all of our attention. It is hard to be sensitive to the needs of our spouse if we are locked in our own inner struggles. Besides, since no one else really understands us, we must keep our defenses up lest we reveal more than we want to show. Who wants someone else knowing what we really like down inside—the resentments, the hurts, the frustration, the failures.

Intimacy is lost also as spouses begin to see each other's faults more glaringly. Over the years, faults may come to loom larger as virtues turn into vices and then eventually become blatantly intolerable. Here, again, spouses usually show a reluctance to discuss the unpleasant aspects of each other's personalities—except, perhaps, in the heat of anger when they couch them in derogatory terms that question the partner's sanity or intelligence.[20]

To add to this we have the emergence of what is referred to as the male mid-life crisis. Jim Conway, in his excellent book **Men in Mid-Life Crisis,** described the situation:

The man approaching mid-life has some strange and difficult times ahead of him. He may negotiate the walk along the unfamiliar top of the brick wall with little trouble, but many men in mid-life feel more like Humpty Dumpty.

The mid-life crisis is a time of high risk for marriages. It's a time of possible career disruption and extramarital affairs. There is depression, anger, frustration, and rebellion. The crisis is a pervasive thing that seems to affect not only the physical but also the social, cultural, spiritual, and occupational expressions of a man's life.

It is a time when a man reaches the peak of a mountain range. He looks back over where he has come from and forward to what lies ahead. He also looks at himself and asks, "Now that I've climbed the mountain, am I any different for it? Do I feel fulfilled? Have I achieved what I wanted to achieve?"

How he evaluates his past accomplishments, hopes, and dreams will determine whether his life ahead will be an exhilarating challenge to him or simply a demoralizing distance that must be drearily traversed. In either case, he is at a time of trauma, because his emotions, as never before, are highly involved.[21]

Daniel Levinson has pioneered the research and practical description of the mid-life time. Here is what he said about this time in the man's life:

Some men do very little questioning or searching during the Mid-life Transition. Their lives in this period show a good deal of stability and continuity. They are apparently untroubled by difficult questions regarding the meaning, value and direction of their lives. They may be working on such questions unconsciously, with results that will become evident in later periods. If not, they will pay the price in a later developmental crisis or in a progressive withering of the self and a life structure minimally connected to the self.

Other men in their early forties are aware of going through important changes, and know that the character of their lives will be appreciably different. They attempt to understand the nature of these changes, to come to terms with the griefs and losses, and to make use of the possibilities for growing and enriching their lives. For them, however, the process is not a highly painful one. They are in a manageable transition rather than in a crisis.

But for the great majority of men—about 80 percent of our subjects—this period evokes tumultuous struggles within the self and with the external world. Their Mid-life Transition is a time of moderate or severe crisis. Every aspect of their lives comes into question, and they are horrified by much that is revealed. They are full of recriminations against themselves and others. They cannot go on as before, but need time to choose a new path or modify the old one.

Because a man in this crisis is often somewhat irrational, others may regard him as "upset" or "sick." In most cases, he is not. The man himself and those who care about him should recognize that he is in a normal developmental period and is working on normal mid-life tasks. The desire to question and modify his life stems from the most healthy part of the self. The doubting and searching are appropriate to this period; the real question is how best to make use of them. The problem is compounded by the fact that the process of reappraisal activates unconscious conflicts—the unconscious baggage carried forward from hard times in the past which hinders the efforts to change. The pathology is not in the desire to improve one's life but in the obstacles to pursuing this aim. It is the pathological anxiety and guilt, the dependencies, animosities and vanities of earlier years, that keep a man from examining the real issues at mid-life. They make it difficult for him to modify an oppressive life structure.

A profound reappraisal of this kind cannot be a cool, intellectual process. It must involve emotional turmoil, despair, the sense of not knowing where to turn or of being stagnant and unable to move at all. A man in this state often makes false starts. He tentatively tests a variety of new choices, not only out of confusion or impulsiveness but, equally, out of a need to explore, to see what is possible, to find out how it feels to engage in a particular love relationship, occupation or solitary pursuit. Every genuine reappraisal must be agonizing, because it challenges the illusions and vested interests on which the existing structure is based.[12]

Frequently the existing structure is changing at the same time and mid-life crisis hits because the children are growing up and preparing to leave home. Children coming into a marriage affect it not only when they arrive, but also when they leave.

Studies show that when the last child grows up and leaves home there is an increased likelihood of marital maladjustment. This event acts as a marital catalyst, demanding that the husband and wife face themselves, each other, and their marriage in a way they have never had to before. And the longer they avoid this task, the faster the gap between them widens.

For one thing, when the children leave, the couple must make adjustments in their parental and spousal roles. This can be especially true for the mother who has devoted herself so completely to her children that she is left with the feeling of being abandoned and thus unloved and uncared for. When her children grow up, the mother literally joins the ranks of the unemployed, where she may begin to sense that she has little reason or justification for her life, little value or worth as a contributor to the process of living. She may experience "post-parental depression" and share the feeling of the mother who said she "felt like dying" when her last daugher got married.[23]

The departure of grown children, according to Gerald Klerman, M.D., of the Harvard Medical School, often necessitates a major renegotiation of the marriage relationship. Suddenly a man and wife are thrown together with no one else to talk to or watch television with. Though the "empty nest" syndrome is described as a maternal problem, it is often the father who suffers most when the last teenager cleans out his closet and takes down the posters. The child who was mommy's little girl at six has become daddy's special pal; and when she goes, he is devastated.[24]

So the experience of the empty nest is always something of a crisis. It leaves a devastating sense of emptiness and purposelessness. Loneliness can set in. The silent house is full of memories. There was once so much to do, and now there is so little. The crowded, busy years seemed arduous at the time. But now, looking back, it is clear that this was far outweighed by the deep, solid satisfaction of being needed.[25] Fathers must also adjust, but they have their jobs and their outside interests. Their adjustments are less severe, and they may feel relief by the children leaving.

The groundwork for this traumatic experience for women is embedded in the conventional notion that in a good marriage the woman lives only for the collective values of being a wife and mother, with emphasis on the latter task since most of the care for the children falls on her shoulders. If she worked before marriage, she usually was expected to put all that behind her upon entering the wedded state. Even if she continued to work after marrying, she was expected to do so without neglecting her family duties. With such an expectation, it is no wonder that the woman, particularly the one who has devoted her life exclusively to motherhood, should undergo a terrific psychological change when all her children are gone. Rooms that once rocked with loud laughter and louder music are now strangely silent and still.

The father must also readjust to the empty nest, of course; but his job and other outside interests usually occupy his attention. Since he has not been as directly and constantly related to the children, his adjustment is less radical. Indeed, he may even breathe a sigh of relief when the children are finally out on their own. As they grew up, the mother's actual work load got somewhat lighter, but he felt increasing pressures for bigger allowances, more clothes, money for college, money to get started with a career or new home.[26]

The empty nest adjustment can move one of two directions as seen in this description.

When all the children leave home and the nest is empty, some parents have no idea who they are or what to do with themselves. Their identity, both as individuals and as family members, has been so tied up in mothering and fathering that they are lost. They feel worthless and useless. They feel robbed of their roles and of their children. The pain of separation often reminds them of other separations, particularly from their own families of origin. Although they mourn the loss of their children, they are also mourning the loss of themselves. The children will be all right; they have everything to look forward to. The parents are not sure that they have anything to look forward to.

On the other hand, parents, and women in particular, know that children grow up and leave home. Indeed, empty-nest theoreticians do not give parents credit for foresight. Watching children grow up and away is an inherent aspect of raising a family, although that does not negate the fact of loss and the very real depression families may experience over separation. But these feelings are not necessarily either unexpected or devastating. In fact, some women and men have very positive feelings about launching their children. It frees them to pursue other interests, to deepen relationships with other people, especially spouses, and perhaps to have different and more successful relationships with their adult children.[27]

The developmental tasks of child launching are twofold. Whether a child is going to college or into marriage, he must be sent away with ceremony and proper equipment. For college, this means a period of shopping for clothes, luggage, and writing equipment. For marriage, it means the hope chest, showers, and wedding preparations. In either case, it is interesting that in the United States, where the rites of passage into adolescence are often minimal, there are rituals that attend child launching. These events have the manifest function of simply preparing the one who is leaving for his or her future, but they have a more hidden function in helping the ones staying home over a difficult transition.

The transition only begins when mother and father put the last boy on the airplane for a distant school or stand on the church steps and wave a final good-by to their radiant youngest daughter. Their next days of behavior are veiled to their friends, but often both parents wander about the home and look at momentos from an exhilarating past— and try to remember how these rooms, now so still, used to echo with rock and roll, loud laughter, or singing. Although they are somewhat comforted to know that their newly marrieds have promised to visit and that their boy will be back for vacation, they are aware that they won't ever really be home again. All the daily tasks taken for granted all these years are suddenly laid aside. The responsibilities, often worrisome, are now relayed to others' shoulders; and the constant dynamo of adolescent activity is abruptly stilled.[28]

But for the wife, in particular, now freed from the cares and concerns of childrearing, the empty nest crisis represents a turning point in her life as she confronts the need to decide what to do with her life and future, perhaps another quarter of a century of good years yet. Now, more than ever, the bored housewife feels trapped and incarcerated in the split-level dream house.[29] If there has been little intimacy and companionship with her husband, then the emptiness is even greater. Companionship is even a greater need for a wife than a husband.

The most profound needs that are involved in companionship are those for tenderness, for emotional support, for contributions from the mates for emotional well-being. We have already indicated that when the wife loses her role as mother, she has no one to turn to but her husband. A wife's great need for emotional support is one of the crises of her middle years, and it is important for us to stress this point as we discuss role change in middle age. Traditionally it has been assumed that an American wife has few emotional resources outside her immediate home.[30]

Retirement

For approximately forty-five years, a man in American society defines himself through his work. He is what he does. Throughout this period he is expected to compete, to overcome obstacles, and to move steadily forward. Suddenly he is sent home with an engraved punch bowl or a watch and told to take it easy. No wonder so many men suffer "retirement shock." It isn't that the retiree has nothing to do. Whatever a man's former job, he misses the distinction it conferred (and often suffers at the thought that someone else now performs his work). The elderly also have the highest suicide rate in the country. The rate among white men from 65 to 69 is four times higher than the national average.

The possibilities of the retirement stage are seen in these two descriptions.

Retiring involves a role loss of major proportions for both the individual and the family. Men are still more likely to feel that their identity is tied to their work, but more women are making this connection, too. To retire is to lose some sense of self, even when we look forward to the freedom we will gain. Some retired people simply do not know what to do with themselves. It's more than just a matter of who we are and what we will do with our lives now. It involves basic questions—what time do we get up in the morning if we aren't going to work, and what do we wear and do during the day? We've lost a routine that buttressed our role. We've lost the co-workers, the clients, the associations and groups to which we belonged.

The underlying theme of retirement is separation — separation from a former identity, from a provider role, from friends and associates, from routine and purpose, and certainly preparation for the separation from life and all one's loved ones. But there is another theme involved. Retirement calls for a new autonomy, a new sense of identity and of family, a new purpose. Many people spend several years after they retire trying to establish a new identity. They mourn the loss of their old self and presume, for a time, that their lives are over. Then, they discover that it's not the end of everything. They still are healthy, they still have family and friends, there still are new roles to be taken on.[31]

For both sexes, certain moments in the life cycle bring conflict and anxiety. Nothing will change that. But men and women can help each other to cope—and grow through coping successfully—by an understanding and sensitive response to needs.

When one looks at marital happiness over the family existence, one might speculate that it would be higher in the aging years. Husbands and wives can look to each other for support in the face of an uncertain future. The concept of limited linkage, however, suggests a contrary view. Couples whose interaction brought little satisfaction in previous marital stages are not likely to experience a sudden upsurge in happiness, particularly given the changes in income, physical competencies, and daily activities that retirement symbolizes.

Noting and attending to the problems affecting marital satisfaction during the family life cycle in marital counseling may be part of the solution toward resolving these struggles.

Perhaps you will see many couples who fit the descriptions in this chapter. You will also see many who have unique problems, which will be a complete surprise to you. No matter who they are or what the problems are, ministers need to be well equipped and aware of their level of competence so they can either provide the ministry or make a referral to one who can assist.

NOTES

All materials quoted are used by permission.

1. As quoted in Clark Blackburn and Norman Lobsenz, **How to Stay Married** (New York: Cowles Books, 1968), p. 196.

2. Mark Lee **Marriage Discoveries** (Chappaqua, New York, Christian Herald Association, 1981) from page 1 of Chapter 13.

3. Diane de Dubovay **Robert Redford** (Des Moines, Iowa, Ladies Home Journal, Oct., 1981) pp. 48 & 52.

4. Bernard Greene. **A Clinical Approach to Marital Problems** (Springfield, Illinois: Charles C. Thomas, 1970), pp. 32, 37.

5. Adapted from Robert F. Stahmann and William J. Hulbert, **Klemer's Counseling in Marital and Sexual Problems—A Clinician's Handbook** (Baltimore, Maryland: William & Wilkins Co., 1977) pp. 21-33.

6. Jane Aldous, **Family Careers—Developmental Change in Families** (New York: John Wiley, 1978), p. 208.

7. Philip Yancey, **After the Wedding** (Waco, Texas: Word Books, 1976), pp. 29-30.

8. David R. Mace, "Marriage as Relationship in Depth," in **Marital Therapy: Psychological, Sociological and Moral Factors,** ed. H. L. Silverman (Springfield, Illinois: Charles C. Thomas, 1972), p. 168.

9. Mace, p. 168.

10. Aldous, p. 217.

11. Alice C. Rossi, "Transition to Parenthood," **Journal of Marriage and the Family,** February, 1968, pp. 35-36.

12. Aldous, pp. 160-169.

13. Ibid., pp. 162-168.

14. Ibid., p. 162.

15. Ibid., p. 163.

16. Ibid., pp. 165, 169.

17. Ibid., p. 179.

18. Ibid., p. 180.

19. Ibid, p. 180.

20. Robert Lee and Marjorie Casebier, **The Spouse Gap** (Nashville: Abingdon Press, 1971), p. 128.

21. Jim Conway, **Men in Mid-Life Crisis** (Elgin, Illinois: David C. Cook, 1978), pp. 17, 18.

22. Daniel J. Levinson, **The Seasons of a Man's Life** (New York: Ballentine Books, 1978), pp. 198-199.

23. Lee and Casebier, p. 132.

24. Ibid.

25. James A. Peterson, **Married Love in the Middle Years** (Association Press, 1968), pp. 52, 53.

26. Ibid., p. 59.

27. Mel Roman and Patricia E. Raley, **The Indelible Family** (New York: Rawson, Wade Publishers, Inc., 1980), pp. 205-206.

28. Peterson, pp. 41-42.

29. Lee and Casebier, p. 135.

30. Peterson, p. 53.

31. Roman and Raley, pp. 214-215.

Chapter 2

A Biblical Perspective of Counseling

Characteristics of Jesus' Approach in Counseling

In any type of Christian counseling—whether it be individual, marital, or family—knowledge and application of a biblical approach to counseling are essential. One way to develop a biblical approach is to study the life of Jesus and His relationships with others. The way He ministered to others is a model for all who counsel.

As we look at the characteristics of Jesus' approach in counseling, we must remember that techniques alone are not effective. Jesus' relationship with the person to whom He was ministering was the foundation of His approach.

An individual or couple coming for counseling needs to know the minister cares about them by his warmth, understanding, acceptance, and belief in their ability to change and mature.

One important observation we can make about Jesus' approach to counseling is that He worked with people through a process. He did not see them for just a few minutes during an appointment. He spent time helping them work through life's difficulties in an in-depth manner. He saw people not only with their problems, but with their potentials and hopes as well.

A basic characteristic of Jesus' approach was His *compassion* for others. We see His compassion expressed in Mark 8:2: "I have compassion on the multitude, because they have now been with me three days, and have nothing to eat" (KJV). Another passage showing His compassion is Mark 6:34: "And Jesus, when he came out, saw much people, and was moved with compassion toward them, because they were as sheep not having a shepherd; and he began to teach them many things" (KJV). His concern was to alleviate suffering and meet the needs of the people.

When Jesus first met others, He accepted them as they were. In other words, He believed in them and what they would become. The characteristic of *acceptance* is seen in John 4, John 8, and Luke 19. When Jesus met the woman at the well, He accepted her as she was without judging her. He accepted the woman caught in adultery and Zacchaeus, the dishonest tax collector, as well.

Individuals were Jesus' top priority. He established this priority and *gave them worth* by putting their needs before the rules and regulations that the religious leaders had constructed. He involved Himself in the lives of people who were considered the worst of sinners, and He met them where they had a need.

One of the ways in which Jesus gave worth to individuals was showing them their value in God's eyes by comparing God's care for other creatures with God's care for them: "Are not two sparrows sold for a cent? And yet not one of them will fall to the ground apart from your Father" (Matt. 10:29 NASB). At the heart of many marital problems is a low self-concept or feeling of lack of worth in one or both of the partners. Helping them to discover their personal worth because of who God is and what He has done for us will help to stabilize many of these marriages.

Another characteristic of Jesus' ministry was His seeing the needs of individuals and speaking directly to them regardless of what they might have brought to His attention. We see *discernment* in the example of Nicodemus coming to Jesus during the night. Whatever might have been his reason for wanting to talk with Jesus at that time, Jesus discerned Nicodemus' real need and confronted him with the need to be born again.

In meeting the immediate needs of individuals, Jesus did not use the same approach with everyone. Gary Collins shared this well in his book, **How to Be a People Helper:**

Jesus not only dealt with people in different ways, but He also related to individuals at different levels of depth or closeness. John was the disciple whom Jesus loved, perhaps the Master's nearest friend, while Peter, James, and John together appear to have comprised an inner circle with whom the Lord had a special relationship. Although they were not as close as the inner three, the other apostles were Christ's companions, a band of twelve men who had been handpicked to carry on the work after Christ's departure. In Luke 10 we read of a group of seventy men to whom Jesus gave special training. Following the resurrection He appeared to a larger group of five hundred people, and then there were crowds, sometimes numbering in the thousands, many of whom may have seen Christ only once and from a distance.[1]

The very words Jesus used in ministering to individuals were important. Sometimes Jesus spoke directly, even harshly. Other times He was soft-spoken. Sometimes He conveyed His feelings nonverbally as in Mark 3:5: "After looking around at them with anger, grieved at their hardness of heart, He said to the man, 'Stretch out your hand.' And he stretched it out, and his hand was restored" (NASB).

Jesus *emphasized right behavior* in the lives of those to whom He ministered. He said to the woman caught in adultery, "Go and sin no more." "Everyone who comes to Me, and hears My words, and acts upon them" Jesus compared to the wise man who built His house upon a foundation of rock (Luke 6:47 NASB).

Jesus *sought to have people accept responsibility* for turning from their present condition. In John 5, He responded to the man at the pool of Bethesda by saying, "Wilt thou be made whole?" (v. 6 KJV). In other words, "Do you really want to get well? Do you want to be healed? Do you want to change?" By asking this question Jesus sought to have the man accept responsibility for remaining sick or being made well. In another instance He asked a blind man, "What do you want me to do for you?" (Mark 10:51 NASB). In any type of counseling the person or couple must see that there is a choice to remain the same or to change and grow, and they must make that choice before much progress will be seen.

To other people, Jesus gave *hope:* "And they were astonished out of measure, saying among themselves, Who, then, can be saved? And Jesus, looking upon them, saith, With men it is impossible, but not with God; for with God all things are possible" (Mark 10:26-27 KJV).

He *encouraged* people as He ministered to them: "Come unto me, all ye that labor and are heavy laden, and I will give you rest. Take my yoke upon you, and learn of me; for I am meek and lowly in heart, and ye shall find rest unto your souls. For my yoke is easy, and my burden is light" (Matt. 11:28-30 KJV).

And He emphasized the *peace of mind* they could have: "Peace I leave with you, my peace I give unto you; not as the world giveth, give I unto you. Let not your heart be troubled, neither let it be afraid" (John 14:27 KJV). All of these characteristics of Jesus' approach in counseling are necessary in helping troubled marriages.

Inspiration was a part of His approach, too. William Crane, in **Where God Comes In: The Divine Plus in Counseling,** talked about the use of inspiration. He said it is more than just encouragement. Inspiration provides the counselee with hope and with the desire to change and to receive.

We can also see that Jesus helped *reshape or refashion people's thinking.* He helped them redirect their attention from the unimportant things of life to the important (see Luke 2:22-25; 12:22-27).

Teaching is a definite part of counseling, and we see over and over again how Jesus taught. He often used direct statements in His teaching. He also used many questions: "And it came to pass, as he went into the house of one of the chief Pharisees to eat on the sabbath day, that they watched him. And, behold, there was a certain man before him who had the dropsy. And Jesus, answering, spoke unto the lawyers and Pharisees, saying, 'Is it lawful to heal on the sabbath day?' And they held their peace. And He took him, and healed him, and let him go; And answered them, saying, 'Which of you shall have an ass or an ox fallen into a pit, and will not straightway pull Him out on the sabbath day?' And they could not answer Him again to these things" (Luke 14:1-6 KJV). (See also Luke 6:39, 42).

Another characteristic of Jesus' approach was expressing Himself with *authority.* He was not hesistant, backward, and bashful, but authoritative: "He was teaching

them as one having authority, and not as their scribes"
(Matt. 7:29 NASB).

Notice how Jesus *admonished and confronted* individuals. "And He said to them, 'Why are you timid, you men
of little faith?' Then He arose, and rebuked the winds and
the sea; and it became perfectly calm" (Matt. 8:26 NASB).
"If your brother sins, go and reprove him in private; if he
listens to you, you have won your brother" (Matt. 18:15
NASB).

Another example of how Jesus admonished and confronted is in John 8:3-9: "The scribes and the Pharisees
brought a woman caught in adultery, and having set her in
the midst, they said to Him, 'Teacher, this woman has been
caught in adultery, in the very act. Now in the Law, Moses
commanded us to stone such women; what then do You
say?' And they were saying this, testing Him, in order that
they might have grounds for accusing Him. But Jesus
stooped down, and with His finger wrote on the ground. But
when they persisted in asking Him, He straightened up, and
said to them, 'He who is without sin among you, let him be
the first to throw a stone at her.' And again He stooped
down, and wrote on the ground. And when they heard it,
they began to go out one by one, beginning with the older
ones, and He was left alone, and the woman, where she had
been, in the midst" (NASB).

Biblical Perspectives in a Secular Model

Another way to develop a biblical approach in counseling
is to compare a current secular counseling model that has
proven effective with the model of counseling in the Bible.
Here is what Gary Collins concluded after making such a
comparison:

... Some see counseling as a highly complex procedure, but more recent writers have simplified the process considerably. Egan, for example, lists four stages: attending to the counselee and building rapport; responding to the counselee and helping him to explore his feelings, experiences, and behavior; building understanding in both counselor and counselee; and stimulating action which subsequently is evaluated by counselor and counselee together.

A psychologist named Lawrence Brammer has a longer but similar list; opening the interview and stating the problem(s); clarifying the problem and goals for counseling; structuring the counseling relationship and procedures; building a deeper relationship; exploring feelings, behavior, or thoughts; deciding on some plans of action, trying these out, and evaluating them; and terminating the relationship.

To a large extent what we do in counseling will depend on the type of problem involved, the personalities of the helper and helpee, and the nature of their relationship. Building on the suggestions of Egan and Brammer, I would suggest that the counseling process has at least five steps, all of which are clearly illustrated in the Bible.

a. Building a relationship between helper and helpee (John 6:63; 16:7-13).
b. Exploring the problems, trying to clarify issues and determine what has been done in the past to tackle the problem (Rom. 8:26).
c. Deciding on a course of action. There may be several possible alternatives which could be tried one at a time (John 14:26; 1 Cor. 2:13).
d. Stimulating action which helper and helpee evaluate together. When something doesn't work, try again

(John 16:13; Acts 10:19, 20; 16:6).

e. Terminating the counseling relationship and encouraging the helpee to apply what he has learned as he launches out on his own (Rom. 8:14).

Much of this was beautifully illustrated by Jesus on the road to Emmaus.

When He met the two men, Jesus used a variety of techniques to help them through their crisis and period of discouragement....

In Luke 24 we see that Jesus first came alongside the men and began traveling with them. Here was rapport-building . . .

As they walked Jesus began asking some very nondirective questions....

As they traveled along, Jesus spent a lot of time listening. He surely didn't agree with what the men were saying, but He listened, gave them opportunity to express their frustrations, and showed them the love which sent Him to die for sinners in the first place.

After a period of time, Jesus confronted these men with their logical misunderstandings and failure to understand the Scriptures. The confrontation was gentle but firm, and it must have begun the process of stimulating the men to change their thinking and behavior...

At the end of the journey, Jesus got close by accepting an invitation from the two men to eat a meal together...

Then an interesting thing happened. It is something that every helper dreams of doing with some of his helpees—especially the more difficult ones. Jesus "vanished from their sight"! In so doing Jesus left them on their own and spurred them on to action. This is the ultimate goal of all helping—to move the helpee to a point of independence where there is no longer any need to rely on help from the helper.[2]

Factors in the Effectiveness of Jesus' Ministry

Jesus' ministry was that of helping people achieve fullness of life, assisting them develop an ability to deal with the problems and conflicts and burdens of life. Perhaps what is really important for the counselor—whether professional or layman—is to consider why Jesus was so effective in His ministry. As we look at His own personal life, the answer is evident.

Foremost in His personal life was *obedience to God.* There was a definite relationship between Him and His Father, and obedience was the mainstay of His life. Two verses from the book of John emphasize this point: "For I did not speak on My own initiative, but the Father Himself who sent Me has given Me commandment, what to say, and what to speak" (John 12:49 NASB). "I glorified Thee on the earth, having accomplished the work which Thou hast given Me to do" (John 17:4 NASB).

Another reason why Jesus' ministry was effective was that He lived a life of *faith* and therefore was able to put things in proper perspective and see life through God's eyes. The example of the synagogue official's daughter in Mark 5 and Jesus' response to his statement that his daughter was dead shows the faith of Jesus.

A third reason for Jesus' effectiveness was the power of His *prayer* life. The example of His prayer life indicates that prayer is a very important element in one's ministry: "So much the more went there a fame abroad of him; and great multitudes came together to hear, and to be healed by him of their infirmities. And he withdrew himself into the wilderness, and prayed" (Luke 5:15-16 KJV). "It came to pass in those days, that he went out into a mountain to pray, and continued all night in prayer to God. And when it was day, he called unto him his disciples; and of them he chose twelve, whom also he named apostles" (Luke 6:12-13 KJV).

Many counselors have found it helpful to pray either at the beginning or the end of their counseling sessions. Others do not, but prayer is still as much a part of their counseling ministry as it is for the one who prays aloud prior to or following the session. Some have developed the practice of praying specifically for each counselee each day and letting the counselee know that this is their practice. Some have also asked their counselees to pray for them that God would give them wisdom and insight as they minister to the counselee.

One pastor shared that it is his practice, when he is completely stymied in a counseling session and does not know what to do next, to share this fact openly with the counselee. He states that he would like to pause for a moment and ask God to reveal to him what should be done next, what should be said, and the direction that he should take. This pastor said that on many occasions, as soon as he had finished praying, what needed to be done or said next was very clear to him.

A fourth reason for Jesus' effectiveness was the *authority* by which He spoke. "For He taught them as one having authority, and not as the scribes" (Matt. 7:28 KJV). Jesus was very conscious of His authority. Those who know Christ and are called to a ministry of helping in counseling have the authority of God's Word.

There is a distinction, however, between using the authority of the scriptures and being authoritarian. Some want to simply pull out a scriptural passage and apply it to any problem without hearing the full extent of the difficulty and knowing whether scripture is necessary at that particular time. Some individuals who are unwilling or fail to examine the problems in their own lives, but attempt to counsel and use scriptural authority, might misapply scripture or distort it because of their own difficulties.

A fifth reason for the effectiveness of Jesus' ministry was His *personal involvement* with the disciples and with others. He was not aloof: He was personal, sensitive, and caring.

The *power of the Holy Spirit* enabled Jesus to be effective. Some have called this power an anointing of the Holy Spirit. We see how His ministry began with receiving the power of the Holy Spirit in Luke 3:21-22: "Now when all the people were baptized, it came to pass, that Jesus, also, being baptized, and praying, the heaven was opened, and the Holy Ghost descended in a bodily shape like a dove upon him, and a voice from heaven, which said, Thou art my beloved Son; in thee I am well pleased" (KJV). The next chapter of Luke indicates that Jesus was full of the Holy Spirit and led by the Spirit, and it says that the Spirit of the Lord was upon Him.

Luke 5:17 states that the power of the Lord was with Him to heal: "And it came to pass on a certain day, as he was teaching, that there were Pharisees and doctors of the law sitting by, who were come out of every town of Galilee, and Judaea, and Jerusalem; and the power of the Lord was present for him to heal them" (KJV).

William Crane, in his book **Where God Comes In: The Divine Plus in Counseling,** talked about the influence and the ministry of the Holy Spirit in the lives of the counselor and counselee:

> The Holy Spirit has access to all the materials that other psychotherapists know and use. In addition, he has direct access to the inner thoughts and feelings of the

counselor. When the counselor becomes counselee in the presence of the Wonderful Counselor and sincerely seeks the honest reproval, correction and training in righteousness which the Holy Spirit promises, then he may find it. Many have.[3]

Biblical Principles of Counseling

Even after years of training and experience, there are many occasions every week when ministers and counselors wonder what they should do or say in a counseling situation. These occasions force the Christian counselor to go back to the Lord and ask, "Lord, what should I do now? What does this person need?" If we begin to help people out of our own strength, mistakes are made. We need to *rely upon the power and wisdom of God.*

In Proverbs 3:5-6 we are instructed to "Lean on, trust and be confident in the Lord with all your heart and mind, and do not rely on your own insight or understanding. In all your ways know, recognize and acknowledge Him, and He will direct and make straight and plain your paths" (Amplified). A similar thought is in Proverbs 15:28; "The mind of the (uncompromisingly) righteous studies how to answer, but the mouth of the wicked pours out evil things" (Amplified).

If there is one problem that counselors suffer from more than any other, it is not knowing when to listen and keep quiet. Most ministers in counseling want to talk and offer advice or exhort from the scriptures. There is a time for advising and exhorting, but how will one know what to say unless he has first listened? *Listening* is one very important principle of counseling.

As we look into the scriptures we see God as our model for listening (Ps. 34:15-18; 116:1-2, Jer. 33:3). The scriptures

have much to say about the importance of listening as
we see in these passages. James 1:9 says that we are to be
"a ready listener" (Amplified). (See also Prov. 15:31; 18:13,
15; 21:28).

Note the difference between hearing and listening.
Hearing is the gaining of information for oneself. Listening is
caring for and being empathic toward others. In listening we
are trying to understand the feelings of the other person and
we are listening for his sake. Hearing is determined by what
goes on inside of me, what effect the conversation has on
me. Listening is determined by what is going on inside the
other person, what my attentiveness is doing for him.

In listening we interpret and try to understand what we
have heard. Paul Wilczak said this about listening:

It is the "heart," however, that is our total emotional
response, that integrates these various perceptions into
full, personal contact, and this is what is needed today.
We can listen with our heads. We can comprehend the
thought content of a person's messages and systematic-
ally analyze what is communicated. This is cognitive
empathy and can be readily learned. But cognitive
empathy has severe limitations.

It misses the dimension of meaning that goes beyond
what is explicitly said. It overlooks the feelings and
experiences usually conveyed without words. These
other messages come from the heart, the center of a
person's experience.[4]

Ecclesiastes 7 emphasizes the next principle of biblical
counseling—*knowing when to speak and when to be quiet,*
when enough has been said. Proverbs 10:19 further emphasizes it: "In a multitude of words transgression is not
lacking, but he who restrains his lips is prudent" (Amplified).
The Living Bible is very graphic: "Stop talking so much. You

keep putting your foot in your mouth. Be silent and turn off the flow!"

The counselor who understands the counselee's problems chooses his words well: "He who has knowledge spares his words, and a man of understanding has a cool spirit. Even a fool when he holds his peace is considered wise; when he closes his lips he is esteemed a man of understanding" (Prov. 17:27-28 Amplified).

Proverbs 29:20 is another passage applicable to the principle of knowing when to speak and when to be quiet: "Do you see a man who is hasty in his words? There is more hope of a (self-confident) fool than of him" (Amplified). Being hasty means blurting out what you are thinking without considering the effect it will have upon others. When you are ministering to a couple who shares something that shocks you, do not feel that you have to respond immediately. Take a few seconds to think, and ask God to give you the words. Then formulate what you want to say.

If you do not know what to say, one of the best things to do is ask for more information. "Tell me some more about it" or "Give me some more background." This gives you more time. You do not have to say something right away. There may be times when you say to a person, "I need a few seconds to go through what you said and decide what to share at this time." This takes the pressure off you and also off the counselee.

Another basic requirement in helping others is *genuine interest and love.* We can listen to the person, we can rely upon the power of God for knowing how to counsel, but little will be accomplished without being truly interested in the other person and loving him. Sometimes a counselor or minister will give an off-the-cuff, superficial answer that does not meet the counselee's need and does not deal with the problem. Counselors must ask themselves, How do I really feel about this person who is coming to me? Am I genuinely concerned?

Timing is a most important principle. "A man has joy in making an apt answer, and a word spoken at the right moment, how good it is!" (Prov. 15:23 Amplified). The right answer, the correct answer, is the word spoken at the right moment.

Keeping confidences is a principle that builds trust. The keeping of confidences is a trait of a trustworthy individual. "He who goes about as a talebearer reveals secrets, but he who is trustworthy and faithful in spirit keeps the matter hidden" (Prov. 11:13 Amplified). "He who goes about as a talebearer reveals secrets; therefore associate not with him who talks too freely" (Prov. 20:19 Amplified). If you have a friend who is a gossiper, who can't keep something hidden, the scripture is saying, Watch out! Don't associate with that person too much. "He who guards his mouth and his tongue keeps himself from troubles" (Prov. 21:23 Amplified).

Another principle of biblical counseling is *saying the right words in the right manner.* A passage that reflects the idea of understanding in choosing words is Proverbs 25:20: "He who sings songs to a heavy heart is like him who lays off a garment in cold weather and as vinegar upon soda" (Amplified). Being jovial around a person who is deeply hurting and suffering is not appropriate. "Oh, you really don't feel that way, come on out of it; let me tell you this story I heard — " can cause the person to hurt even more. This person is hurting so much already he is unable to focus on what is happening. On some occasions casual or off-the-subject conversation can help lift a person.

Advice-giving, in the proper manner, is a part of counseling. If you give suggestions in counseling, try to draw them from the couple or give tentative ones. "What if you did—?" "Have you considered—?" "What possibilities have you come up with?" A safety factor we can employ if we are going to give advice is to give several choices.

Do not say to a person, "This is exactly what you need to do." If you do, you are assuming the responsibility for the solution. If your suggestion does not work, he may come back and say, "You really gave me a stupid idea. It didn't work. It's your fault." Giving several tentative suggestions is not only safer for you, but it causes the person to think through the alternatives. Most people have the ability to resolve their problems but need the encouragement to do so.

Edifying and helping are also involved in counseling. Galatians 6:2 teaches the concept of bearing one another's burdens: "Bear (endure, carry) one another's burdens and troublesome moral faults, and in this way fulfill and observe perfectly the law of Christ, the Messiah, and complete what is lacking (in your obedience to it)" (Amplified). Romans 14:19 reads: "So let us then definitely aim for and eagerly pursue what makes for harmony and for mutual upbuilding (edification and development) of one another" (Amplified). The word edify, which is part of helping, means to hold up or to promote growth in Christian wisdom, grace, virtue, and holiness. Our counseling should include edification.

Helping means assisting a person do something for his betterment. We have to ask ourselves, "Is what I'm sharing with that person going to cause him to grow in the Christian life and assist him to be strong?" A person might come to you and say, "I really want you to help me." What does he mean by "help?" He might mean agreeing with his point of view, especially if it is a marital dispute, or even taking sides. This is where the counselor gets into difficulty—taking sides.

Another way of helping others is to encourage them. "Anxiety in a man's heart weighs it down, but an encouraging word makes it glad" (Prov. 12:25 Amplified). "Therefore encourage (admonish, exhort) one another and edify— strengthen and build up—one another, just as you are doing:" (1 Thess. 5:11 Amplified).

Encouraging means urging forward, stimulating one to do what he should be doing. It is saying to the person, "I believe in you as an individual. I believe that you have the ability and the potential to follow through in doing this. Now, can we talk about this together so that you would feel more competence in yourself?"

Empathy is a scriptural basic for counseling. Empathy is one of the most important commodities for effective counseling, but, unfortunately, the word empathy, like so many others, has many meanings to many people. What does empathy mean in the counseling relationship? The word comes from the German word *Einfühlung*, which means to feel into or to feel with. It is as though we are in the driver's seat of the other person and feeling and sensing with him. It is viewing the situation through his eyes, feeling as he feels. Galatians 6:2 and Romans 12:15 admonish us to bear one another's burdens, to rejoice with those who rejoice, and to weep with those who weep. To do that is to have empathy.

Girard Egan has said that empathy involves discrimination—being able to get inside the other person, looking at the world through his perspective or frame of reference, and getting a feeling for what his world is like. Not only is it the ability to discriminate, but also to communicate to the other person this understanding in such a manner that he realizes we have picked up both his feelings and his behavior. We must be able to see with his eyes what his world is like to him. It is like being able to see another person's joy, to understand what underlies that joy, and to communicate this understanding to the person.[5]

Joshua Liebman described the function of empathy:

It serves us in two ways. First, it helps us to understand the other person from within. We communicate on a deeper level and apprehend the other person more completely. With this kind of communication we often find ourselves accepting that person and emerging into a relationship of appreciation and sympathy. In another sense, empathy becomes for us a source of personal reassurance. We are reassured when we feel that someone has succeeded in feeling himself into our own state of mind. We enjoy the satisfaction of being understood and accepted as persons. It is important for us to sense that the other person not only understands our words but appreciates the person behind the message as well. We then know that we are recognized and accepted for the particular kind of person we are. When friends fail to empathize, we feel disappointed and rejected. When empathy is lacking, our self-awareness and self-respect are diminished. We then experience ourselves more as objects and less as persons.[6]

Donald Houts wrote of empathy in terms of involvement in the lives of others:

Love is the capacity to involve oneself, unselfconsciously, in the lives of other men—without using these relationships primarily to minister to oneself. To understand their weaknesses, to suffer with them, to hate the things that hurt them, to grieve over their hard-heartedness—these are manifestations of the kind of relationships which contribute to new life in those whose lives have been so touched.[7]

William Crane described empathy in this way:

The person who practices the presence of the Holy Spirit and learns to love God through focusing upon His demonstration of love in the gift of His only Son becomes increasingly mature and capable of ministering to the needs of others. As Dr. Reuel Howe and others have said, nothing will take the place of love in the heart of the counselor for his counselee. This kind of love is more concerned with giving than with getting; it is the basic factor in establishing an empath(ic) relationship between counselor and counselee. True empathy must have its roots in agape love, for only this kind of self-giving concern is capable of entering into the deeper areas of the counselee's problems.

For a better understanding of the meaning of this "larger love" in empathy, let me quote from J.B. Phillips' translation of I Corinthians 13:4-8: "This love of which I speak is slow to lose patience—it looks for a way of being constructive. It is not possessive: it is neither anxious to impress nor does it cherish inflated ideas of its own importance.

"Love has good manners and does not pursue selfish advantage. It is not touchy. It does not keep account of evil or gloat over the wickedness of other people. On the contrary, it is glad with all good men when truth prevails."

"Love knows no limit to its endurance, no end to its trust, no fading of its hope; it can outlast anything. It is, in fact, the one thing that still stands when all else has fallen."

First of all, there can be no empathy when one loses patience quickly with a troubled person. This can happen when one is more concerned about his own affairs than about his counselee's interests or needs. Lack of patience may destroy any possibility of empathy; it can easily be detected by the counselee whether through words or through actions and attitudes.

Sometimes the counselor shows his impatience by "pushing" the counselee too fast to get on with his problems, so that, presumably, the counselor may begin his "important work."

The basic love from which empathy springs "is not touchy." "Touchy" implies a degree of oversensitivity on the part of the counselor, which really means that he is more concerned about receiving the counselee's praise and approval than he is of giving his attention to the counselee's needs. Here is an area where lack of insight and failure to be aware of the counselor's own emotional blocks may cause trouble and destroy empathy or make it impossible to establish empathy in the first place.

A touchy counselor is one who listens primarily for things that might reflect upon his own character or worth rather than seeking for constructive ways to be helpful to the counselee. A neurotic counselor is inclined to become extremely touchy and to be thrown on the defensive by any slight, word, or act on the part of the counselee which would insinuate that the counselor is not as important as the counselee.

Love also refuses "to keep an account of evil or gloat over the wickedness of other people."

Rather than having a judgmental attitude, the counselor is "glad with all good men when truth prevails." This is to say that the counselor is responsive to the counselee wherever he sees in him potential for good and evidence of truth. The counselor's joy is a contributing factor in the deepening and strengthening of empathy.

There is an ongoingness in love which "knows no limit to its endurance." The counselor must learn to endure all sorts of things in his counselees.

But the next factor is even more difficult at times. Love knows "no end to its trust." Every counselor and especially every pastoral counselor has people who come to him clothed in hypocrisy, insincerity, and falsehood. Their neurotic problem makes them need to test the sincerity of the pastoral counselor by their very insincerity.

The smiling face, smooth words, and overly pious attitude which some counselees bring to their counseling relationship with their pastors may be deceptive for a while. Eventually the real nature is discovered—and then the counselor has a real problem. He needs to trust his counselee, but how can he trust one who is so false, deceptive, and insincere?

Actually he cannot. Nevertheless he must learn to trust his belief in and knowledge of his counselee's need for help. Above this he must have an unfailing trust in the presence and power of the Wonderful Counselor, the Holy Spirit, who is ready and willing to change the counselee from an untrustworthy person to a person of integrity and honor, through the instrument of the counselor. This basic personality change is impossible without the work of the Holy Spirit within the heart, but the pastoral counselor need never doubt it is an unfailing possibility and desirable result in the counseling relationship.[8]

The word confrontation is used frequently in discussions of counseling techniques. What is confrontation? When should it be used? Confrontation is really part of everyday life, and it can be used effectively when we are involved in helping another individual. Confrontation is not an attack on another person "for his own good." Such a negative and punitive attack would be detrimental to the counselee.

William Crane has said,

A judging confrontation, unprepared for, may end any relationship which would make counseling possible. The person already feels guilty and ashamed, and to be judged and condemned rather than understood and accepted is nothing less than absolute rejection. A person laden with guilt already feels cut off and rejected by all that stands for rightness and justice; he surely does not need to be condemned more by the one to whom he goes seeking help.[9]

Girard Egan has suggested that confrontation at its best is an extension of advanced, accurate empathy. That is, it is a response to a counselee based on a deep understanding of his feelings, experiences, and behavior. Such a response involves some unmasking of distortion and the client's understanding of himself and some challenge to action.[10]

William Crane has suggested that "Only when empathy is established is the climate ready for confrontation; until then it is neither wise nor helpful."[11] The relationship between confrontation and empathy is very important, yet so many never have attempted to link the two together and have failed to see the relationship between the two. A counseling confrontation has been defined as an act by which a counselor points out to the counselee a discrepancy between his own and the counselee's manner of viewing reality.

Confrontations have also been called "acts of grace." Girard Egan has defined confrontation as "a responsible unmasking of the discrepancies, distortions, games, and smoke screens the counselee uses to hide both from self-understanding and from constructive behavioral change."[12]

Confrontation also involves challenging the undeveloped, the underdeveloped, the unused, and the misused potentials, skills, and resources of the counselee with a view to examining and understanding these resources and putting them to use in action programs. Confrontation is an invitation by the helper to the counselee to explore his defenses, those that keep him from understanding and those that keep him from action.

Our purpose in confronting a person would be to help him make better decisions for himself, to become more accepting of himself, and to be more productive and less destructive in his life. There are times when professional and nonprofessional alike hesitate in confronting because it involves a commitment. There is also the risk of the possibility that the counselor could be wrong or the other might misunderstand and feel rejected. In confronting the person we also need to be careful that even though the confrontation is given with proper intentions, it does not work against what we are actually trying to accomplish in the counselee's life.

When is confrontation appropriate? Earlier it was mentioned that empathy must be a part of the relationship. The quality of the relationship between counselor and counselee is very important. Generally speaking, the stronger the relationship, the more powerful and intense the confrontation can be. A confrontation must come about because the counselor cares about the counselee. If we do not care about him or his improvement, confrontation can be harmful.

Another factor involved in confrontation is the ability of the counselee to understand and see what we are saying. Does he have the ability to accept the confrontation? Can he follow through with what we are suggesting?

How should confrontations be made? A confrontation should be made with empathy. The caring approach is so vital, for when care is expressed and perceived by the counselee, he can accept the confrontation much more readily. Confrontations can be made in a tentative manner with statements such as "I wonder if—," "Could it be—," "Is it possible—?" "Does this make sense to you?" and "How do you react to this perception?" There are also times as seen in the following example that a confrontation is used to shake and motivate a couple.

The confrontation in the example took place in a counselor's office. The wife was very upset because her husband was going to leave her for a two-month trip to the Orient and would not give her the assurance that he would not become involved with other women. The marriage had a history of the husband's involvement with several affairs a year for each of the ten years that they had been married. The counselor had seen them for eight sessions and had established an open relationship with the couple. In a quiet, calm voice he spoke to the husband:

Counselor: At the present time I think it is only fair to share with you that if you proceed as planned and take the trip without reassuring your wife that you will be faithful, there is every possibility when you return that your wife will have left and will have filed for a divorce. This is just a natural consequence that may follow what you are intending to do.

You have complained earlier about your wife becoming upset with you, yet I can see from her perspective why she would feel upset at this particular time. You have also said earlier that you would like to have further testing done on your wife to see if there isn't something psychologically wrong with her because of how upset she becomes. Frankly, I am not sure the problem at this time rests with her. I think it might be better for us to take a look at what is going on inside of you that has caused you not to be faithful to your wife over the past ten years. Since you have also shared with me that you are a born-again Christian, I think we need to consider your relationship with the Lord and begin to discover how His presence in your life can bring a turnaround.

The following is another example of confrontation that was directed at both husband and wife. It is taken from the fifteenth session with a couple in their mid-thirties. It begins about thirty minutes into the session.

Janet: I really would like to get out of this apathetic, indifferent state that I am in toward my husband. I would also like to see him really begin to make some changes that we have been talking about for several weeks.

Jim: I am really getting frustrated because I feel I am making some changes, and yet I never hear any recognition. I am beginning to think my wife is a nymphomaniac. She wants more sex. We had sex three times this week. I haven't heard one word about whether or not she liked it. All I hear is negatives. I perform and she doesn't seem to care.

Counselor: Jim, I hear you making an assumption. Have you checked this out with her? Have you asked her how she felt about the increase in your sexual activity?

Jim: No, I haven't.

Counselor: How did you feel about the increase in the relationship this week?

Janet: I really liked it.

Counselor: Janet, did you share with him that you liked

it? Did you let him know that you were pleased?

Janet: No, I didn't.

Counselor: I would like to stop at this point and just share with you some of my own feelings. I feel frustrated and have felt this way with you the past three sessions. There are three things that I would like to say about your marriage. Number one: I believe that the two of you have the basic potential that is needed to put together and to develop the type of marriage that you are both wanting.

Number two: Janet, you have a defnite tendency to focus on the negatives, to see just the problems and not to give recognition to Jim when he begins to change. When people change, the process is slow and maybe the improvement is only 5 to 10 percent. Instead of concentrating on that 5 to 10 percent improvement, it appears you are focusing on the 90 to 95 percent that has not changed, and you are actually looking for about 60 or 70 percent change. It doesn't happen like that. I feel that it is necessary and vital for you to begin focusing on those positive changes. Letting him know that you appreciate them, that you know that he is trying, reinforces them in a positive way. Then quit focusing mentally and verbally on some of the defects and the lacks that you think are there.

Jim, on your part I would like to see you triple your efforts. You have made some changes, but usually they are about 10 or 20 percent of what we discuss here in counseling. I really feel that it is necessary for you to intensify and perform even more.

Janet: I didn't realize counselors had feelings. I thought that they were totally objective or they insulated themselves.

Counselor: No, I have very definite feelings. I have

positive feelings and negative feelings. I have to be totally aware of my feelings. If I totally insulated myself, then I probably wouldn't care. I am frustrated with the two of you because I do care about both of you and I see you as having potential. I needed to let you know my frustration because I would like us to begin really moving.

Janet: I guess I didn't realize that.

Jim: Nor did I.

How might a counselee respond when confronted? Girard Egan has suggested several possible responses. The counselee might try to discredit the counselor. He could do this by attacking the counselor, showing that he knows better than anyone else. If this occurs, it could mean that we have been wrong in our confrontation and have not been perceptive. A counselee might attempt to persuade the counselor to change his views. He might employ reasoning. He might try to show the counselor that he is really not that bad or that he is being misinterpreted. He might also try to minimize the importance of the topic being discussed in the form of rationalizing. As often happens in pastoral counseling, the counselee might seek support for his own views from others.

Often a counselee will agree with the counselor. His agreement could be valid or it could be a game. He could agree in order to get the counselor to back off. If the agreement does not lead to behavioral change, the sincerity of the counselee should be questioned. Our goal in confrontation is not necessarily to have the person agree with us, but to have him reexamine his behavior so that he can understand himself better and act in a much more effective manner.

One example of a direct confrontation in scripture is in 2

Samuel 12:7-14. Nathan confronted David with his sin against Uriah and his wife Bathsheba. David openly admitted his sin and Nathan responded by saying, "The Lord also has taken away your sin; you shall not die. However, because by this deed you have given occasion to the enemies of the Lord to blaspheme, the child also that is born to you shall surely die" (NASB). Because of the wrong that David committed—against Uriah, against his position as King of Israel, against Bathsheba, and against the unborn child—David had to be confronted with the total picture.

William Crane noted that

> ... the judgment placed upon David for his sin was not without an expression of the love and mercy of God in providing pardon and forgiveness. When Nathan was able to say, "The Lord has also put away your sin; you shall not die," he was giving reassurance to David of his acceptance by God and his pardon as a result of his true repentance. Had David not been confronted by Nathan in this way it is doubtful that he would have come to recognize or admit the fact of his sinfulness and need for forgiveness.[13]

When you work with people you cannot use the same approach every time. You must be sensitive to their needs. The need for *adaptability* is stated in 1 Thessalonians 5:14: "We earnestly beseech you, brethren, admonish (warn and seriously advise) those who are out of line—the loafers, the disorderly and the unruly; encourage the timid and faint-hearted, help and give your support to the weak souls (and) be very patient with everybody—always keeping your temper" (Amplified).

How do you confront a person when he is doing something wrong? In John 5 Jesus asked the man at the pool, "Do you really want to be healed? Do you really want to change?" When I work with people I ask that question in one way or another. In John 8 Jesus responded to the woman caught in adultery by saying, "Go, and sin no more."

Honesty is yet another principle of counseling. Proverbs 28:23 states: "In the end people appreciate frankness more than flattery" (TLB). In Proverbs 27:5 we read: "Open rebuke is better than hidden love" (TLB).

Finally, *acceptance* is involved in helping others. "Brethren, even if a man is caught in any trespass, you who are spiritual, restore such a one in a spirit of gentleness; looking to yourself, lest you too be tempted" (Gal. 6:1 (NASB). "But when they persisted in asking Him, He straightened up, and said to them, 'He who is without sin among you, let him be the first to throw a stone at her'"(John 8:7 NASB).

NOTES

All materials quoted are used by permission.

1. Gary Collins, **How to Be a People Helper** (Santa Ana, California: Vision House, 1976), p. 37.

2. Collins, pp. 51-53.

3. William Crane, **Where God Comes In: The Divine Plus in Counseling** (Waco, Texas: Word Books, 1970), p. 28.

4. Paul F. Wilczak, "Listening as Ministry," **Marriage and Family Living Magazine,** LXII, 3 (March, 1980), p. 4.

5. Girard Egan, **The Skilled Helper** (Monterey, California: Brooks/Cole Publishing Co., 1975), p. 76.

6. Joshua Loth Liebman, **Peace of Mind** (New York: Simon & Schuster, 1946), pp. 7-8.

7. Donald C. Houts, "Sensitivity, Theology and Change: Pastoral Care in the Corinthian Letters," **Pastoral Psychology,** XX, 193 (April, 1969), p. 25.

8. Crane, pp. 31-36.

9. Ibid., p. 57.

10. Egan, p. 158.

11. Crane, p. 60.

12. Egan, p. 158.

13. Crane, p. 56.

Chapter 3

The Initial Interview, How To Begin

Many pastors and marriage counselors use the first session with a couple to gather information about them and their relationship. This may not be the best approach for the first meeting. If the first session is devoted entirely just to identifying the problems of the marriage, you could be reinforcing a defeatist attitude about the marriage and hindering progress. The couple is well aware of the pain and conflict, which they have probably hashed over for weeks and months before coming in to see you. If anything is to be magnified at this time, it is strengths rather than weaknesses. Part of the first session may be used for gathering assessment information, but the main purpose is to build positive expectancies, establish a commitment for change, and begin the process of change.

Most of the assessment information can be gathered outside of the counseling setting, thus releasing this time for productive efforts. Not all couples can verbally define their difficulties in specific objective terms, and some are embarrassed to discuss some topics initially with a counselor. Responding to an evaluation survey or questionnaire may be much easier and offer more complete information.

The pastor's or counselor's objective is to relieve pain

and to provide hope for the possibility of positive growth. Picture yourself as a couple going for help. What would encourage *you* to return week after week? What would keep *you* going during the difficult times? What would encourage *you* to cooperate with the counselor?

Precounseling Contact and Assessment

The assessment information should be obtained prior to the first interview if possible. By having the information beforehand, the pastor can structure the first session according to the needs of the particular couple because he is aware of their strengths, weaknesses, conflicts, and areas of concern. He can also save several hours of counseling time.

One of the most helpful tools is the Marital Pre-Counseling Inventory.[1] This inventory is eleven pages in length and collects information in the following areas: the daily activities of both spouses, their general goals and resources for change, their satisfaction and targets for change in twelve areas of marital and family functioning, the bases for their decision making, and the level of their commitment to the marriage.

The completion of this inventory serves several important purposes. It provides the counselor with most of the data needed for planning intervention prior to the first counseling session. It helps the couple to anticipate the kind of concerns that will be discussed by the counselor, and in that way it helps to introduce them to counseling. Answers to the inventory questions also initiate changes in the ways in which spouses think about their objectives and can bring about some change before the first interview.

By placing each person's form side by side, you can

quickly see areas of conflict, difference, concern, strength, and weakness, all of which will help you to formulate questions prior to the first session.

Here are two sample sections from the Marital Pre-Counseling Inventory. In the first section (Figure 2) note the progression of the questions from evaluation of self to evaluation of the spouse. Because questions are specific, they help a person evaluate his relationship in specific areas of the marriage. The inventory then focuses each person's thinking upon what each can do to change his own behavior for positive improvement. This section not only gives you information in some of the critical areas, but measures their level of importance to the individual and each person's own motivation and sense of responsibility.

Figure 2

Marital Pre-Counseling Inventory, Section H

H. The following series of questions relates to the level of satisfaction which you usually find in your interaction with your spouse.

   1. How happy are you with the way in which you and your spouse usually handle each of the following aspects of your family life? Please *circle* the number which best represents how happy you are in each area.

		Mostly Happy		Moderately Happy		Mostly Unhappy	Does Not Apply
_____ a.	Social interaction with each other	1	2	3	4	5	—
_____ b.	Affectionate interaction with each other	1	2	3	4	5	—
_____ c.	Sexual interaction with each other	1	2	3	4	5	—
_____ d.	Trust in each other	1	2	3	4	5	—
_____ e.	Management of children	1	2	3	4	5	—
_____ f.	Management of free time	1	2	3	4	5	—
_____ g.	Management of chores or other responsibilities at home	1	2	3	4	5	—
_____ h.	Management of finances	1	2	3	4	5	—

_____ i. Social interaction with friends   1   2   3   4   5   —

_____ j. Social interaction with in-laws   1   2   3   4   5   —
and other relatives

_____ k. The way spouse manages   1   2   3   4   5   —
himself personally

_____ l. Management of jobs outside   1   2   3   4   5   —
the home

2. Please look back over each question. This time draw an X through each answer which you think your spouse will select in answering each question for himself/herself.

3. Please read over the list of areas. In the blanks at the left of the list, please indicate whether the item is:

> 1. Most important to you
> 2. Highly important to you
> 3. Fairly important to you
> 4. Unimportant to you

4. Looking back over this list once again, please suggest ways in which a change in your own behavior might improve your satisfaction in any areas which you rated as "4" or "5," that is, less than moderately happy or unhappy.

Source: Richard B. Stuart and Frieda Stuart, **The Marital Pre-Counseling Inventory** (Champaign, Illinois: Research Press, 1973), p. 7.

Figure 3

Marital Pre-Counseling Inventory, Section L

L. These questions concern your general commitment to and optimism about your marriage. Please answer them with your present feelings in mind, leaving out of consideration the way you used to feel or think that you should feel.

1. Everything considered, how   95%+   75%   50%   25%   5%—
happy are you in your
marriage?

2. Everything considered, how   95%+   75%   50%   25%   5%—
happy do you think your
spouse is in your marriage?

3. Everything considered, do you   95%+   75%   50%   25%   5%—
expect to become happier as
time goes by?

4. Everything considered, do you think that your spouse expects to become happier as time goes by?	95%+	75%	50%	25%	5%—
5. How committed are you to remain in your marriage?	95%+	75%	50%	25%	5%—
6. How committed do you think your spouse is to remain in your marriage?	95%+	75%	50%	25%	5%—
7. What proportion of the time spent with your spouse is happy for you?	95%+	75%	50%	25%	5%—
8. What proportion of the time which your spouse spends with you do you think is happy for him or her?	95%+	75%	50%	25%	5%—
9. Everything considered, do you expect to continue to grow personally as time goes by?	95%+	75%	50%	25%	5%—
10. Everything considered, do you expect your spouse to continue to grow personally as time goes by?	95%+	75%	50%	25%	5%—

Source: Richard B. Stuart and Freida Stuart, **The Marital Pre-Counseling Inventory** (Champaign, Illinois: Research Press, 1973), p. 11.

In the second sample section (Figure 3) you will be able to discover the level of commitment and optimism concerning the marriage. Questions 5 and 6 provide practical values in giving direction to the emphasis within counseling.

For example, if a husband indicates for Question 6 that he thinks his wife is 75 percent committed to stay in the marriage, and yet on her inventory she responds to Question 5 with an answer of 25 percent, one of the apparent problems has already been discovered. This husband does not understand the full extent of her hurt and discouragement with the marriage. Her motivational level to stay in the marriage and work on it is low, which means she will need more support, encouragement, and hope during the initial counseling session just to keep her working. A definite emphasis upon the strengths and possibilities of the marriage will be important to stress with her. Her husband may be shocked as he discovers what she is feeling and what her intentions are at this time.

Each section of this inventory contains valuable information that will help both the counselor and the couple.

The Taylor-Johnson Temperament Analysis (TJTA) is another helpful tool in assessing the couple's needs in counseling. This test will provide you with information about several important areas of each spouse's personality and his/her perception of the other's personality. The results of the TJTA may indicate a need for individual counseling concurrent with or in some cases prior to the joint sessions. (See the appendix for details on the use of the TJTA.)

Naturally there will be times when couples walk in for counseling or must be seen immediately. But most will call for an appointment. At this time both the Marital Pre-Counseling Inventory and the TJTA can be introduced to the couple. These tests are used in this manner by pastors as well as by professional counselors. Those who call a pastor will respond to the pastor's use of the tests just as they would to their use by a counselor.

As you tell them about these forms, it is important to give the person calling a brief summary about each form. The Marital Pre-Counseling Inventory consists of eleven pages and measures a number of important areas of the marital relationship. It will take between 1½ and 2½ hours to complete. By completing the inventory the couple will have done a thorough analysis of their marriage and probably will be surprised at what they discover. By completing this form prior to seeing you, they will save several hours of counseling time and will be able to focus on some areas of help in the first sessions of counseling.

Also, share that you want to offer them as much help as possible, and therefore you have established a policy of asking them to complete these evaluations. As they hear the reasons, most couples are very responsive and thankful for this assistance. Either on the phone or during the first session, you can share with the couple or person that you will also be asking them to complete outside assignments or projects during the week. This will be done in order to bring about positive change in their marriage as soon as possible and to reinforce what occurs in the counseling session.

Even if just one member of the marriage seeks counseling, the same policy and procedure are used.

From time to time you will find couples and individuals who do not want to complete one or both of these forms. It is important to share firmly and calmly that this is your policy, and in order to give the most help to the person or couple you need to have these forms completed. Usually the caller will respond affirmatively. Their willingness to complete these forms will also be a possible measure of their motivation to work on their relationship.

John Gottman, in his excellent demonstration film **Behavioral Interviewing with Couples,** shares his assessment approach.[2] He waits until the first session to gather information. At that time he asks each person to fill out an "Initial Goals" evaluation form (Figure 4) and a "Problem Inventory" (Figure 5). By completing these forms a couple is able to determine specifically what some of their main difficulties are. The forms also give the counselor pertinent information about the couple and topics that need to be discussed.

Upon completion, the Initial Goals form is given back to the counselor. He can then ask for additional information concerning any of the problems indicated, or he can ask each person which of these they would like to discuss during the first session. Often couples will have checked the same issues, and you could begin with these. Or you may want to ask each of them to share what each could do to bring about a positive change in the indicated area.

The Problem Inventory, which is available in a form for the husband and a form for the wife, can be used in a similar manner to identify specific problem areas.

Figure 4

Initial Goals Form

INITIAL GOALS

Name: _____ Date: _____

Instructions: Below you will find a list of goals you may consider important for the two of you to work toward at this time. Please read each item. Select *the one* most important goal *for you at this time.*

_____ 1. I would like to get some relief from the constant arguing and unpleasantness between us.

_____ 2. I would at least like things to be a bit more peaceful and pleasant.

_____ 3. I would like to see more politeness in our day-to-day relationship.

_____ 4. I would like to avoid violent quarrels.

_____ 5. I would like us to be more civil and respectful toward each other.

_____ 6. I would like to be able to work together better as a team, to take better care of the daily chores.

_____ 7. I would like to know that if I do something positive it will count and mean something to my spouse.

_____ 8. I would like to be able to come to agreements better in which there is give and take on both sides.

_____ 9. I would like there to be more exchange of affection between us.

_____ 10. I would like my spouse to share more in the responsibilities we both must meet.

_____ 11. I would like my spouse to accept me more and to express more liking for me.

_____ 12. I wish we could be better at being each other's friend.

_____ 13. I would like my spouse to find me more attractive.

_____ 14. I would like to have more influence in making decisions.

_____ 15. I would like to have my spouse be more interested in me.

_____ 16. I would like to be better able to get my messages across to my spouse.

_____ 17. I want my spouse to be better at discussing problems and helping to solve them.

_____ 18. I want my spouse to improve at listening to me.

_____ 19. I wish my spouse were more understanding and considerate of my feelings.

_____ 20. I would like to better understand my spouse's feelings and reactions.

_____ 21. Other (please specify) _____

Source: John Gottman, **Behavioral Interviewing with Couples** (guidebook accompanying the film) (Champaign, Illinois: Research Press, 1976), p. 34.

Figure 5

Problem Inventory, Husband's Form

HUSBAND'S PROBLEM INVENTORY

Name: _____ Date: _____

Instructions: A list of areas of disagreement experienced by many couples is provided below. In the first column, please indicate how severe the problem is by placing a number from 0 to 100. A zero indicates that the problem is not severe and a 100 indicates that it is a very severe problem area.

In the second column, please write the number of years, months, weeks, or days that this area has been a problem.

For example:

	How severe?	How long?
Alcohol and Drugs	90	2½ yr.

This indicates that alcohol and drugs are in your opinion a serious problem and that it has been a problem for about 2½ years.

	How severe?	How long?
1. Money		
2. Communication		
3. In-laws		
4. Sex		
5. Religion .		
6. Recreation		
7. Friends		
8. Alcohol and Drugs		
9. Children		
10. Jealousy		

Please feel free to write down any other problem area(s) which you may feel is (are) relevant.

11.		
12.		

Source: John Gottman, **Behavioral Interviewing with Couples** (guidebook accompanying the film) (Champaign, Illinois: Research Press, 1976), p. 45.

How To Begin The First Session

One of the greatest frustrations of beginning counselors is how to begin the first session. There is no "right" way to start a session. Several different approaches may work, and in many cases the couple themselves begin with the difficulties they are encountering.

One approach is to tell the couple what you and they will be doing during the session. By presenting an informal outline of the session, you can relieve some of the anxiety and stress that couples normally feel. Here is an example of such an introduction:

Before we get started tonight, I want to tell you a little bit about what we'll be doing. My goal is to get to know you a little and I'll be asking you some questions about the past and the present to get an idea of what your relationship has been like over the years. Then I'll tell you a bit about me and what I do so that you can get to know me.

I want to make it clear that you have not committed yourselves to therapy by coming here tonight. There will be a thorough evaluation period before any of us have to decide whether or not we would like to work together. Tonight's interview is part one of that evaluation. After tonight I will give you some forms to fill out which will give me a great deal of information about the difficulties that you're having. After you have finished those and returned them to me, I will see you again. During that second visit I will evaluate your communication by having you talk to each other about some of the problems you've reported.[3]

In this approach a commitment to work together with the counselor has not yet been made. Couples who come to a pastor for counseling may already be committed to working with him.

Another way to begin the first session is to explain the counseling process. For example, "I'm glad that we have this opportunity to get together. I appreciate your concern about your marital relationship, which has led you to come in. As we work together, we will be looking at, evaluating, and then developing plans to build your relationship."

If you have not previously met this couple or don't know them well, share with them information about yourself such as training, time in the ministry, family, and anything that will help them get to know you as a person and relieve some of their anxiety. Then ask, "Have you ever been for counseling before?" If they have, ask for information concerning where they went, when, for how long, what their experience was or the outcome, and the reason for going.

If they never have been for counseling before, you could share the following: "When a person or couple seeks counseling for the first time, they naturally have some questions and concerns about what is going to occur. Let me tell you something about what we will be doing. I would like to know what your perception of your marriage is at the present time, and I will be asking you some questions concerning the development of the marriage to the present time."

"I would like you to be as open and honest as you can in these sessions together. If you have fear, anger, worry, or any other feeling—whether it is directed toward the marriage, yourself, your spouse, me, or others—I encourage you to bring it out so we can discuss it together. If you have any questions during these sessions, feel free to ask them. At first we will meet each week for an hour (or whatever you are comfortable with for your sessions). Later we will work together every other week or every third week."

Many pastors and counselors like to establish a set number of sessions during the first visit. Often they ask the couple to commit themselves to four, six, or eight sessions. This gives both the pastor or counselor and the couple a goal to work toward and lets the couple know that they will be assured of a certain number of times together. It is important to share that at the end of the number of sessions the three of you will evaluate what has occurred and decide whether to set another number of sessions and continue counseling.

A third way to open the first session is to ask the question, "Why have you come for counseling?" Shirley Luthman, a professional counselor, conducted the following interview during the first session, which focused upon the couple's feelings and the way in which they interacted rather than the actual content of the interview. The emphasis was on how the couple was trying to make contact with each other and how they were handling their differences.

Therapist: What brought you to us?

Husband: Well, I am a weakling. I drink periodically. I don't come home when I say I'm going to. I don't always keep my word.

Wife: Oh, he is not as bad as he says. He is always overdoing things. The truth is . . .

Therapist: You are speaking for him.

Husband: She usually speaks for me. She is more articulate.

Therapist: I don't have any trouble understanding you.

Husband: Well, it is easier to let her talk for me.

Therapist: You don't look happy about it.

Wife: Well, really doctor, we are here because of our daughter who is taking drugs and we can't seem to control her.

Therapist: I appreciate your concern about your daughter, but I do not understand your changing the subject.

Husband: She often changes the subject in the middle of a conversation.

Therapist: Could you say that to her and let her know how you feel about that?

Husband to Wife: It makes me angry when you change the subject in the middle of a conversation.

Wife: Well, darling, I . . .

Therapist: You are interrupting. (To husband): You are letting her interrupt.

Husband: Let me finish. I can never keep my train of thought. You are always off somewhere else. Why don't you stick to one thing?

Wife: Well, I was concerned about our daughter because . . .

Therapist: There you go again.

Wife: What do you mean?

Therapist: Changing the subject. Could you respond to what your husband said to you?

Wife: What did you say, dear?

Husband: I said, why don't you stick to one thing?

Wife: Well, you know I always have so many things hanging over me, right?

Husband: Right.

Wife: Well, you never seem to be around when I need you, right?

Therapist: You just did it again.

Wife: What?

Therapist: You set him up. Do you notice what is happening? You constantly cut your husband off from expressing himself by talking for him, by presenting him with conclusions—'that is the way it is, isn't, dear?'—by interrupting him, by telling him he does not mean what he says, by defending yourself, and presenting your case instead of exploring his feelings. You (addressing husband) cooperate beautifully in this by withdrawing, agreeing, keeping your feelings to yourself. It is as though the two of you are operating like you have an agreement not to make any real contact. What are you afraid of?

Husband: (after long pause) I am afraid I could kill her.

Therapist: You are sitting on a lot of anger.

Husband: Yes, all my life.

Therapist: Then part of your anger that has never come out is connected to your wife, and part, perhaps, to your family before her?

Husband: Yes, I used to have temper tantrums when I was a young child . . . (discusses family's difficulty in expressing or accepting anger during his childhood).

Wife: I have felt this and I am very frightened of it— more that he would leave me if he got angry enough at me.

Therapist: I feel that both of you have many strong feelings that have never come out and that you are frightened of them. That is understandable. If you have never experienced expressing strong feeling in a constructive way, it seems overwhelming and catastrophic. However, the route to being in charge of your feeling is to let it out and find out it is not as overwhelming as you thought.

So, I would like to recommend that you come into a married couples group. The group makes it possible for you to begin to learn how to express your feelings with others who are not connected so deeply to you and such expression serves as a bridge to beginning to express to each other. Also, if the expression does get out of hand, which it sometimes does in the beginning because it has been building up for so long, there are enough people in the group so that we can exert controls from outside so you don't have to worry about hurting yourself or someone else.[4]

As you read through this brief account, perhaps you saw how much was accomplished during the first three to four minutes of the initial session. The therapist was directing the couple's attention to their typical style of interacting and helping them begin the process of change and freeing up the husband to express his hidden feelings. Some of the statements appear very confrontational, yet with a proper, soft, and supportive tone of voice, such statements will be accepted by the couple.

Several other important techniques are illustrated in this interview:

1. The counselor did not allow the wife to sidetrack the husband by interrupting and/or changing the subject.

2. The husband's responsibility in this game was openly shared for both to see.

3. The counselor quickly moved the couple into direct face-to-face communication and did not allow herself to be the vehicle of communication between them.

4. She also summarized what was occurring or being felt on two occasions. Note the skill of taking the husband's statement of being angry all of his life and clarifying it in such a way that his wife did not have to carry the feeling of responsibility for all of his anger.

Here are some other questions you could ask to open the

first session:

"What brings you here, and which of you was most concerned about coming?"

"Why did you choose to come for counseling at this time in your life?"

"Often when couples come for counseling they are experiencing dissatisfaction and pain. What is the pain and dissatisfaction you are experiencing in the relationship?"

"What do you want from your marriage and what will it take to get it there?"

"Let's think about the goals you have for counseling. What would it be like if the counseling were completely successful?" Then: "What is the worst possible thing that could happen to you in counseling? What do you fear most?"

As I said before, there is no one "right" way to open the initial session. You may have a structured plan that you want to follow yet find yourself changing it because of other needs that the couple presents. In developing your own way of opening the initial interview, you will find yourself combining approaches from time to time. This is why a pastor or counselor must be able to think on his feet, be insightful and sensitive, and rely upon the ministry of the Holy Spirit in his life.

As you open the first session, you must make sure the couple is aware of the extent and limits of privileged communication or confidentiality. You may explain it to them or handle the matter routinely by having them read and sign an "Intent or Duty to Warn" form prior to the first session.

This is an example of a form which many professional counselors use to inform clients of their procedure concerning confidentiality.

DUTY TO WARN:

Confidentiality and privileged communication remain rights of all clients of MFC counselors according to state law, however, some courts have held that if an individual intends to take harmful, dangerous, or criminal action against another human being, or against themselves, it is the counselor's duty to warn appropriate individuals of such intentions. Those warned may include a variety of persons such as:

1. The person or the family of the person who is likely to suffer the results of harmful behavior;
2. The family of the client who intends to harm himself or someone else;
3. Associates or friends of those threatened or making threats;
4. Law enforcement officials.

Before informing anyone who should be warned, the counselor will take all possible steps to first share that intention with the client. Every effort will be made to resolve the issue with the client so as to prevent any such breach of confidentiality.

_____

Counselor

I have read the above and understand the counselor's social reponsibility to make such decisions where necessary.

_____   _____

Date   By

Know what your church or denominational policy is on confidentiality as well as the laws of the state in which you minister. Your limits may vary depending upon whether you are a licensed counselor, ordained minister, or licensed minister. Your state laws may also require notification of law enforcement and/or public health agencies in situations where indications of suicide or child abuse are present.

An example of this is one of the laws of the State of California which pertains to ministers and necessitates breaking confidentiality. 11161.5: *Injuries by other than accidental means, sexual molestation or injuries to minor.*

In any case in which a minor is brought to a physician and surgeon, dentist, resident, intern, podiatrist, chiropractor, marriage, family or child counselor, psychologist, or religious practitioner for diagnosis, examination or treatment, or is under his charge or care...and it appears to said person from observation of the minor that the minor has physical injury or injuries which appear to have been inflicted upon him by other than accidental means by any person, that the minor has been sexually molested, or that any injury prohibited by the terms of Section 273a has been inflicted upon the minor, he shall report such fact by telephone and in writing within 36 hours, to both the local police authority having jurisdiction and to the juvenile probation department; or, in the alternative, either to the county welfare department, or to the county health department.

No matter what approach you use for the initial interview, it is important that you create warmth, concern, openness, and empathy at the onset of counseling and maintain it throughout the counseling process. A relaxed tone of voice, direct eye contact, and a comfortable body position will help the couple to relax and respond positively.

It is important also at the onset of counseling to create an attitude of hope and optimism in the couple concerning their relationship. At the same time, you must let them know that change and improvement is their responsibility and will require a concentrated effort, dedication, and a substantial amount of time on their part. They may be expecting you to wave a magic wand and cure them.

Often I say something like the following to a couple: "I appreciate your desire to do something about your marital relationship. From the information that you have already shared with me, I see a number of strengths and positive qualities in your marriage. You may not see it that way because of the hurts and frustration you are presently experiencing. I believe improvement is possible, but it will entail a time commitment and concentrated effort on your part.

"You have spent a number of years bringing your marriage to this state. Therefore, it will take time to relearn some new positive responses, and this relearning will be your responsibility. I will work with you as a guide and assist you, but I am not here to do your work for you or rescue you. I will be making observations and suggestions based upon the areas of your relationship you would like to change.

"It is also important for you to realize that as we take a microscopic look at your marriage and confront some issues head on, you may feel the relationship is getting worse rather than better. If so, don't despair, for this is a normal pattern. It means that we are bringing everything into the open so that the difficulties can be resolved. As you then begin to progress in your relationship, improvement is not a steady upward movement. You will find it going up and down, forward for a while and then perhaps backward a little.

"You may even experience a time when you are delighted with some positive changes in your relationship or you and your spouse assume you are on the path to

satisfaction. Then one of you messes up the next week and
you are shattered and discouraged and may feel like
throwing in the towel. Don't expect perfection from yourself or the other. We're all human. Positive change is a hard
struggle, but it's possible. When the upsets and problems
occur, don't focus on them like you have been doing.
Remember the times of progress. I want you to be aware of
this in advance so that you're not thrown if it occurs in this
way for you.

"It will also be important for each of you to exert the same
amount of effort and not rely upon the other to carry the
load. It is crucial that each of you complete the outside
projects or homework that we work out together as this will
accelerate the process of counseling.

"Do you have any questions at this time based upon what
I've just shared with you?"

During the intial interview and throughout the counseling
relationship, the couple will express various feelings. It is
important that you know how to reflect these feelings in a
positive manner so they don't hinder the progress of
counseling. Billie Ables suggested the following approach
for handling feelings:

It is important to acknowledge whatever feelings
spouses are expressing in their opening comments, be
they discouragement, helplessness, or whatever. Although one can recognize that the spouses have lost faith
in their own abilities to solve their problems, one can also
point out that since they have chosen to come, it is to
their advantage to use the time to see how they can work
together with the therapist to better their relationship.[5]

Dr. Ables had these further thoughts about beginning the
counseling process with a couple:

The therapist should not promise to take over but

should convey the willingness to use therapeutic skills to help the couple, stressing that all three will be working together. The stage is being set for the spouses to assume more responsibility in the therapy. The therapist is also trying to convey that help lies in the mutual work, not with the therapist. One should be careful to avoid making promises which may feed into omnipotent wishes. The therapist attempts to foster hope and provide encouragement, but the promise is not help *per se*, but help to aid the spouses to learn how to deal more effectively with their problems.

In a case where the couple say that they cannot talk to each other, one might respond that this probably means that they cannot agree when they do talk together and perhaps have given up trying. At any rate, the therapist should encourage them to begin talking together now.

The next common stage is that the couple will appear confused and say, "But we don't know where to start; there is so much." The therapist can agree that there must be much going on between them that cannot be quickly conveyed, and then suggest that they decide on something that is uppermost in their minds at the moment that is particularly troublesome in their relationship and that they can begin to talk about together. The therapist may add that in time it will be possible to talk more about the many things that are contributing to their dissatisfaction, but that it is necessary to start somewhere. Sorting out which are the most important issues to work on is part of the therapeutic task. The therapist hopes to give a couple the feeling that although it may all seem complicated and hopeless, "We will take our time and do what is necessary to see if we can get things going better."

It is preferable to let the couple decide what to begin talking about; a specific topic is rarely suggested. It makes little difference what material the couple choose to begin with; what is important is that they accept the responsibility for beginning and are free to begin with whatever problem they wish to focus on, however they may see it. If need be, it might be added, "You both have told me that things are not going well—maybe you can begin by each of you telling the other how you see the things that are going badly."

One of the most common errors by beginning couple therapists is the tendency for too little intervention in directing and structuring how the couple are to work. If one listens to tapes of beginning therapists, one usually hears the couple flooding each other with complaints while the therapist is left behind. It is the therapist's task to slow down the interchange and to help the couple focus on a particular issue. With experienced therapists, often half or even all of a session may center on one or two major issues.[6]

NOTES

All materials quoted are used by permission.

1. The **Marital Pre-Counseling Inventory**, published by Research Press, is now titled **Couple Pre-Counseling Inventory**. It is available through Christian Marriage Enrichment, 1913 East 17th Street, Suite 118, Santa Ana, CA 92701.

2. John Gottman, **Behavioral Interviewing with Couples** (film and accompanying guidebook) (Champaign, Illinois: Research Press, 1976).

3. Neil S. Jacobson and Gayla Margolin, **Marital Therapy** (New York: Brunner & Magel, 1979), p. 6.

4. Shirley Luthman, **Family Therapy: The Growth Model in Marital Therapy** (Family Therapy-The Journal of the Family: Therapy Institute of Marin) (Libra Publishers, 1972), pp. 63-83.

5. Billie S. Ables, **Therapy for Couples** (San Francisco: Jossey-Bass, 1977), p. 41.

6. Ibid., pp. 41-42.

Chapter 4

Focus On The Couple's Courtship

A Courtship Analysis

After the initial preliminary interchange, it is important to focus on the couple's courtship. It is during courtship that couples experience some of their most intimate and romantic feelings toward each other. This is the time when hopes, dreams, and expectations for marriage are most intense. Because most couples build their relationship on romance, they rarely articulate what they expect in a relationship. You need to help them discover what these expectations were during their courtship.

There are two reasons for reviewing the courtship. First, couples need to remember the intense feelings of love toward each other. Many couples begin counseling with questions of "Why did I marry him/her in the first place?" and "Did I ever really love him/her?" By reviewing their courtship, you can help establish hope for what can occur in the marriage now. Couples who were quite romantic during courtship may now feel led to exert more effort to commit themselves to redevelop their relationship.

Second, the couple needs to discover what each felt the other had intended to do in terms of responsibilities and behavior and what each had intended to give.

One therapist described his approach in focusing on the courtship period in this way:

I ask the couple, "When did you last touch one another affectionately?" A brief follow-up to this question brings out the current state of the couple's affections. Unless there is a clear indication not to, I ask the couple to hold hands and inquire how this makes each feel. The following dialogue is excerpted from a session with a couple who requested treatment for alleviation of conflicts over marital infidelity and abandonment:

Therapist: When was the last time you touched each other? Do you remember?

Wife: This morning . . . this morning we did.

Husband: This morning.

Therapist: Affectionately? Or just accidentally?

Wife: Affectionately.

Therapist: When did you hold hands last? (Both shrug their shoulders and look questioningly at each other.) Do you think you could do that now?

Wife: Sure (laughingly).

Husband: Sure.

Therapist: How does it feel to hold hands?

Wife: Okay, I guess.

Husband: Just fine.

First early impressions of character traits of the spouse-to-be are rather significant indicators of qualities important to the spouse who reports these traits.

Therapist: What did you think of Nancy (his wife) the first time you kissed her?

Husband: (Long pause) I saw her as someone who was full of life. . . just who was a very enjoyable person. . . just someone who I could relate to. . . attractive and vivacious and outgoing.

Another question that could be asked at this time is, "What attracted you to the other person?" In this question you are looking for positive responses, and often one or both may be resistant to the question. They are primed to give you the negative complaints about their spouse. One might begin by sharing a positive remembrance and then continue on by saying, "but he changed and . . ." This is the time to interrupt and reflect the positive statement. Husband: "I really enjoyed her company because she listened to me and was outgoing, but after . . ." Counselor: "At first you thought she was outgoing and attentive to you. What else did you like?"

The spouse-to-be often perceives in the other traits that may prove useful in complementing character traits of his own about which he does not feel comfortable. He expects assistance from the spouse in either developing qualities similar to hers or learning to deal with his own.

Therapist: How did this compare to your own personality at the time? Were you as active as Nancy. . . were you as full of life?

Husband: I think I was. I was a little more guarded. I sort of hold my feelings inside, which I am trying to get out because I've been looking back recently. . . I held back a lot of things which were bothering me. . . which popped out the last two months.

The husband is vaguely alluding to his implicit expectations of Nancy. The therapist would take note of this for exploration later on in the interview.

Therapist: How did you see Ernie (the husband) at that time at the fair? Do you remember?

Wife: Yeah, I remember that... I saw him as a real nice looking, sophisticated... he knew a lot more things than I knew... he had a lot more experiences than I.

Therapist: He was a lot more sophisticated and assured than you were?

Wife: Yes.

Therapist: This was something rather important to you?

Wife: Yes... ah... yeah, it was... he had, I felt, he had... a lot of strength of character... which I did not have at the time. (This issue was explored in some detail.)

Next, I ask the couple to close their eyes and fantasize about what their courtship was like. For partners who experience blocking in recalling these memories, I ask specifically about when they met, where they met, what the other was wearing, what the circumstances were, etc., whether there were any unusual circumstances in the situation, what their first impressions of the others were, and how the spouses-to-be resembled partners in earlier relationships. After the partners have had some time to get into their fantasy memories, I ask them to share the fantasy with me.

Therapist: Do you remember back when you were courting?

Husband: Yes.

Therapist: That was more than six years ago. (They had been married six years.)

Wife: Nine years ago!

Therapist: Nine years ago! It was a long courtship, was it?

Wife: Yes, it was.

Therapist: What was it like? Where did you meet each

other?

Husband: We had known each other for a long time. I guess the first time I saw her she had this sexy hat... at a party I think her sister was giving... and she smiled sort of warm and I saw her again at a dance in the country. I can remember the first time I kissed her. (The husband went on to describe this event in some detail.)

When asking questions like this, you are helping couples relive enjoyable experiences. Your goal at this point is to help them enjoy this interchange, which may be humorous, for people differ in what they remember. If the interchange is positive, the couple may feel better about the relationship and the beginning ray of hope may have started.

My next step is to inquire on what basis did each decide to marry the other. I follow up with the questions, "Who did each first tell about their decision?" and, "How did this person react?" I then ask about specific thoughts and feelings each spouse had about himself and his spouse-to-be at the moment he or she decided to marry the other. Specifically, what did each spouse hope would happen for himself as a result of being married to his partner? What would his spouse be like in 5 years? (Or whatever number of years the couple have been married at the time they are being seen in treatment.) What would each do for the other in fulfilling their marital life?

At this juncture, I ask for reactions and fantasies about what the marriage is actually like at the present time. This is the point at which many marital therapists begin their interview of the couple in distress. A major difficulty in beginning at this stage is that the content and the expression of material is extremely conflict-laden, confused, contradictory, and hostile. The therapist, there-fore, frequently finds himself either having to act as a referee to calm down the spouses in order to elicit relevant material or simply trying to weather it out. Starting with the courtship period—because it helps the spouses get in touch with many of the constructive, pleasant, and gratifying elements experienced in their re-lationship, or at the very least at positive things they had hoped for—creates a climate more conducive to con-structive marital treatment. Moreover, by the time the therapist asks the spouses to discuss their present situation, he has a wealth of clinically and socially relevant information to help the couple sort out their conflictual issues.

Finally, I ask the couple to synthesize what they have been reexperiencing and discussing in the interview(s) to determine what seems to be missing in the marriage.[1]

I often ask two additional questions as we finish reviewing their courtship: "What was the dream that you had for your marriage?" and, "What would it take on your part for your dream to become a reality now?" This leads into a time of plan-making and a commitment for positive change during the coming week.

Expand On The Couple's Responses

What you do and the direction you take from here will vary because of the different responses from each couple you counsel. You may want to expand on the responses of each spouse individually in order to understand how their marital problems developed over a period of time. A question like the following can be helpful: "Think back to when your marriage began having major difficulties. What happened to make you feel that way, and what did each of you do about it?"

Each person should be given the opportunity to respond to the question. You should look for similarities and/or differences in the evaluation, whether they dealt with the conflict or withdrew from it, and how successful their efforts were. Remember that each person will be reporting the situation as he/she remembers it, and the report may be subjectively distorted.

The following is an excerpt from the first session with a couple in their twenties who had been married for four years. No testing or evaluation forms had been completed prior to this session. As the excerpt begins, some of the preliminary interchange had occurred and the counselor is directing his attention to why they have come for counseling:

Counselor: I am sure there are some expectations that you have for what will transpire here. I am wondering if each of you could summarize what it is that you would like to see happen to you personally and for the relationship by us working together.

Jane: Well, the way that I imagine it is that you are going to be kind of like the middle man in helping us to communicate to each other and to develop that better, because sometimes we aren't too good at communicating with each other. I know I a lot of times assume he knows what I am thinking or what I want, and that's not always true. And it is the same the other way, too. So I feel like I want to learn what he is thinking, to let him know what I am thinking, and to learn maybe through all of this how to do that better, too.

Counselor: You started out by saying I *imagine* that this is what we are going to be doing. Is that another way of saying I hope this is what we are going to be working on?

Jane: Yeah, I guess that is more like what it is.

Counselor: Ken, I would like to hear what it is that you're perhaps hoping will occur as we work together.

Because Jane shared more than one thought as she spoke, the counselor wanted her to be more precise about what she wanted, not just for his sake but also for the sake of her husband.

The initial reasons for coming were shared by her husband, and then the courtship period was reviewed. As the couple finished describing their courtship, Jane began talking about how they had opposite characteristics. At this point the counselor chose to pursue this topic and allow it to lead into other areas. This exchange lasted for about fifteen to twenty minutes.

Counselor: Can you recall back to some of your thoughts or dreams at that time, as to how the relationship would be complementary if you were married?

Jane: I mostly thought I just didn't want to go through life with anybody else but Ken. I thought that he would add so much spice to my life, that I needed spicing up and I felt like my quietness was . . . I felt like there were a lot of opposites, and that we would complement each other with those opposites, and that we would come to a happy medium.

Note the strong expectations that were present at the onset of their marriage. She was looking for Ken to enrich her life and trusting that a balance would be attained.

Counselor: Did you enumerate all of those opposites ahead of the marriage so that you were both aware of them?

Jane: We did a lot of talking. Ken usually had to drag everything out of me because I did have a hard time expressing or even collecting my thoughts, to where I could say something or tell him all about it, because most of my reactions were mostly on feelings and not on definite thoughts. So we did a lot of talking, and I felt like mostly everything was talked about ahead of time.

Counselor: As we compare now to the way you were a few years ago, does Ken still need to drag things out of you? Does he still need to be the one to encourage you as much, or have you seen any kind of change?

Jane: I feel like I have come out a lot, and it has been a lot easier for me to talk with him. He doesn't need to drag as much out, but in other areas, well, he still has to drag a lot out of me; and I think that is what I meant that I don't say a lot of things, and I want him to talk with me about a lot of things, but yet we don't do a lot of talking now.

Here the counselor is looking for a continuation of this pattern within Jane. Jane is telling what she feels is occurring. During this time it is important to observe the husband's nonverbal responses. These responses may indicate agreement or disagreement with what Jane is saying.

Often individuals describe a situation or tendency at the onset of marriage but do not tell you whether it has changed.

Jane is still voicing a need here for more communication. At this time it is important to discover what topic areas Ken still needs to draw from her.

Counselor: I think what I would like for you to do at this point is to talk with Ken. Are you aware of the areas where Ken still needs to drag this out of you? Begin sharing those areas with Ken, what they are and if you can somehow put into words why it is so difficult for you to mention them on your own and why it is usually necessary for you to have Ken draw it out. (She turns toward Ken and begins to talk with him.)

As soon as possible couples should be guided to talk with each other in the session. The counselor's questions were quite specific and again were for the benefit of both Jane and Ken. Hopefully this will help to clarify the issue for them and for the counselor.

Jane: We can still do a lot of talking but not about, well, we do a lot of talking about everything. I don't like to talk about...I don't know where to start or what to say. I don't like to, I'm afraid of the tendency to become a, oh, a nag or referee. I am afraid to say or to complain about things ...usually he hears about when I complain about the house, or say at work, or something about myself or not so much about myself but things concerned or that I don't like to talk about because I don't want to hurt you and make you feel like I'm on your case, because I feel like you have enough people on your case at work and different places and so I don't like to say anything because I want to be on your side. I would probably be more on your side if things—I guess I could give constructive criticism. But I don't want to because I guess I feel that you don't need that the way I would do it. I feel that I don't know how to do it very well. (Her voice becomes continually softer and she begins to cry.)

Counselor: What are you feeling right now, Jane?

Jane: I don't know; I do this everytime I talk.

Counselor: We were aware of that ahead of time because we had talked about it. I'm wondering if there is a feeling that you are experiencing. It's hard to mention to Ken that there might be some things you would like to give him as constructive criticism. That is a big first step even to come out and say that.

Jane: Yes, that is hard to do.

Counselor: Are you concerned with how Ken will accept you? His reaction to it?

Jane: I am more concerned with what he will think of me. That he will feel like, oh you have got enough to take care of yourself without coming in on my case.

Counselor: Has this ever occurred?

Jane: More in my mind than probably actual.

Counselor: So, in reality this has not happened but it has sort of built up and maybe you have told yourself that "If I do this, if I say something to Ken, then he is not going to like me."

During this exchange the counselor was speaking in a soft, supportive voice, attempting to help her continue exploring her thoughts and feelings. Gently the questions proceeded to help her discover what she really thought and what had occurred. The last statement summarized what she had said so she could continue to explore her feelings.

Jane: Partly I think, too, I feel that it won't do any good if I say it. I would be blowing hot air and it wouldn't change anything, and he would be upset with me and nothing would have changed, so I might as well not say anything.

Counselor: Did you talk with Ken once again about this feeling that, if I tell you it is not going to make much difference?

Jane: Well, a lot of times when I feel like there is something I want to tell you that I don't like or that I would like to see changed or something, I'm hesistant to do so because I feel like it wouldn't do any good. That is not fair for me to say that because I need to give you the chance to at least tell me if you're going to do anything about it or not, but I feel bad that a lot of times that I don't like to say anything because I feel like I have enough—or thinking that you would think that I have so many things to change before I come to you, that I feel that I have a lot of things to change. So I shouldn't come to you and try to get you to change before I put an effort to try and change myself. It takes a lot of effort, and I am pretty stubborn. So I don't like to change and since I don't like to change, I feel like I shouldn't expect you to change. But yet I still get upset that I am not accepting of those things not getting changed. You know it's kind of a vicious circle.

Ken: I have some assumptions but I think the assumptions are all based on her past, and I am curious as to parts of a message I have maybe sent to her that would indicate that I am that way, because I don't feel like I am that way. I feel like I am the other way and it really, this portion is a surprise to me here, that she would be afraid to tell me because she is afraid I won't change. I know some of her past is influential there, but I don't want to put it all in the past. I want to know if there is something I've done.

Counselor: Okay, as we are talking about this, I am wondering what kind of a feeling you have when you hear that she may be thinking that "If he tells me then I won't change."

Ken: Perplexed, excited, because I wasn't sure whether or not she perceived anything that she would want to have changed, and it's really an enriching thing to hear that they are for me.

Counselor: When you started out earlier you say you couldn't imagine Jane being critical, and yet here we are where there are some things inside her that could be said. I am wondering if there is anything that you could say to Jane now that would sort of free her up a little bit and open the door for her to be willing to venture out and at least try to say some things that perhaps could be changed.

Ken has already indicated that he is open to these new expressions on the part of Jane. He is defending himself a bit in his statements, but the counselor's intent at this point is to proceed as though there is something Ken could do to assist Jane in sharing herself with him.

Ken: I can say some things that I think would encourage her, but I am not sure that they will encourage her.

Counselor: If you are uncertain, then what options do you have to find out what you really could do?

Ken: What would it take for me to be able to encourage you to share those things that you would like to see changed? I would really like to be able to encourage you to be able to do that. And I am not sure what would be the best way right now.

Jane: Well, I think that the biggest thing that stops me is—from my perspective—is that I have too much to change myself, and I express something that I want changed, you will make an effort to change; and so when I am upset about something I just won't keep it in necessarily because I let you know that I am upset, but yet I don't want to say anything because of my low self-esteem or something. I feel like I shouldn't be asking you to change when I have so much to change.

Ken: Is there some way that I can encourage that? To change that area?

Jane: Seems like encouragement on things that you appreciate a lot about me. Maybe if you could encourage me on the areas that you do like then that will give me the, make me feel good enough about myself to feel like going ahead and kind of trying to do better. I guess I need courage. I feel like there are some pretty broad things, some good things about me. I need to know. You do tell me small things but sometimes, I would like to hear a lot.

Counselor: I hear you saying, Jane, that this positive feedback you want from Ken is going to encourage you to do what? Change some of the other areas of your life? Or have the courage to say to Ken, "Here is what."

Jane: I think both, because when I feel like I am actively doing something to change something that I know that pleases him. Then I feel maybe I would have the right to say something to him. I would expect him to change.

Counselor: What if Ken were to tell you it isn't dependent upon you changing first?

Jane: I wouldn't believe him.

Counselor: It is almost like having to earn the right, that "I am not worthy enough to say anything to you because of all these defenses." Have you ever tried it the other way?

Jane: What other way?

Counselor: Sharing with Ken first without being so concerned about the various defenses as you call them in your life. What would happen if you tried that?

Jane: I can't remember if I have or not.

Counselor: I guess that is why I asked.

Jane: I'll be glad to do it.

Counselor: What would be the worst thing that could happen, Jane, if you were to go ahead and say, "Well, here is something, Ken, that really does concern me, and I would like to discuss it with you." What could happen that would be really detrimental?

Jane: Well, I guess about the worst thing is that he would say that I don't have the right to ask him to change. It was just what I was saying for him to give back a reason why I haven't. I don't want to hear that.

The counselor was trying to help Jane discover that she has little to fear from Ken. By working through her fears and helping her face them realistically, he was helping Jane to be able to open herself more in the communication process. Challenging assumptions about consequences is a technique that usually assists people in seeing that their fear is perhaps unrealistic and not likely to happen.

Counselor: You're really certain that that would occur?

Jane: No, but that is the worst thing that could happen.

Counselor: It could happen, but you really don't perceive Ken as being that type of a man?

Jane: No.

Counselor: What do you think he would say?

Jane: He would probably say I will do the best I could to change.

Counselor: How would you feel about that?

Jane: I would be glad that he was going to, but yet I would feel bad even asking him.

Counselor: So your feelings about yourself are really sort of blocking the building of more of a two-way communication pattern. I would also guess that a number of these things that you would like to share with Ken are not monumental or gigantic; they are just little things.

The summary statement here was directed toward helping Jane see how her feelings were blocking the communication process. In a tentative manner the magnitude of the problem was lessened as a means of encouraging Jane to reach out.

Jane: No, they are just dumb little things, and even right now if you were to ask me, what would you ask him to change, I couldn't come up with anything. Just little feelings that have built up, but it is nothing big, no big deal, just little things that come up that irritate me. I think that a lot of it is just my, oh, when I am displeased with myself and the progress I am making in self-improvement then I don't find fault. Then it is easier to get along with me and I get along with Ken easier and so much of it hinges on how I am doing on self-improvement and self-control.

Counselor: So again we come back to the issue that really what is going on with you is the real key to what is going to be shared. I am just wondering about what you said right now as compared with a few minutes ago. I think I heard you mention that if Ken would give you more positive statements and you felt better about yourself, then maybe you would have greater courage to reach out and say something to him about the constructive criticism. Yet right now you have mentioned that, well, when I feel better about myself then I am actually *less* critical.

Jane: Because my feelings make me feel like I am not so bad, and he shows me some good points about myself then that makes me feel more like, well, when he tells me good things about myself, then it is easier for me to see the good things when he tells me, and then that makes it seem like other things would be easier to conquer in myself, and then that would give me, when I feel like I'm not doing so bad, then it would make it easier to go to him.

Counselor: So it actually wouldn't work against you going to him. Here is somebody who is giving you positive statements and all of a sudden you have a feeling which is...

Jane: Well, that too. Yes, it could backfire. Here he is saying good things about me, and I wouldn't want to tell him anything bad when he has been saying good things to me.

Counselor: Right. That is what I was trying to see, if that wouldn't occur. It is almost as if you are caught in a bind. I do have these feelings and earlier it was almost indicated that you give part of the message maybe nonverbally. But verbally would really clarify it for him and allow him the freedom and the opportunity to go ahead and do something. Have you ever thought that if you were to share a suggestion with Ken in a positive way that it wouldn't be nagging? I wonder if you are associating every time you give a criticism it has got to be in a nagging, detrimental manner. What if you were to show your criticism in a positive way that, "Ken, I would appreciate it if you would do such and such" and point it out in that way. You're not forcing him to do it. It's still up to him to go ahead and respond. So you're not manipulating, not forcing.

This statement was designed to encourage Jane to be bolder and reach out and at the same time it showed her a new way of voicing a concern. New concepts such as this one are more likely to be accepted when the need is felt by the counselee.

Jane: That sounds good. A lot of times I feel like the request that I would have would be just out of selfishness or selfish motivation. Like I said, they are not biggies; they are no big deal. They are not any big problems, but just little things that I would like, but maybe that is not the best thing for him.

Counselor: What would happen if you would assist Ken or allow him to assist you in making the value judgment, whether or not it is something that he would like to change? It is almost like you have made up his mind for him in a sense. You are evaluating this as "selfish." Maybe Ken wouldn't.

Jane: I don't know what to say.

Counselor: That is all right. Ken, in these issues that Jane has brought up tonight, even though she keeps saying that they are little small things, do you think there is some importance attached to them?

Ken: Oh, yeah. The importance that I see to them is that I want to do what I can to help you, and I am hearing that these little things that you might point out to me if you could verbalize those, it might help you to feel more able to deal with you. I just want to encourage you to be selfish if that's what you would call it. The only person who has the right to be selfish in telling me or requesting from me is you, and you are the only person in the world who has that right, and I would like for you to exercise that. I promise I'll let you know when I have had enough. I would like to hear it.

Jane: I think that what I am afraid of, too, is that when you do, I do tell you something and you decide that that is

not what you would like to do. It is not a big thing and it is not
a life-changing decision but you would rather do it the way
you have done it and I am not accepting of that. I still want it
the other way.

Ken: I would like to hear when you are not accepting of
it. Because I don't always know when you are not accepting
of it. I don't know how big an issue is to you until you
magnify it for me to the size it feels like to you. What you say
are little things, my guess is that they are not little when you
feel them. They are little when you look at them in hindsight
or retrospect. But at the time they are big things to you.
When you do bring them up, maybe I take them too lightly.
Sometimes if you will help me see that they are important to
you and press that, and you have some clout that nobody
else has, you can say, look, I am your wife, and that will
rattle my cage real quick. I think you know that. I want you
to pull that rank once in a while. That is the relationship that
I want to have with you.

Counselor: I hear Ken saying two things. First of all I
hear a lot of perceptiveness on Ken's part and sensitivity
toward you. I hear some frustration on Ken's part like, "I
really would like to help or to change but it is almost like I
have go to be a mindreader" and then I heard him offer you a
gift of openness of "please tell me." Jane, I am wondering if
this week, you would be willing to try to share one concern.
We will call it a complaint. I am not always sure it's a
complaint, but I'm just wondering if we do need to relabel it. It is a constructive concern that you have for Ken.
Would you be willing to run that risk of doing it and see what
happens? (She nods yes.) I think you know we are going to
start small and maybe open some cracks in the wall because
you have some feelings, Ken has some feelings, and we will

sort of test the water by putting our foot in it. Just a little bit.

Jane: I'm scared of cold water.

Counselor: I wouldn't say it is so cold.

Ken: It is going to be cold no matter what temperature the water is.

Jane: Sure, that sounds good.

Counselor: It is maybe a small item, but maybe from your perspective and from the issue it's a big step, but I think you can accomplish it. Ken, as we close this evening, can you think of one behavior on your part that Jane has asked for from you that you could make it a point to perform toward her?

Ken: Yes.

Counselor: Do you want to say what it is?

Ken: I'm going to enjoy reinforcing the good qualities; that's something I love to do.

Counselor: She has a number of good qualities?

Ken: Yes, she does.

Counselor: Jane, how do you feel when Ken says that?

Jane: Oh, I like it.

Counselor: Do you believe him?

Jane: Yeah.

Counselor: Fine.

Jane: He makes me feel, he tells me what good qualities I have. He makes it a reality. He doesn't use a bunch of fancy words, but I feel that way when he tells me.

Counselor: You place a lot of stock in what he thinks and feels?

Jane: Yes.

At this time several details were handled and then the session concluded.

Most of the time was spent in encouraging Jane to drop some of her assumptions and protection and communicate her feelings and concerns to Ken. A commitment for positive change was also encouraged throughout, and Ken was asked for a verbal commitment to change during the coming week, which would reinforce Jane to continue to change.

Conclude The Interview

There are many ways to bring the first session of marital counseling to a close. Often you will find the couple themselves are aware of the time and will mention it. There will be other occasions when you might want to say, "I notice that we have just a few minutes left, and I am wondering if we can review what we have been talking about and what you will be doing the next week." On other occasions the sharing of feelings or even making plans for the next week will lend itself to a natural stopping point.

You may find individuals or couples who bring up very significant items right at the end of the counseling session or even as they are walking to the door. In this situation you could say, "I can see that this is important to you. Let's talk about that the first part of our next session."

The close of every session will vary, and again it is important for the minister or counselor to be sensitive to what is appropriate in each situation. Often just sharing with the couple that you will be praying specifically for them and their needs during the week can be very supportive. On a number of occasions you may find it fitting to conclude your session with prayer. Although prayer during a session should not be a rote habit or a way to mark counseling Christian, it is a very important part of the counseling process.

NOTES

All materials quoted are used by permission.

1.   Carl Goldberg, **Therapeutic Partnerships** (New York: Springer Publishing Co., 1977), pp. 145-150.

Chapter 5

Selecting An Approach

One decision to make is whether to work with a couple together for marital counseling, to see them separately for individual counseling, or both.

Four of the more common approaches to working with couples are the following:

Concurrent marital counseling or therapy. Each person is seen individually by a counselor. From time to time there will be sessions when the couple is seen together. Major problems involving marital issues are worked through at the same time.

Conjoint marital counseling. The couple is seen together by one or two counselors. This type of counseling has a higher rate of success when both individuals are motivated to work and both desired to come for help. Often within the context of this counseling, individual work will occur in the presence of the other partner.

Individual counseling or therapy. Each person is involved in counseling with either separate counselors or the same therapist. They do not meet together as a couple with the therapist. Sometimes during this approach the couple's relationship is dealt with but it is not the major concern.

Couples group counseling or therapy. This approach

involves several couples meeting together with one or more counselors. This is often used to diffuse a tension-filled relationship. A couple can learn from the others' comments and by observing how they interact.

Some of the indications for individual counseling could involve the following:

1.) When one partner needs to discuss any deviant behavior which is yet unknown to their spouse, seeing them alone is necessary. Confession, acknowledgement, and deciding which direction to turn may take considerable time.

2.) If one partner is totally weakened and shattered by the partner, or if his or her anxiety and tension level is so high that little productive work can occur, seeing the couple individually may help.

3.) If there is severe mental disturbance, a person is best seen individually. This type of case is generally not handled by a pastor, but is referred to a professional counselor. Making the referral in a session may be done with just the person present, or it may be best accomplished with the spouse present for support.

Some basic indicators can help a counselor to decide in favor of using the conjoint counseling method:

1. If you have been working with both husband and wife individually and you do not see any carryover or effect upon the marriage, you may find it more effective to see them together.

2. If the relationship is explosive and changes and agreements need to be made quickly, seeing both may be more efficient and productive at this time.

3. If there is a need to enhance communication, the decision-making process, or the sexual relationship,

working with the couple is easier and more productive in most cases.

4. If one individual is suspicious or somewhat paranoid, then meeting together will lessen the possibility of distortion, misrepresentation of what one or the other said, misinterpretation, or siding.

5. In order to help couples accept and adapt to their differences and see them in a complementary manner, working with the couple will be more effective.

Each pastor or counselor will have to make his own decision concerning the direction of their work with couples, but the ideal is for most couples to be seen together. When individual counseling is necessary, many times it can be handled in the presence of the spouse. In fact, you will often find yourself alternating between a focus upon the relationship and the personal as you work with most couples.

It may be helpful for the partner to observe how you relate to and communicate with their spouse. Often statements which you make toward the one partner also contains a message for the listening spouse as well.

Counselor: "Why don't you reach out to your husband again?"

Mary: "I can't. I've reached out to him so much and have been rejected so often that I'm torn up inside."

Counselor: "Why don't you reach out again? You seem to both want and need him."

Mary: "Oh, I'm just too discouraged and afraid of the same old reaction."

Counselor: "Reach out to him again. I think he knows how much you hurt and he will be more sensitive and accepting now."

Mary: "I just don't know..."

The counselor's last statement was for reassurance to her and more of a direct statement to her husband.

One couple I saw for six months included a very hostile, dominant, controlling wife who was adept at elevating her husband's guilt level and diminishing his self-esteem. She manipulated and degraded her husband. Her scores on the Taylor-Johnson Temperament Analysis included low scores in nervous, depression, sympathetic, objective. She had high scores in active social, expressive responsive, hostile, dominant, and self-discipline.

Her husband had a very low self-concept, characterized by anger and receptivity to manipulation. All but one of his scores on the TJTA were in the white area which indicates improvement urgent. The crisscross TJTA which his wife took upon him as she saw him had an attitude score of 0, which indicated an excessively low opinion of him. In fact, she saw him as a zero and treated him likewise.

For the initial two months of counseling the majority of each session was spent in direct confrontation with the wife. The purpose was to expose some of her own insecurity and need for control and to work with her to take her strengths and use them in a constructive manner with her husband. He observed another person responding to his wife in a new and different manner, which served as a model for him. Soon she began to respond in more of a supportive manner to her husband, and then most of the time in counseling was directed toward him. Here the focus was upon his self-concept, submissiveness, anger, and his tendency to allow himself to be manipulated. The wife observed a new way of response to her husband and through quiet listening, heard for the first time about his inner struggles and hurt. She could then respond to them in a more positive manner. As time went on, more attention was given to their marital relationship.

The following verbatim is an example of focusing upon an individual problem as it reflects upon the marriage. Often in a single session there is a shifting back and forth between the couple and the individual, with an emphasis on the intertwining of their own personal difficulties. The responses of one partner can either help to free the spouse, or they can intensify the spouse's insecurities.

NOTICE THE FOLLOWING:

1. The counselor reinforced Liz in feeling good about what she accomplished.

2. The counselor asked her to clarify her thoughts and her sense of responsibility for others' emotions.

3. He pointed out how her "shoulds" need to be re-evaluated and how she limits herself.

4. When Jim began to share his inner feelings for the first time this was reinforced and encouraged by the counselor.

Liz: Well, I think it is a step in the right direction. I felt like it was the right thing *I* needed to do to bridge a communication gap. We had kind of a silent period there for awhile. Well, we need to talk about it but I don't want to say well, "why didn't you do this or that" but to start it out with, "well, what can I do different," like you were saying. And so I feel like I'm going in the right direction. I should have followed through and maybe next time that thought comes to me I could go ahead and follow through even though it feels awkward.

Counselor: The feeling awkward is normal. It is like you give yourself permission to feel awkward. That is all right. I want to point out the fact that you have that thought on your own. Which means . . .

Liz: That was exciting.

Counselor: It goes back to this same thought that I have had time and time again. You don't give yourself credit for what is going on inside of you. You have got much more capability than is coming out. I would really like to encourage you to overcome that intimidation. Blurt it out!

Liz: That happens a lot where I will think of words or phrases or something I want to say, and I think, "oh, that will be too corny," but it is what I am thinking and a lot of times I don't because I think it will just sound awkward.

Counselor: Who is judging you? (softly)

Liz: Me.

Counselor: You are a harsh judge?

Liz: Yes.

Counselor: But Jim is not judging the way in which you say it?

Liz: No.

Counselor: So you don't have to worry about outside interference. It is you. Let's talk about Jim's anger. On some of these issues where Jim says he has anger, how do you feel about him having anger over them in the first place?

Liz: Curiosity. I wonder why or what the anger is about. I wonder what I have done to him to contribute to that anger.

Counselor: Your statement "what I have done" . . .

Liz: I always feel like there is something I have done . . .

Counselor: Like the bad little girl.

(Pause)

So you are taking away Jim's responsibility for his anger and you are saying, "I am the one responsible for Jim's anger.

Liz: Yes, a lot of times I guess.

Counselor: You guess...

Liz: I am trying to think of instances where he has been angry and I can't think of any.

Counselor: But I hear that uncertainty that Liz is really responsible for the anger.

Liz: Yes. Like I need to be doing something different. If I did it different then he wouldn't be angry.

Counselor: Well, let's say that you purposely did something offensive to Jim. When couples are married they know how to push each other's button, and so you purposely really pushed him. Who is responsible for Jim's anger?

Liz? Oh, in that instance I would be, I would think. If I did it on purpose.

Counselor: But are you really responsible? In other words, *must* he get angry because you did that?

Liz: No, I guess not, not necessarily.

Counselor: So Jim has a choice at how he is to respond.

Liz: I would really be pushing him though, boy.

Counselor: Well, whether you did it on purpose or inadvertently, Jim is still responsible for his anger. You can be the worst person all day long, and it is still his responsibility how he responds. Earlier Jim mentioned that he made a very cognitive logical choice not to come out with the anger and frustration. That cognitive choice goes back even further, where we can have something occur, and even though that reflex action is the initial anger, we can either feed it or we can begin to talk ourselves out of it.

Liz: Yes, that is true.

Counselor: So who is responsible?

Liz: Well, when you put it that way, he is. If he can make a choice. But the responsibility...

Counselor: It took you about four seconds. I could see the word "but" forming on your lips.

Liz: But it still seems like I would be responsible, because I had done something especially on purpose!

Counselor: Take away the "on purpose," because I am sure that is not what we are talking about. Some things just happen.

Liz: Well, I should know better.

Counselor: See, when you put it like that...

Liz: It sounds good when you say that...

Counselor: You say that, "I should know better." I am wondering somehow if that doesn't cripple you from doing some things better. It is like you have something hanging over your head. Instead of wanting to do this better myself, I *must* do it. Otherwise it makes Jim angry. You don't allow yourself the freedom to grow. It is almost a growing out of fear, or "I *must*, to please him."

Liz: Yes. I do because I feel like that is what I should do, not because I wouldn't want to necessarily.

Counselor: Do you ever identify those shoulds? List them?

Liz: No, not really. Not specifically.

Counselor: With all your lists, it might be another one. As we look at our lives and we find these "shoulds," maybe we need to question "where did I get this? Where did this 'should' come from? Is it some sort of parent inside of me, something that I have incorporated from others, or is this something that I have come up with myself?" It is like any time that there is a "should," perhaps it needs to be challenged to put it in a proper perspective...

Liz: That sounds like a good idea.

Counselor: And begin to evaluate it. Can you do that on your own?

Liz: Evaluate it? I can list them. I am not sure if I can evaluate them.

Counselor: What would keep you from evaluating them?

Liz: Just a mental block, thinking I should because that is the way that it is supposed to be.

Counselor: I have got a hunch, and I would like to throw it out to you. I think that one of the ways that you could possibly be crippling yourself is by statements, "Well I have a mental block", "I don't think I could do it" and you say that to yourself. You sort of put yourself into a bind, and maybe if we didn't make that statement and we had another statement like, "Gee, that is nothing I have ever done before, but I think I could give it a try." If you wouldn't begin to loosen up some of that creative potential that all of us know is there but somehow blocked.

Liz: Yes. I could always try.

Counselor: Not a lot of failure in trying.

Liz: Usually I will score at least one point.

Counselor: And that is what we focus on. Not the other nine. It is the one point.

Liz: One point always feels good.

Counselor: I would like to throw another concept at you, Liz. Usually when we talk about anger, we talk about it as a sort of a symptom, the end result of something else. In fact, a lot of anger is not really the true emotion. In most cases we can either find that that anger has come about because of fear, hurt or frustration. Liz, you have been married to Jim for how long?

Liz: Four and one half years.

Counselor: During that four and a half years you have come to know him pretty well. What do you think most of Jim's anger stems from, of the three that I have mentioned?

Liz: Fear, Frustration, and Hurt. Oh, probably frustration.

Counselor: How does frustration occur? Are you aware of the reasons?

Liz: Sometimes.

Counselor: Often people are frustrated because they have expectations or needs that aren't being met. But if frustration is really the main cause, it is one of the easiest ones to counter, because things can go wrong or occur differently than we plan on. But you don't have to become frustrated. It is . . .

Liz: It is one of those choices.

Counselor: It is a very definite choice. There is less reflex or instinctive response to the frustration than maybe to the fear or to the hurt. It is one of the most rational components that can be dealt with. In fact, the book **Overcoming**

Frustration and Anger by Paul Haulk is the book that goes into this with great detail. A very, very helpful book from what they call the rational emotive approach. That would be a helpful book to recommend to Jim to read sometime.

Liz: I have experienced that just in the last three weeks or so in making a choice not just to get frustrated because I allow myself a lot of times to get frustrated and that—not talking about Jim now but myself in different things, I see where it really is a choice and not something that I just got to be that way. And when something happens, I automatically get frustrated, and "isn't life terrible," but I can really make a choice not to be frustrated. Sure makes the day go a lot nicer.

Counselor: In doing that did you find that you were burying or denying your anger?

Liz: In doing what, in not getting frustrated? No. It just eliminated a lot of anger. I just didn't cause it to even be there.

Counselor: Is Jim capable of doing that?

Liz: Oh, yes.

Counselor: So actually we come back to the issue that Jim can choose a lot of his emotional responses.

Liz: Oh, I am sure that he does that now.

Counselor: How then do you feel about yourself in light of that?

Liz: It still seems like if I . . . I don't know. If I am the cause of a lot of that frustration, he—even though he has a choice not to get frustrated—I don't know. It still seems like that I should change or something.

Counselor: What would it be like, Liz, if you saw yourself

as a person where "I am not the cause of his frustration or anger. I am free from that. That is not my responsibility." And you didn't have that weight?

Liz: That would be nice.

Counselor: How would that make you different?

Liz: It seems like it would . . . I would be freer to make whatever choices I wanted to make, instead of the fear of my choice might not be what Jim necessarily wants. It seems like I would have a lot more freedom . . . Mostly that.

Counselor: In having freedom you would be more verbal, more outgoing, or what?

Liz: Yes, probably both of those.

Counselor: Could you feel as secure being that way as you do at the present time, with this belief that you are responsible for Jim's anger?

Liz: A different kind of security. Like right now my security lies in Jim's approval, but if I had my own approval maybe that would be a security that is different, but there.

Counselor: Interesting that you put it that way. Maybe that would be even a greater security, and then Jim's approval would be like the icing on a cake.

Liz: Yes.

Counselor: Can you tell me your feelings?

Liz: Well, it was just a good thought. I need to give myself approval. It seems like it should be an easy thing, but it is not. You are right, that would be the icing on the cake if that security that I depend on now could be so much better if I would use that as the icing and not the basic part.

Counselor: Did you hear your phrase a minute ago?

(Pause) "It should be easy but it is not." I guess I wonder why should it be easy if we never had that experience that much. What would it do if you could say "It is difficult, it is hard but I can certainly learn how to do it. I have got that capability."

Liz: Yes. I could do it. But it would be hard.

Counselor: Maybe I would like to see that reversed. "It would be hard, but I *could* do it." Otherwise you are ending up with "but it could be hard" . . . that defeats you. Even that switching will make a difference. What can you do with yourself to give greater confidence in you? I didn't say what I could do or Jim could do, it is what can you do?

Liz: I am not sure other than . . . just making decisions and going ahead with it and not doing it because I would think well, maybe someone else wouldn't approve, but to see more validity in my opinion and to do what I want to do, just to trust myself more. But other than that I don't know . . . it seems like the main thing to trust my decisions and go with it.

Counselor: Jim, what did you learn about yourself this evening?

Jim: That I am not satisfied with me, where I am at and the things that I am feeling. I am not satisfied with our relationship. It is ok not to be satisfied at this point. I learned . . . or I am learning that I don't know Liz all that well, and that is pretty sad for me. Just listening and trying to figure out what I can do to make it different, and then having to stop myself and recognize that I am not going to do anything different yet. I am just going to wait and not try to fix it, because I am not convinced that it is broken. A lot of things about me, and that I am still very frustrated with our relationship. How can I walk by faith with confidence that what appears to me right now to be something that I could regret our maybe doing this at all—that I can walk with the confidence that I don't have to run, that I don't have to regret it, that even regret's a choice and that I have always believed you're only beat when you say you are beaten. Again I get the opportunity to exercise that choice not to be beaten. The rebel in me won't admit defeat, and a lot of things as I was listening. A lot of things. (Pause) I don't know what I will do with them all. Sometimes they are very discouraging. Sometimes I wonder where we will be at in five more years down the road, and I recognize quickly that speculating when I am not feeling real good about our relationship produces in me a sense of not wanting the relationship. It is self-defeating. I really work out of specula-tion for the future when I am not feeling real good about my relationship with Liz.

Because I feel like Satan really operates real hard to convince me that, "see it is not all that great," and I don't believe that. What I believe and what I feel conflict, and a lot of times that is what causes the tears. Conflict. But I am winning the fight.

Counselor: I really appreciate your letting us see the tender side of Jim tonight. I don't think that it is a broken relationship. All relationships need growth and nurture and attention. I don't think that it *is* a matter of fixing it. I think tonight you focused on both of you focusing upon yourself and growing, developing. I think that is essentially where the emphasis needs to be placed, that as each of you grow and develop that it is going to feed the relationship even more. There have been some adaptive patterns that have devel-oped, and there has been a security in that. We are sort of tearing those away and gradually building.

Jim: I am feeling . . . I was just thinking today that I am not going to wait any more to grow. Buying into a maladaptive pattern that I have got to wait for Liz to grow and I am not going to wait any more and I am going to go ahead and grow with the belief that the growth in me will be good for our relationship. I had a friend who had me concerned because they were talking about my losing our relationship because if Liz didn't keep up in growth I was just going to out-distance her. Of course it took me by surprise, and I was sitting here when you said that statement, the growth will be productive for the relationship. The only way that I can grow out of a relationship is if I point my growth away from the relationship rather than point my growth back into it. That is not my goal, so I can only grow into the relationship, not out of it. I don't have to believe what this person says.

Counselor: I also think Liz could grow even faster.

Jim: I believe that but I have been waiting for her to get the belief going, thinking I am not just going to wait anymore. She will catch up. She *will probably* pass me.

Counselor: That is good to hear you say that.

Jim: That would be nice.

Counselor: Liz is beginning to catch that belief. There is a lot of potential for growth, and she is beginning to believe it a little more, I think. I think she needs to hear your affirmation.

Jim: About her ability to grow.

Counselor: Even more. Not that you have to talk her into it, but just the statement. Liz, you are going to be the one in charge of your life, talking yourself into it. Two things that I want to mention, Jim. The book that I mentioned to Liz about overcoming frustration by Paul Haulk. I would really like to encourage you to get into that. If you can't find it call me and I will send a copy. Secondly, I would like the two of you to take some time and talk about what some of the phrases are that we can begin to develop to decrease our anger and increase our productivity. When we begin to feel the anger, the coming of the frustration or the intimidation, what can we say to lessen its occurrence. I think that will keep you moving ahead instead of retreating.

The session concluded a few moments after this.

Chapter 6

An Apologetic For
The Positive Behavioral Emphasis in
Marital Counseling

When couples come for counseling, the focus is upon two aspects of their life: behavior and thoughts. These two aspects are the areas of emphasis in the model of marital counseling presented in this book. This model does not deny the existence or validity of feelings; it simply does not focus directly on feelings as the source of marital conflict.

Despite this emphasis upon behavior, feelings cannot be ignored entirely. There is a need for their expression throughout the entire counseling period. If, in fact, you are working with a person who is very cognitive-oriented and does not respond to his own or others' feelings, it is necessary to give a greater concentration to feelings and emotions during the counseling. Dr. Billie Ables described the use of feelings in this way:

> The therapist must not challenge feelings; rather, they are important data to be given attention. Nor can they be readily legislated. Respecting this principle is important for both spouses, who hope to change not just behaviors but also feelings. Behaviors are easier to change than feelings. This does not preclude acknowledging that

given behaviors may in fact stem from certain feelings and often do cause difficulties with the spouse. Once the importance of respect for each spouse's feelings has been emphasized, there is a greater chance for the triad to focus on troublesome behaviors without the judgmental implications that cause difficulty. Spouses will then be less defensive and be able to address behaviors that they feel they can and should change.[1]

It is difficult to formulate criteria by which to determine whether to focus first on behavior or on thoughts in a particular counseling situation. I have found, however, that immediate change in the marital relationship is often necessary, and that behavior is easier to change than thoughts. Behavior is voluntary and can be changed at will by the individual. Thoughts, although the initiators of behavior, often are involuntary, automatic, or very highly refined and are not therefore as easily controlled as behavior.

Behavior changes can, however, be the catalyst for thought changes. A change in one's behavior can affect not only his own thoughts and feelings, but those of his spouse, too. A change of behavior can be recognized; a change in thoughts cannot be known except as manifested through behavior.

Therefore, much of our approach can be summarized as follows:

1. A person or couple is encouraged to change their behaviors regardless of their attitude and feelings.

2. Changed behaviors should involve an increase of positive behaviors.

3. A change in attitude or thought needs to occur early, in the sense of accepting the belief that a change in behaviors will effect a change in feelings.

4. Behavior is easier to change because it is voluntary. Often thoughts are automatic, although many behaviors do stem from purposeful contemplations and chosen thought.

5. It is important to focus upon one's thought life (or what is sometimes called "selftalk") while one is making a change in behavior.

6. It is difficult to determine a criteria that would clarify whether one should start with thoughts or behavior. Discussions with the couple will therefore often be a combination of discussing behaviors, thoughts and feelings.

Whenever possible, change or solutions should occur on the part of both individuals. People who are not alone in having to do all the work are more willing to change. When two are involved, each benefits from the other's feedback and assistance. Also, each person's participation can be a positive reinforcement for the positive changes which the other person is attempting. Each person's behavior is directly related to the other's, and mutual change has a greater opportunity to become permanent.

Positive Emphasis

As you talk with distressed couples you will soon discover that loving behaviors between them are probably limited or noncreative. They have been the same which have been emitted for years. And even though outsiders would see these activities in a positive light, their value for the couple has diminished and lost its potency. New and creative responses must be discovered and deployed.

This initial emphasis in the first session has been described as a doorway for the entire change process. Jacobson and Margolin describe it like this:

One of the primary functions of accelerating the rate at which spouses exchange positive behaviors is to maneuver the couple into a position of readiness for more demanding changes. Upon entering therapy, spouses often feel deprived by the partner of gratification, depleted in their reservoirs of relationship energy, and unappreciated for the efforts they do expend. Before these spouses are ready to negotiate and resolve major issues, they must first be convinced that the relationship is worth their additional efforts and they, in fact, can be on the receiving end of relationship benefits. This initial intervention is designed to provide spouses with an immediate "shot in the arm" of marital pleasures to revitalize their debilitated stores of relationship energy. If successful, this intervention makes spouses aware of the inherent worth of their relationship and encourages them to persevere through the remainder of therapy.[2]

Therefore, our first stress in counseling will be to identify and emphasize positive behaviors which will build the marital relationship. Little attention is given to the problem behaviors in the early stages. Instead, it will be important to discover three factors within the relationship:

1.   Existing strengths and positive responses.

2.   Positive behaviors which the couple would like to have increased.

3.   Areas of agreement between the couple.

Some couples may be both surprised and resistant when the negative areas are deemphasized. Some of their responses might include hesitancy, caution, and even relief. Comments and reactions of this time might include:

"This isn't what I thought we would talk about."

"How will this help? It's his drinking and running around

that's the problem."

"I guess what you've suggested sounds a bit risky to me. What if I cooperate and do this and there is no response from him?"

Risk is involved. For some couples this focus upon positive rather than negative could be experienced as threat because most couples come to marital counseling expecting to talk about the problems, irritating behaviors, or negative attitudes of the other person. Yet some of the conflicts the couple is experiencing may loom out of proportion and consume all available energy.

If the couple is allowed control of the direction of counseling and moves the pastor or counselor into a position of dwelling upon negatives, progress is hindered. In many cases marital difficulties can even be perpetuated by this concentration, and positive changes delayed. Consequently, the couple is asked to identify positive qualities within their marriage. This provides them with a firm foundation upon which they can build their relationship, and at the same time it develops a more realistic perspective.

Reactions to the Positive Behavioral Approach

There will be counselors who will disagree with the positive behavioral approach. Some feel it is difficult to build positive behaviors and a healthier relationship while the negative behaviors are alive and well. Often both behaviors do exist side by side, and most individuals and couples know what is right to do. Yet they do not always follow through. Paul spoke about this in Romans 7:15: "For I do not understand my own actions—I am baffled, bewildered. I do not practice or accomplish what I wish, but I do the very thing that I loathe (which my moral instinct condemns)." (Amplified).

The traditional assumption underlying an immediate focus upon negative behaviors is that when negative behaviors decrease, other positive behaviors increase. But this relationship is not automatic. The elimination of the marital problems is not the only goal of counseling (although it is one main objective). Increasing the satisfaction level in the marriage is a more important objective. The potential for rapid immediate recovery is greater with the approach recommended here.[3]

Research has given indication that an emphasis upon the positive has an effect of diminishing negative without direct attention being directed toward them.[4]

Some couples will also resist the positive behavioral approach. Somewhere along the way they have developed the belief that "insight"—or understanding the historical beginning of their problem—must occur before behavioral change can happen. This concept is theory and not necessarily fact. Insight is not an absolute must. Nor does it help the emphasis of direct attention upon future positive changes.

It is also important to realize that some couples may want to concentrate upon the past in order to avoid a direct confrontation of present problems. Detailed information about the present problems, not an historical search of the past, is what is needed.

Another resistance which may occur concerns the area of responsibility. It is true that each individual is responsible for his own emotions or feelings, but there are those who refuse to take any responsibility for behaviors which bother their spouse.

One example of this would be the husband who daily returns from work and piles his briefcase and other paraphenalia in the middle of the dining room table just as his wife is setting it for supper. He sees her frustration as "her problem," and leaves it to her to solve in whatever way she can.

Or perhaps the husband came from an alcoholic home and is upset by the wife's use of alcohol. She refuses to control her drinking, even though it disturbs her husband, on the grounds that it's his responsibility to learn to cope. In both cases the resistant partner projects the problem back to his/her spouse, using the projection as an excuse for refusing to make necessary changes.

Another criticism heard frequently is, "the only reason my spouse is changing is because you've suggested it and not because he feels anything or wants to. I want him to sincerely desire to make these changes. They've got to be genuine." Sincere and genuine desire will come through changing behavior which then reinforces more positive thoughts.

It is important then in working with the couple to encourage them to behave in a positive manner. Many therapists and counselors have suggested this for years. Probably all who have done so have heard the same criticism, which is; "to encourage an individual or a couple to behave in a way that is not in harmony with their feelings is a deceptive and manipulative approach." This is a false criticism. The motivation for a positive approach is based upon the belief that behavior *is* an antecedent of attitudinal and emotional change.

As with all theories and approaches to counseling, there will be exceptions and changes to the approach described here. Numerous couples come with immediate problems that will take precedent. Some have financial questions and decisions which must be made within ten days. An impending job change, to return to school or not, a step child in a second marriage coming for a visit in three days are typical. More serious matters such as spousal abuse, incest, suicidal threats or attempts, emotional disturbance will need immediate attention. Wisdom and discernment on the part of any person doing counseling is a necessary quality. Blind adherence to any one model of counseling with no creative variations can be detrimental.

Nevertheless, to bring about positive changes in the relationship, the easiest place to begin is with behavior. Acting out positive behaviors tends to provide sufficient reinforcement for the couple to continue to exhibit additional positive behaviors. This, in turn, builds a more positive attitude. Merely hearing that this approach can raise the level of marital satisfaction usually produces a willingness to move ahead. Such willingness either stems from belief that a behavioral change produces attitudinal and/or emotional change, or it is a step taken on faith.

Specific Plans for Increasing Positive Behavior

Much of the pastor's or counselor's effort is directed toward making plans, with the couple, to increase positive behaviors. Whatever is decided upon, significant attention must be given to developing specific plans sufficiently so there is little chance of failure.

There are several approaches which can be implemented for these purposes.

Richard Stuart, who developed the Marital Pre-Counseling Inventory, uses a concept which he calls *caring days.* He describes it as follows:

In introducing the caring-days procedure, it is important for the therapist to do three things. First, it is essential to recognize that the couple faces conflicts that must eventually be resolved. As enumerated in Scale H of the Marital Pre-counseling Inventory (Stuart & Stuart, 1973), the therapist should mention the challenges but should point out that change must be undertaken as an orderly process, and that the first step in the process must be the development of the request and acknowledgment skills and the simple behavior exchanges about to be described. Second, it is essential for the therapist to stress that the initiation of the change process depends upon the willingness of both spouses to make investments in relationship enhancement independently of the other. Each must act "as if" she or he cared for the other (see Chapter 2) if true caring is ever to be experienced. Generally, the spouse who has the most to lose if the relationship does not improve will be the one who is most willing to be committed to this change effort. It is therefore wise for the therapist to concentrate efforts on the other partner, who should be encouraged to view the caring-days process as a low-cost method of assessing the feasibility of relationship change. Treatment cannot proceed beyond this point without the concurrence of both spouses, but fortunately, factors such as the "halo" effect in the first session and the reasonableness of the request will lead to at least hesistant agreement by both partners for the one or two weeks needed for the couple to net some of the gains expected from this technique. Finally, it is essential for the therapist to use the word "caring" and not "love." "Caring" is a very positive word that does not have the complex mythical associations of "love." Couples are usually more willing to commit themselves to act as if they care for each other than to act as if they love one another. Love may or may not be the end point of treatment, but it can never be its start. Thus, delay of confrontation of conflict, adoption of an as-if-strategy, and pursuit of caring and tenderness rather than love are a trio of antecedents, the absence of which is very likely to undermine any hope of success through the caring-days technique.

In caring days each spouse is asked to answer the question: Exactly what would you like your partner to do as a means of showing that he or she cares for you? Answers to the question are written in the center column of a sheet of paper specially ruled for that purpose. To be entered on the list, the behaviors should meet the following criteria:

1. They must be positive.
2. They must be specific.
3. They must be "small" behaviors that can be emitted at least once daily.
4. They must not have been the subject of recent sharp conflict.

A positive request aims for an increase in constructive behaviors, not a decrease in unwanted responses. "Please ask me how I spent my day" is a positive request that should be used in place of the negative request "Don't ignore me so much." A specific request is one that can be very easily understood. "Come home at 6 P.M. for dinner" is a specific request that might replace the vague "Show more consideration for the family." Small, potentially high-rate responses are needed at this stage of treatment if partners are to enjoy the immediate changes that they need in order to gain confidence in the treatment process. "Please line the children's bikes along the back wall of the garage when you come home" is a much more manageable request than "Please train the children to keep their bikes in the proper places." It is important to include relatively conflict-free requests on the caring-days list because neither spouse is likely to concede major points at this stage of treatment, that is, before both have made a durable commitment to maintaining their relationship. Conflict affords some immediate reinforcement in two forms: many enjoy the catharsis inherent in the expression of anger, and conflict sometimes succeeds in coercing immediate, if short-lived, change in the other's behavior. Neither partner is likely to forego these gains before developing trust in the longer life of their relationship, a time during which they can expect longer-range reciprocation of the positives that they invest. Therefore, if the couple have been having arguments over when to turn off the television set and go to bed—one wishing to watch the late show through to the end, while the other wishes to retire much earlier—this would not be an acceptable item to include on the list.

It is typical for the clients to begin by making requests that are negative, vague, large, and conflict-embedded. It is the responsibility of the therapist to model desirable request lists, perhaps by showing clients acceptable models. It is also appropriate for the therapist to coach the partners' facilitative responses and to edit requests when writing them on the list. The couple should also be encouraged to add to the list during the week between sessions. The list should include *at least* 18 items for several important reasons. The items are contributed by both spouses, and some are of much greater significance to one spouse than to the other. Some of the items will seem much more relevant and feasible on some days as opposed to others. The actual opportunities to express caring and commitment are virtually limitless, and stimulating thinking about a range of these alternatives helps to overcome any stereotypical or monotonous tone in the daily exchange between spouses. Finally, interests shift over time, so keeping the list open-ended allows the list to keep pace with evolution in the partners' preferences. Coaching the couple to initially select 18 items and encouraging them to add several items to the list each week is an effective means of building a list with sufficient breadth and responsiveness.

When the list has been completed, each request should be discussed. The spouse making the request should state precisely what, when, and how he or she would like the other to respond. The spouse hearing the request should ask for clarification about any ambiguities during the treatment session. This process of making and clarifying requests prefigures the communication treatment that is the second stage of treatment.

Each spouse should be asked to make a commitment to emit *at least five of the behaviors on the caring-days list daily*. This number will provide frequent demonstrations of the couple's willingness to meet each other's expectations. Moreover, each should be asked to make these positive investments in improving their relationship *irrespective of whether or not the other has made similar gestures*. This condition is important because partners in distressed marriages tend to inhibit constructive interaction through their reliance upon what might be termed the "change-second principle." According to this principle, each decides that he or she will act positively only *after* the other has offered a positive. However, as each awaits a positive commitment from the other before acting, neither ever takes the constructive steps that are needed to improve their relationship. Therefore, the caring-days procedure asks each to abide by the "change-first principle," according to which each person is expected to change before the other, initiating that process of reciprocal change fundamental to the approach to relationship management based on social learning theory.

In addition to taking frequent, independent action, the spouses should also be encouraged to record on the sheet the date on which each has benefited from positive gestures by the other, the husband entering the date beside the behaviors emitted by the wife under the column headed "Husband," with the wife using the "Wife" column for the same purpose. These written records have several functions. Distressed couples tend to take for granted the positives that are offered to one another. Asking for written notation of these events helps to pinpoint their acknowledgment. Also, the written notations help each person to identify the behaviors that may have been overlooked. In addition, the record serves as a visual reminder of the amount of change that has taken place as a means of overcoming the pessimism that blights so many couples' belief in the possibility that they might improve their relationship. Finally, the record is also a source of data for use by the therapist in evaluating the willingness of each partner to take constructive, assertive action in response to therapeutic instigations.[5]

Figure 6

An Operant Interpersonal Program For Couples
Sample Request List for Caring Days

Wife's Requests
1. Greet me with a kiss and hug in the morning before we get out of bed.
2. Bring me pussywillows (or some such).
3. Ask me what record I would like to hear and put it on.
4. Reach over and touch me when we're riding in the car.
5. Make breakfast and serve it to me.
6. Tell me you love me.
7. Put your things away when you come in.
8. If you're going to stop at the store for something, ask me if there is anything that I want or need.
9. Rub my body or some part of me before going to sleep, with full concentration.
10. Look at me intently sometimes when I'm telling you something.
11. Engage actively in fantasy trips with me—e.g., to Costa Rico, Sunshine Coast, Alaska.
12. Ask my opinion about things which you write and let me know which suggestions you follow.
13. Tell me when I look attractive.
14. Ask me what I'd like to do for a weekend or day with the desire to do what I suggest.

Husband's Request
1. Wash my back.
2. Smile and say you're glad to see me when you wake up.
3. Fix the orange juice.
4. Call me at work.

5. Acknowledge my affectionate advances.
6. Invite me to expose the details of my work.
7. Massage my shoulders and back.
8. Touch me while I drive.
9. Hold me when you see that I'm down.
10. Tell me about your experiences at work every day.
11. Tell me that you care.
12. Tell me that I'm nice to be around.[6]

Increasing these behaviors is a practical application of Biblical principles of loving and caring for another person. This approach is based upon the mutual cooperation of the couple. Some have found it beneficial to explore with the couple what may occur if one of them fails to follow through on their caring day. Whenever a failure occurs, discouragement will follow. Giving careful attention to the possibilities which could occur, and the means by which an individual might sabotage himself into not following through, will lessen the possibility of failure.

Another approach for increasing positive behaviors is for each person to commit himself to give a specific number of pleasing behaviors to his spouse every day. As with the caring days, this approach is not to be on a reciprocal basis. Each person is committed to pleasing behaviors, regardless of what the other does. To insure that the correct number of positive behaviors are occurring, the number of times they occur at the present must be ascertained.

This information can be derived in two ways. Through careful discussion with the couple, you may be able to obtain some idea of the current frequency of these behaviors. Realize, however, that the person in question will possibly overstate how often they have been occurring, and the spouse will deemphasize the amount. For this reason there may be a definite discrepancy which will continue to hamper progress.

In that case it will be necessary to establish an accurate frequency ration. In doing this, a husband or wife is asked to pay careful attention to the number of times a behavior occurs at the present, and to record each occurrence on a three-by-five card. Upon determining past performance, gradual and realistic increases should be determined. The information derived from page 3 of the Marital Pre-marital Counseling Inventory will also be helpful.

One way to begin establishing a positive atmosphere is to ask the couple how they greet one another at the end of the day. Attentive time of conversation and touch for just two or three minutes at this point will help set a positive tone for the evening. Too often the dinner, dog, T.V. or paper receives the immediate attention and the spouse feels like a non-person. Each person is encouraged to stop what he is doing, to go to the other person, and to attend to him in a positive manner. (Leonard Zunin in his book **Contact — The First Four Minutes** has also emphasized this approach).

Evaluation of Approaches

There are criticisms of a structured behavioral approach. One is that it is too directive. The directiveness of this approach, however, is activated only occasionally and does not violate the free will of the couple. Most of the instructions are given as recommendations. The couple makes their own decision whether what they want or need is in harmony with the suggestion of the minister. There will be times of countering, when one or both displays resistance to change. There will also be occasions when new goals and behaviors will need to be incorporated or accepted by the couple. No matter how strong a suggestion or directive is given, the couple still has the right to accept or reject it.

Couples need a resource person or catalyst to assist them. Part of the process will be to help the couple develop new responsible roles and behaviors which reflect a consistency with a scriptural pattern for life. A minister or counselor is not secretly manipulating the couple, but is helping them work toward goals they have all agreed upon. The resource individual will gradually fade into the background as the couple learns to take charge of their own life, since such counselors operate under the conviction that those they work with have the capacity and potential to learn, change and mature.

The second concern of focusing just upon outward and perhaps superficial behaviors is an issue which needs clarification in two areas: first from a scriptural perspective and then from a permanent change perspective.

Some show concern since scripture talks of internal causes of behaviors. Examples of such passages include "out of the heart of man...", (Mark 7:21); "the heart is deceitful above all things," (Jer. 17:9); "as a man thinks in his heart so is he," (Pro. 23:7). Yet scripture actually speaks to *both* issues: that of the internal life and outward behaviors. The approach I am suggesting is a careful blending of the two. This is readily seen in several passages.

Ephesians 4:31-32 (Amplified): "Let all bitterness and indignation and wrath (passion, rage, bad temper) and resentment (anger, animosity) and quarreling (brawling, clamor, contention) and slander (evilspeaking, abusive or blasphemous language) be banished from you, with all malice (spite, ill will or baseness of any kind). And become useful and helpful and kind to one another, tenderhearted (compassionate, understanding, lovinghearted), forgiving one another (readily and freely), as God in Christ forgave you."

Colossians 3:12-13 (Amplified): "Clothe yourselves therefore, as (God's own picked representatives,) His own chosen ones, (who are) purified and holy and well-beloved (by God Himself, by putting on behavior marked by) tender-hearted pity and mercy, kind feeling, a lowly opinion of yourselves, gentle ways, (and) patience—which is tireless, long-suffering and has the power to endure whatever comes, with good temper. Be gentle and forbearing with one another and, if one has a difference (a grievance or complaint) against another, readily pardoning each other; even as the Lord has freely forgiven you, so must you also (forgive)."

Ephesians 5:1-20 indicates behaviors which Paul states are important for a Christian to put on if he is becoming an imitator of God. James 2:17 states, "Even so faith, if it has no works is dead." Behavior is a criteria of our faith. In the Gospel of Matthew behavior again is stressed: "You shall know them by their fruits." (Matt. 7:16).

Concentrating initially upon outside behaviors means neither that treatment will be superficial nor that change will only be temporary. The belief that insight or understanding must occur before behavioral change can occur and become permanent is a theory. This debate between these issues has lasted for many years and will continue to occur.

Some have questioned the emphasis upon behavior and positive reinforcement from a theological perspective as well. Edward Bolin and Glenn Goldberg, in their article "Behavioral Psychology and the Bible: General and Specific Considerations" have addressed themselves to this issue.

Even though behavior theory relies upon the principles of reinforcement to shape a person's behavior, many Christians believe that a person should be motivated by higher, intrinsically spiritual desires and not by external rewards—in this case, eschatological rewards. Many believe that the use of rewards to change behavior is analogous to using a bribe or a power ploy; others claim that reinforcement is ineffective because it cannot change complex behaviors or foster inner-directed responsibility. Still others maintain that rewards as a motivator induce selfishness and self-interest.

These arguments fail to recognize that motivation by positive reinforcement is inherent in the social system that God has established. They overlook the fact that behavior is strongly influenced by praise, approval, monetary incentives, and social recognition. That rewards are a primary factor in motivation is apparent in the warning: "Each will receive his own reward according to his labor" (I Corinthians 3:8). We would not work if we did not receive a salary, yet we do not consider our salary a bribe but merely an incentive. God has created man so that rewards are part of the natural fabric which motivates him (Adams, 1973).

Hebrews 11:6 establishes God as a positive reinforcer by stating, "He is a rewarder of those who seek Him." It is obvious that God gives rewards, and that they are usually contingent upon appropriate behavior (e.g., seeking Him). In fact, the word "reward" occurs over 100 times in the New Testament and is used most commonly for purposes of operant conditioning. Notice how frequently the emission of correct behavior results in a reinforcement so that that behavior will be maintained: "if any man's work remains, he shall receive a reward" (I

Corinthians 3:14); "if a man perseveres under trial, he will receive the crown of life" (James 1:12); "he who shepherds the flock will receive the crown of glory" (I Peter 5:1-4).

Heaven itself, along with God's eternal presence, is one of the strongest positive reinforcers Scripture uses to maintain motivation. Notice that the incentive of the heavenly reward resides largely in the fulfillment of human desire: the wealth of nations (Revelation 21:26); happiness (Revelation 1:9); no more grief, crying or pain (Revelation 21:4). If there were danger in goodness being ruined, certainly God would not appeal to our pleasure in the heavenly reward. But, in Psalm 16:11 He promises, "In Thy presence is fullness of joy; in Thy right hand there are pleasures forever." The longing for eternal happiness is not to be suppressed so that God can be honored out of some higher, less selfish motive. "Christian hedonism does not put us above God when we seek Him out of self-interest... On the contrary, the one who is actually setting himself above God is the person who presumes to come to God in order to give rather than to get" (Piper, 1976, p. 5). The Apostle Paul was honest enough to admit that if there were no expectancy of heavenly reward there would be little incentive to maintain his Christian service (I Corinthians 15:19). If Paul needed more than "higher virtues" to sustain him, how much more do we?

But, if the believer's motivation for conversion and for sanctification is initially controlled in part by the external contingencies of eschatological rewards, this is not to say that righteous living never becomes intrinsically reinforcing. Behavior theory assumes that, through extrinsic reinforcements such as praise, hugging, recognitioin, and encouragement, a person adopts intrinsic reinforcement such as feelings of pride and approval, feelings which are motivating in and of themselves. Behaviors that have been acquired through reinforcing techniques have a tendency to become intrinsically reinforcing (Rimm & Masters, 1974). For the believer, conversion and good deeds are often initially acquired through the attraction of the heavenly rewards. Yet, good deeds have a tendency to become intrinsically reinforcing so that the believer derives satisfaction out of simply obeying God.

Although heavenly rewards are described as a primary reinforcer for believers, this is not to suggest that it is the only primary reinforcer that Scripture provides. For instance, the internal working of the Holy Spirit in a believer's life is also consistent with reinforcement principles of behavioral psychology. Paul states that our experience of the fruit of the Spirit is contingent upon our walking in the Spirit. In addition, abiding in Christ is a strong motivator since we are attracted by his love and the prospect of our joy being made full (incentives which are described in John 15:9-11). The eschatological rewards provide a strong incentive for godly living, yet this is not to deny the motivation that is presently given in Christ and through the Holy Spirit.[7]

It is vital to comprehend and fully investigate the concepts discussed in this chapter during the counseling process. What occurs early in counseling will affect the direction future sessions will take.

NOTES

All materials quoted are used by permission.

1.   Billie S. Ables, **Therapy for Couples.** (San Francisco, CA: Jossey-Bass), 1977, pp. 66-67.

2.   Neil S. Jacobson and Gayla Margolin, **Marital Therapy.** (New York, N.Y.: Brunner and Mazel, Inc.), 1979, p. 160.

3.   S.R. Orden & N.A. Bradburn, **Dimensions of Marriage Happiness,** American Journal of Sociology, 1968, pp. 73, 715-731.

4.   D.R. Follingstad, S.N. Haynes & J. Sullivan, **Assessment of the Components of a Behavioral Marital Intervention Program.** Unpublished manuscript, University of South Carolina, 1976.

5.   Richard B. Stuart, **Helping Couples Change — A Social Learning Approach to Marital Therapy.** The Guilford Press, New York 1980, pp. 198-199, 201-202.

6.   David Olson, (edited), **Treating Relationships.** (Lake Mills, Iowa: Graphic Publishing Co.), 1976, pp. 124-125 — **An Operant Interpersonal Program for Couples** by Richard Stuart.

7.   Edward P. Bolin and Glenn M, Goldberg, "Behavioral Psychology and The Bible: General and Specific Considerations", **Journal of Psychology and Theology,** Fall, 1979, 7 (3) 167-175, pp. 173-174.

Chapter 7

How Expectations And Needs Disrupt Marriages

Most marital journeys begin with high romantic intensity. As couples approach marriage they usually have only a superficial awareness of each other's wants and needs. During this time (and unfortunately for many even after marriage) the least important and obvious needs get the attention.

At the same time, both partners enter marriage assuming that certain events will transpire and that their relationship will develop in a certain way. Many times these expectations remain unspoken. Often unfulfilled expectations are at the heart of marital disruption, even though most expectations are not necessities but desires.

Expectations Which Hamper The Marriage

One of the common expectations is that things should stay the way they were in the early days of marriage. Unfortunately, change overwhelms many individuals and couples, especially if the change is negative or unexpected.

Another expectation, somewhat related to the first, is that honeymoon fever can be maintained or recaptured.

But life is not static. The additional tasks and responsibilities of marriage and parenting make this expectation unrealistic. Yet, while the honeymoon excitement wanes, the love experienced later in marriage can be a deeper love.

A third expectation involves narcissistic mind reading. "If my spouse loves me, he or she will know what my needs are and do everything he can to meet them." A subtle corollary to this is, "If this doesn't occur, then you don't love me." It would be nice if all this occurred spontaneously, but such an expectation is impractical.

Finally, there are some couples who enter marriage *expecting* to have problems because of their differences. Such couples believe having marital problems is a predetermined fact. They focus on their differences whether or not such differences are the initial problem. In such cases the counselor should ask, "What would it be like if you were married to someone just like you? Would you like it?" We can agree that they are different from one another and say, "This is probably what attracted you to one another in the first place." Being different is not the problem, for differences exist with all couples.

Problems *do* develop, however, when expectations are not met. Unfulfilled expectations generate frustration and anger.

The higher our expectations, and the more numerous our needs, the more often will we find ourselves blocked. So anger in civilized man is much more often aroused by frustration than by fear. People differ greatly in the amount of frustration they can tolerate, but all of us have a flash point at which we experience a surge of anger. In marriage, as we have seen, this can easily happen, because we find ourselves in a situation in which expectations are high, and frustration can often occur.

We would venture the opinion that for normal people, being married probably generates more anger than any other interpersonal situation in which they normally find themselves.[1]

A further result of unfulfilled expectations is that they eventually evolve into demands. The spouse senses the demanding tone and is offended by it. I sometimes ask "could it be that inside of you, you are saying that Jim *should* do this? He has got to do this? He must? It sounds like a demand to me. Is this how you feel?" Restating the expectation as a demand often helps to define it. These can be shared verbally or written out. Some examples might be:

"I demand that she get up first and cook my breakfast."

"I demand that she always be at home when I arrive after working all day."

"I demand that she dress the way I've suggested in order to please me."

Dr. Joseph Maxwell described the negative effects of demandingness in this way:

> Most of us are aware of the demands we make on our spouse to exhibit certain traits or behaviors. What we are aware of is the feeling of anger or annoyance we experience when we are frustrated in realizing our demands. The feeling is so strong, so dependable, so apparently autonomous that we think it is not only justified, but unavoidable. We believe that the feeling is caused by our spouse's failure rather than our demand. This occurs because we are very aware of the failure but are largely unaware of the demand which designates the failure as a bad event.
>
> Demandingness is a formidable barrier to marital growth because the person doing the demanding is likely to spend most of his or her time and energy catastro-

phizing and pitying self, and to spend little creative energy in planning ways to develop the relationship. Since every behavior of a spouse necessarily evokes a responsive behavior from the other spouse, such personally upsetting behavior as is produced by demandingness will usually have significant effects on the actions and feelings of the partner. In most cases, when one partner reacts negatively the other one responds by behaving equally negatively, creating an endless cycle of demandingness that leads away from growth and development of the relationship.

If only one spouse is willing to give up his or her demandingness, the cycle can not only be stopped, but reversed toward strengthening the marriage.[2]

What happens internally to a person whose expectations are not met? The sequence flows something like this:

A wife makes a demand of her husband, but he does not meet it. She then becomes angry because she believes he "should" or "ought" to do what she demanded. (It is not he, but she who generates the anger.) Every time he fails to respond to the demand she says to herself "It is awful." She then feels anger toward him and self pity toward herself. Each time he fails to meet her demand, her emotional responses become more intense.

When expectations are unmet there are two ways to resolve the problem. Naturally, one is to increase performance so that expectations are met. But another approach which can greatly lessen the frustrations and anger is to change one's expectations about one's spouse.

To do this, it is important to identify expectations which have developed into demands. As you talk with a couple, determine which area of the marital relationship would be helped by direct attention to the demands. These may be in the area of roles, decision making, sex, child rearing, personal habits, or others.

It is also helpful for couples first to define areas in which they have expectations and then to submit them to these questions:

1. Do we both have expectations in this area?

2. Do we have the same expectations for ourselves as we do for our spouse? Why not?

3. How are our expectations of each other alike or different?

4. Whose expectations are the strongest?

5. Whose expectations are most often met? Why? Is that person the oldest, strongest, more intelligent, male, more powerful?

6. Are one person's expectations more worthy of fulfillment than another's?

7. Where do your expectations originate? From parents, books, church, siblings, neighbors where you grew up?

8. Do all the people you know have the same expectations in a given area?

9. Does a married person have a "right" to his expectations of a spouse?

10. Is a person obligated to live up to a spouse's expectations?[3]

To aid one or both partners in eliminating unrealistic expectations, it often helps to assist them in seeing the futility of demands. It is also beneficial to identify the negative effect demanding has upon the marriage. The goal is to eliminate, reduce, or change demands.

One way to reduce demands is to challenge or counter them to see if they are rational or realistic. One means of doing this is to ask the following questions of each demand:

1. Is this expectation I have of my spouse supported by objective reality? Is it objectively true that he or she should act this way?

2. Am I hurt in any way, shape or form if this expectation is not fulfilled?

3. Is this expectation essential to the attainment of any specific goal I have for my marriage?

4. What does this expectation do to the perception my spouse has of me?

5. Does this expectation help me achieve the kind of emotional responses I want for my spouse and me in marriage?[4]

If the answer to the first and any other two is negative, it is obvious that this expectation is invalid. Remaining expectations can be phrased in a new manner such as "I would appreciate if you would..." or "I would really prefer you to..."

Another evaluation exercise which can be conducted during the counseling session is the following: Ask each person to list twenty of his expectations of his partner. Then ask each one to write on a separate sheet of paper, a two or three line paragraph about each expectation. The paragraph should tell what the effect on his own life and on the marriage will be if that expectation is never met. (You may want the couple to go to another room while they complete this exercise, since it can take 15-20 minutes.) Ask the couple to exchange their lists of expectations, but not to exchange the paragraphs. Now each person has an opportunity to look at and to evaluate each expectation. They can respond to each expectation by making one of the following statements:

1. "I can meet this expectation most of the time, and I appreciate knowing about this. Can you share with me

some of the reasons for this being important to you?"

2. "I can meet this expectation some of the time, and I appreciate knowing about this. Can you share with me some of the reasons for this being important to you? How can I share with you, when I cannot meet this, so it would be acceptable to you?"

3. "This expectation would be difficult for me to meet and these are the reasons. Can you share with me some of the reasons for this being so important to you? How will this effect you? How can some adjustment be worked out?"

By going through this evaluation the couple will probably be talking about these issues in detail and in a rational constructive manner for the first time. This process could continue for homework purposes. In some cases it may be necessary to ask the couple not to discuss this during the week, but continue the process in the safety of your presence during the next session.

Needs

Realistic need fulfillment is essential for a person's satisfaction and development. It is necessary for both the husband and the wife to analyze both their needs and their wants in order to determine which are realistic and which are not. Sometimes people confuse their needs with their wants.

For the purposes of this study we will not focus on physical (air, water, food, etc.) or safety (security, freedom from danger) needs, nor on self-actualizing needs such as being creative or fulfilling potential. Instead we will concentrate on the needs to be loved, to belong, to feel self-esteem, and what happens to a person and to a marriage when these needs are unmet.

Unmet Childhood Needs as a Source of Conflict

Sometimes people enter adulthood with needs that were not adequately met in childhood. Such needs might include love, security, belonging, or acceptance. Frequently such unmet needs develop into rigid behavior patterns. These patterns are called *frozen needs*, and they are like recordings that play over and over. Frozen needs cannot be met in the present.[5]

There will be occasions in marital counseling where the marital relationship is severely hampered because one or both members are crippled by their past. Unfortunately, too many have rejected the influence of the past upon their lives because they associate an emphasis upon the past with Freud's Psychoanalytic approach. Rejecting this influence without a careful assessment and analysis is a mistake.

While it is true that some Christians have been able to overcome emotional abuses, rejections and hurts, far too many have not. In many cases Christians have allowed the past to influence and affect their Christianity instead of allowing their faith to heal the effects of the past. Often they have not known where to turn for help nor have they had anyone available to assist them. There will be many cases where difficulties of the past will need to be worked through, either in the presence of their partners or individually. To help this process, several resources have been found to be especially helpful. (A minister or counselor needs to be knowledgeable of the content of these to aid in their application). Several tapes by Dr. David Seamands have proved very beneficial.* Their titles are, "Damaged

*(These are available from Dr. David Seamands, Wilmore United Methodist Church, Wilmore, Kentucky).

Emotions," "Healing of the Memories," "The Hidden Child Within Us," and "The Hidden Tormentors." The two most helpful books are, **Your Inner Child of the Past** by Dr. Hugh Misseldine, Simon and Schuster Publisher, and **Healing Life's Hurts** by Dennis and Matthew Linn, Paulist Press. Prior to conducting any type of counseling ministry it is essential for the minister to read or even take a course in abnormal psychology in order to be able to identify and recognize various disorders and severe deviations.

Two books which are used as texts in many colleges are **Abnormal Psychology and Modern Life** by James C. Coleman (Scott, Foresman and Co.) and **Abnormal Psychology, Current Perspectives** (Communications Research Machines, Inc.).

To gain greater insight into personality problems and styles that you will encounter, Paul Schmidt's brief but helpful book, **Coping with Difficult People** (Westminster) is a starting point. It is difficult to assist a marriage when one or both partners have serious individual problems, and this resource discusses some of these, including the paranoid, obsessive, hysterical, aggressive, apathetic, impulsive, dependent, manipulative, etc.

In most cases when a couple enters marriage, each person is demanding little but receiving much. Under the influence of very intense feelings, each responds to the other's needs. But in time this changes. There are more demands upon them now, whereas previously most of the attention could be focused upon their partner. As the demands increase, attention transfers from the needs of the spouse to the fulfillment of one's own needs. The couple moves into the stage of giving less and expecting more. Thus, needs begin to be the source of conflict, because each desires the fulfillment of his own needs. One therapist described the problem in this way:

To be able to balance one's own needs along with all that is required of one, to remain attuned to another's needs, to be able to give when one feels more like getting, to be able to protect one's own interest, all these require a certain level of maturity, that is, a resolution of the various developmental tasks along the road to adulthood that may not have been completed. Thus, many individuals who enter marriage are often looking for a way to resolve unmet needs and are handicapped in their capacity to give. The normal stresses of a changing relationship affect these people more intensely.

One other fact should be mentioned because of its frequent occurrence. The very characteristics that are the most appealing initially and that pull the couple together inevitably become sources of major irritation later.[6]

Sometimes the unmet need is for security or attention. There are times of fulfillment, but the emptiness returns. Then the person places unrealistic demands upon his partner to fulfill the needs. He tends to see the partner as someone to be used.

There is no way that any one person can meet all the wishes of another. Desires and needs accompanied by the notion that one deserves to have what one wants must be acknowledged for what they are: archaic feelings and wishes from the past which impede realistic expectations in the present. Once spouses can accept this, one can stress the importance of diversifying ways in which each spouse gains satisfaction, lest they be overly dependent on each other and accrue resentments. This is not to say that they should not expect some of their desires to be met; expectations that some needs be satisfied are both legitimate and appropriate. The difficulty is when expectations exceed realistic possibilities (and this, of course, varies with spouses). The persistence of infantile fantasies presents major, and sometimes insurmountable, obstacles to achieving mutuality in the relationship.[7]

Some people are raised in an atmosphere of neglect, which deprives them of needed attention. A person from this background may develop in such a way that he lacks the capacity to feel important. Sometimes he is unable to be concerned with others and how they feel. He may run from one person to another, hoping that each person will supply the necessary ingredient. He is perpetually dissatisfied with his relationships with others, including his spouse.

He longs for a deep, intimate relationship, but the need is so deep that he wants constantly to be parented. He has an excessive need for warmth, love, and attention. But even if his spouse were able to get that close, he would be fearful that she would not like him if she really knew him intimately. He would be unable to accept the attention he needs. (This is also true of some women.)

Occasionally I counsel someone who has an excessive need to be "perfect." The need to be perfect was created in this person by his parents when he was a child. He soon learned that in order to gain acceptance, his behavior had to be superior to others. Acceptance from the parents was held out in front of the child like a carrot before a horse—he must always forge ahead and do better. This person has learned to belittle his own efforts. He must always strive to do better, but he does not accept his own efforts.

The perfectionist could be a person who was rejected as unaccepted, unwanted, or a nuisance. He has an intense need for two commodities—affection and approval, but he has difficulty believing that the other's love is really sincere! Thus, the spouse must continue to give and give and prove his love. The perfectionist sets up "tests" of love which his partner must pass. There is an insatiable demand for love, which can become a pain in time. If the spouse inadvertently or purposely slacks off, the rejection occurs again.[8]

Hugh Missildine described the perfectionist behavior in this way:

The perfectionist person has great trouble in finding an acceptable marriage partner, for he wants a perfect mate, not a human one. Thus, he tends to reject potential mates, often until he has delayed marriage for years. He has difficulty forming a relationship that would be close enough to lead to marriage. Some such persons give up the attempt to form close human ties and devote themselves to work, not realizing that it lies within their power to alter their attitude toward themselves. This is the situation of some of our successful bachelors and striving career girls.

The perfectionist person often looks upon marriage as another achievement. Once married, he does not know how to enjoy it. He generally continues his old perfectionist attitudes, demanding perfect order. He becomes anxious if the house is not in order at all times, with eggs done to a split-second three minutes, toast to a certain shade of tan, shirts starched a certain way, and perfect children from his perfect wife. His anxiety leads him to demand these things because anything less than what he considers "perfect" arouses his childhood patterns of self-belittlement. Many a husband silently accepts his perfectionistic wife's demands that he not wear shoes in the living room because she fears marks on her perfect rugs, endures her corrections of his speech, and indeed never feels comfortable himself.[9]

Whenever a person brings a frozen need into a marriage, he invests most of his energy in having that deficiency met. People with frozen needs require a release of the painful feelings associated with them. If there is hurt or resentment, inner healing and forgiveness will meet the need.

Another kind of need that people bring into a marriage is the *false need*. Most false needs stem from hurts or even myths perpetrated on a person in childhood. Two examples of false needs are related: the need to be taken care of, and the need to take care of someone else. Some believe that their lives will be all right if they find someone to take care of them. When the feelings of inadequacy or helplessness are disposed of, and when the person discovers he can take care of himself, the need to be looked after or taken care of goes away.[10]

Unmet Needs Within Marriage

Although every couple brings unique characteristics and perspectives into counseling sessions, you may begin to notice some common themes and common frustrations that occur with counseling couples.

One of the main frustrations involves blocking the fulfillment of one another's psychological needs. Each one is probably involved in a destructive pattern of response which could drain the other's self worth. Each downgrades the other, which creates a "fight withdraw" pattern. In counseling each will try to convince the minister of their "rightness" and hope the counselor will "straighten out" their partner. At this point a minister may feel like a referee or a labor negotiator. Each spouse may insist that the majority of responsibility for marital problems rests with his partner.

It is important to express awareness and concern for their hurt, frustration and anger. But it is just as important to share that they have a common problem which will need attention from both of them. Their expectations of counseling may need clarification at this time. The issue will not be who is right or wrong, but what is the best way of responding to one another. The reason they are at this point in their marriage is that they have not yet learned to relate to one another effectively.

It is important to point out to a couple how they are mutually frustrating one another. One way of sharing this is to explain to them in simple language that all people have needs. Two of the most vital are the need to feel worthwhile and the need to be liked and accepted by others. People need to feel self-respect and self-appreciation. When both partners feel this way they are both contented and satisfied. And each then is better able to share with their partner that he or she is worthwhile and likeable.

When this essential need for self-esteem is unmet, one or both will begin to feel unworthy. They will each find it difficult to share their good feelings and sense of worth with their spouse. Instead they will set up a *blaming pattern* manifested by rejection, ridicule, and the tendency to nag.

Consequently, each feels even more unlikeable and worthless. They begin to defend themselves through a process called the *fight-flight* pattern. Each begins either to hurt or to attack the other as much as possible and in as many ways as possible. Most fights include blame, criticism, and putdowns.

The second stage of this pattern is flight, and is often referred to as a "cold war." Each feeds his own feelings of hurt and rejection and probably begins to fantasize or plot ways of inflicting hurt and downgrading upon their spouse. They find many escapes.

Some retreat into silence and refuse to speak to their partners. Some withhold sexual intimacy. Others retreat into their jobs as they find their self-esteem being built by success there, and by retreating they retaliate against their partner by their excessive absences. Others escape into drinking or drugs. Many find another person who appears to appreciate them and sees them as a worthwhile person. Each of these patterns continues to frustrate the other partner. This is often referred to as a *vicious circle pattern*.

The vicious circle pattern, which is common, can be seen with this illustration. A man who feels pressure at work decides to get rid of some of this pressure by stopping at a bar with his friends for a couple of drinks before coming home. He lets the time go by and arrives home an hour and a half later than usual. His wife, who has been waiting for him, has strong feelings. These include frustration (he didn't call and let her know), rejection and worthlessness because of his coming home so late. He spoiled her dinner and all her hard work. So she verbally attacks him. He doesn't care for this because his feelings of worth and acceptance are lessened. He becomes resentful. He may shout at her, and then he may leave without eating the dinner.

Later that week or the next, the behavior is repeated. He stops off for a couple of drinks and enjoys the atmosphere and acceptance felt in the bar. It's better than a nagging wife waiting at home! Now she feels even more neglected and uncared for as she realizes he would rather be with his friends than at home with her. So she attacks and blames him even more. And the vicious circle continues.

On Sunday he decides to play an early morning round of

golf but promises his wife that he will be home in time to take her to the 11:00 service. But after the game he goes into the clubhouse bar for a drink or two with his golfing partners. The time slips to 11:30. She calculates where he might be, calls the bar and has him paged. She then berates him over the phone while he is in the presence of his friends.

Embarrassed to think that some may have sensed what was occurring, he wants to prove that he is not dominated by his wife. He suggests another game of golf and does not return home all day. This is a mutual self-destructive pattern which each is feeding.

One of the key elements to observe is how the couple sets up the vicious circle. Each person's behavior and the consequences of that behavior need full and careful exploration. As each person begins to see what his behavior is triggering in his partner and what a different response may do, then the cycle can be broken. In many cases changing the pattern of behavior even without a full insight can lead to the discovery of a better way of relating. Part of the process of counseling is to discover more effective ways of responding to one another.

Sometimes the idea that both partners share responsibility for the vicious-circle pattern in their relationship meets with resistance. Dr. Billie Ables has formulated the following approach in dealing with such objection:

Even if one can get each spouse to accept that objectionable behavior of the mate would not have occurred if the spouse had not behaved in some way to provoke it, one often encounters stiff resistance from both, which results from their competitive tug-of-war. Neither wants to be the first to change, which is often viewed as accepting all the blame. One strategy for dealing with this tug-of-war is to say, "It seems to me that there are some changes that you want to make that will make things a lot better for both of you. As I see it, the best chance you both have for getting some of these changes you want is to decide what you personally are willing to do for your spouse which will meet some of the needs your spouse feels are important. This will then give you better odds on the possibility of your spouse's effecting the changes which you want. This is something each of you will have to decide—what you can and are willing to do (assuming that the couple have already discussed what changes they want). Now there is no guarantee that even if you make a serious effort to do some of the things your spouse wishes that you will get everything or even anything in return. Your efforts may net you nothing. But I can guarantee you from this vantage point that you will have increased your odds considerably. I can also guarantee both of you that what you are doing now (present behavior patterns that are grievances to each) is absolutely guaranteed to fail. What I am stressing is that a certain amount and kind of risk taking is necessary.[11]

Expressing Needs

The problem of mind reading is not only frustrating, it is a total impossibility! But this is exactly what has to occur if one will not share his needs openly. In marital counseling, the procedure is to ask each person to specifically define his/her needs, to describe how the spouse can meet them, and then to share these with one another.

Here is an example of how one woman in premarital counseling shared her needs and how she thought her future husband could specifically meet them.

EMOTIONAL

MY NEEDS	*HOW KEN CAN MEET THEM*
To feel loved, cherished	Call me, prepare me for sex, hold me, kiss me, look at me with a glimmer in his eye, take naps so he will feel refreshed to be with me.
To feel supported, believed in	Pray for me in front of me and secretly as well. Challenge me, praise me, see my potential in specific situations.
To feel comforted when down	Hold me, let me cry on his shoulder, feel my hurt with me, be gentle and sensitive to my moods, let me know he notices them.
To feel not alone	Share my daily life's joys and sorrows, enter into the conversation about my day, be interested in daily details that help him understand me.
To feel free to be myself, to be genuine	Be himself, be genuine, see through my masks and let me know it. Know that I love him deep down so he can take my present anger. Accept my goofy antics as me but when he doesn't like them, let me know gently what he prefers instead and give me the opportunity to change it.

SOCIAL

MY NEEDS	*HOW KEN CAN MEET THEM*
To get together with other women	Encourage me to get to know friends and neighbors when I feel timid, and ask me what I learned afterward.
To get together as a couple with friends	Be himself, laugh at himself, at me, at us, and share it with others. Be as uninhibited as he dares.
To do something spontaneous	Go out to dinner, movies, friend's house, miniature golfing, TV show, something new—surprise me!
To get away from the house and schoolwork regularly	Notice when I am useless and suggest a change of pace, just as if he felt cooped up and needed a change.[12]

One difficulty in sharing needs is how each partner verbalizes the requests. How the desired behavior is communicated will probably influence the response from the partner. Well-chosen and articulated words can have a negative effect when the accompanying tone of voice and non-verbals are sending yet another message. A flat, negative, demanding tone will over-shadow the well-chosen words of a positive statement. An indifferent look, scowl, frown, or even the lack of expression can sabotage a request.

Couples need to share their initial requests of one another in the presence of the counselor so you have an opportunity to evaluate and/or comment upon the mode in which the message is sent. The use of a tape recorder or even a video recorder has proven to be of immense help in showing an individual or couple these areas, of which they are probably unaware. Frequently it is helpful to share with a couple information from Dr. Albert Mehrabian derived through his studies of face-to-face communication. He determined that 7% of our message is conveyed through our words, 38% through our tone of voice and 55% through our non-verbals or body language.[13]

The realization of this along with concentrated effort can make a message palatable.

Requests should be made with a positive indication of what is desired. There must be no criticism or reference to the past. The counselor might suggest prefacing requests with statements like "I would like you to ..." or "I would really appreciate it if you would ..."

Requests should be about such behaviors which are somewhat easy for the spouse to perform. If there has been one central or main issue that brings the couple in for counseling, this should not be the substance of the request at this time.

It is probably obvious to us that when a positive behavior is performed toward another person, it should be positively reinforced. But such awareness is not always obvious to a counseling couple, so it needs to be mentioned along with some examples or illustrations of what to say.

Objections To Expressing Needs

Sometimes one or both partners will object to expressing needs to their spouse, so it is important to be aware of common problems and to know how to answer the objections. Three statements typify reactions one might hear. These statements might also give an insight into previous occurrences between the couple in their day-to-day life.

1. *Expecting spouse to be a mind-reader*

"Why should I tell him? We've been married for ten years and he ought to know what I want."

Even if it were possible for one spouse to read the other's mind, 100% accuracy would be unlikely. It frustrates the partner and places unrealistic demands on his ability to perform.

2. *Not giving spouse the benefit of the doubt*

"The only reason that he's going to do this is because of your recommendation. He doesn't really want to. That's hypocritical."

Even if the person performing the positive behaviors is hesitant and not fully committed, at least he is willing to try to see what improvements may occur.

3. *Lack of belief*

"It won't do much good to tell her. She's been aware for some time but has never responded. Why now?"

In some cases this hesitancy may be based on years of broken promises, and consequently there may be valid justification for it. If the spouse (whose ability to change is being questioned) shows a very low score on trait I (Self Discipline vs. Impulsive) on the TJTA or has a pattern indicating a "con artists tendency," there will be reason to question present commitments. This type of person will need much assistance and structure in order to follow through and in some cases individual therapy may be in order.

Nevertheless, this lack of belief in the partner's ability to change or to mature presents a definite roadblock to the future of the marriage. It is highly discouraging to the partner. This is a time to counter the attitude gently and to move the objecting spouse to a point of belief.

There are numerous ways of responding to this lack of belief. It's important here, as with other reactions, to value and respect the person's perspective of the relationship. Preface each comment with "I can understand your hesitancy based upon your present feelings," and then move to whatever response you plan to make. Here are some examples of responses:

"Let's explore the future, say, the next two or three months. If we don't believe that John will be any different, what will it be like?"

"I'm wondering what John is feeling right now as he's sitting here listening to us. Would you like to hear from him?"

"John, could you share with your wife your feelings about what she has said?"

"I get the impression from what you have shared with me earlier that you have a concern for a Biblical model of marriage. Could I direct you to a passage which might assist you in achieving that goal? How would I Cor. 13:7 as expressed here in the Amplified Version give us a basis for the marriage you seek? How could this passage be applied?"

One of the characteristics of love as expressed in I Cor. 13 is "Love bears up under anything and everything that comes, is ever ready to believe the best of every person . . ." (Amplified). This thought is one which is basic to the improvement of any relationship.

NOTES

All materials quoted are used by permission.

1. David & Vera Mace, **How to Have a Happy Marriage.** (Nashville, TN: Abingdon), 1977, p. 111.

2. Nick Stimeti; Barbara Chesser; John DeFrain, **Building Family Strengths.** (Lincoln, Nebraska: Univ. of Nebraska Press), 1979, p. 112.

3. Nick Stimeti; Barbara Chesser; John DeFrain, **Building Family Strengths.** (Lincoln, Nebraska: Univ. of Nebraska: Univ. of Nebraska Press), 1979, pp. 118-119.

4. Nick Stimeti; Barbara Chesser; John DeFrain, **Building Family Strengths.** (Lincoln, Nebraska: Univ. of Nebraska Press), 1979, pp. 118-119.

5. H. Norman Wright, **The Pillars of Marriage.** (Ventura, CA: Regal Books), 1979, pp. 68, 69.

6. Billie S. Ables, **Therapy for Couples.** (San Francisco, CA: Jossey-Bass), 1977, pp. 3, 218.

7. Billie S. Ables, **Therapy for Couples.** (San Francisco, CA: Jossey-Bass), 1977, pp. 3, 218.

8. H. Norman Wright, **The Pillars of Marriage.** pp. 73-74.

9. W. Hugh Missildine, **Your Inner Child of the Past.** (New York: Simon & Schuster), 1963, p. 91.

10. H. Norman Wright, **The Pillars of Marriage,** pp. 73-74.

11. Billie S. Ables, **Therapy for Couples.** (San Francisco, CA: Jossey-Bass), 1977, p. 110.

12. H. Norman Wright, **The Pillars of Marriage,** pp. 74-75.

13. Albert Mehrabian, **Silent Messages.** (Belmont, CA: Wadworth Publishing Co.), 1971, pp. 42-44.

CHAPTER 8

Variations Of Behavioral Approaches

There are numerous behavioral approaches and procedures which can be implemented with couples. While some counseling styles rely on subtle, indirect suggestions and directives which are left in their subtle form with no clarification, the behavioral approach is structured and didactic in nature. In many cases the approach is to teach couples relationship skills from an open and direct format. As a result, the counseling couple will be able to generalize the principles they've learned concerning a specific conflict area to other areas of their life.

Numerous books and articles describing the multitude of behavioral approaches are available. A few of these approaches include Richard Stuart's Intervention Approach, Behavioral Exchange Programs, Positive Reinforcement Emphasis, and Contract or Covenant Therapy.

Intervention

The intervention program developed by Richard Stuart involves a five-step approach.

First the counselor or minister begins the discussion with the couple by helping each of them identify positive changes in his or her behavior and in the behavior of the other which would significantly increase both individual and marital satisfaction. This can either be done orally or by having each write a list of changes.

To accomplish this process it may be necessary to assist the couple in developing a new vocabulary. This is because most couples seeking counseling have learned to describe and label their behavior and that of their spouse in a faulty manner. Absolutes, generalizations, assumptions, name calling, and mind reading are just a few of the difficulties which should be tackled. In place of focusing upon why problems or negative behaviors occur, the couple is encouraged to share, in a positive manner, what they desire and how positive changes and exchanges can occur. These positive behavioral changes have two objectives: To maintain an adequate level of personal and mutual satisfaction, and to rebuild trust in the relationship at the same time.

The *second* step involves discussion in which the couple is helped to develop a new method of sharing. It may be necessary at this point to identify and change *coercive* methods. Often couples have developed this approach when nothing else has worked, but coercion builds suspicion rather than trust.

Coercion can involve controlling, forcing or manipulating the other person for personal benefit. In coercion one partner seeks positive reinforcement from the other while giving negative reinforcement in exchange. A frequent example of this is the husband who wants more affection from his wife but rarely receives the desired response.

How does he behave when he reaches out to her for affection and she doesn't respond? He may become verbally abusive, sulk, accuse his wife of being indifferent, sexually cold, or interested in someone else. Only when he receives his affection does he settle down.

But in responding in this manner he is actually sabotaging his own desires. If he makes himself unpleasant by what he says and does, he is less likely to receive the desired affection. On the other hand, if he is abusive and demanding and she finally responds, her affection has less significance since it was not a genuine gift on her part. He loses both ways, but he still persists. How can these often long term patterns of response be broken? Richard Stuart said:

> To overcome the excessive use of coercion, it is necessary to convince both partners that the exchanges which they enjoy in their marriage are privileges and not rights. A privilege is 'a special prerogative which one may enjoy at the will of another person upon having performed some qualifying task' in contrast to a right which implies inalienable access to a reinforcer. To earn privileges, one must reinforce the other; to enjoy rights, one need only insist upon his due. By conceptualizing preferred marital pleasures as privileges, reciprocity becomes the only means of gaining access to them, replacing coercion as the means of security rights.[1]

During the *third* step, the counselor assists the husband and wife in developing their verbal and nonverbal communication skills so each can verbalize both their desires and their satisfaction to one another.

This involves discovering and cultivating new styles of communication. All couples communicate in one way or another. Since communication is made up of verbalization and nonverbalization, communication is constantly occurring. When couples state that their problem is "we don't communicate," they are really saying their style and mode of communication is not functional. Four basic communication principles need to be shared and reinforced at this time:

1)   One cannot *not* communicate. Even without words the nonverbal communication still exists. As couples become aware of the impact of their nonverbal communication patterns and begin to work at them, such patterns can become positive.

2)   Sensitivity and measured honesty are necessary in order to build the relationship. For this reason each spouse is encouraged to ask the other only for those changes which can reasonably be granted. The elimination of condemnation and criticism relieves tension.

3)   Only positive information can bring about changes in a marital relationship. The husband and wife are encouraged to be selective in their interchange.

4)   As couples describe their interactions, it will be important for the person speaking to describe specifically what each person did and what the consequence was of each response. Often the spouse describing the other's behavior leaves out what he, himself, did or didn't do. This gives a very incomplete picture. Sharing what both contributed can increase the possibility of the exchange of constructive information. These four principles will probably have to be reinforced from time to time.

The *fourth* phase involves assisting the couple in developing their program of decision-making. New decision-making techniques must be constructed and the power structure clarified. All couples develop a style of making decisions. Some styles are effective; some are self-defeating. For many, decision-making is one of the least enjoyable and even one of the most painful aspects of marriage. A couple who has never developed skills for competent decision-making suffers the consequences.

During this time you may find it helpful to share the following decision-making patterns with the couple, asking them to identify which of these may be operating in their relationship.

There are at least three basic decision-making patterns. One is the *stepwise* pattern, in which the decision is made according to a specific order. For example, a couple could agree to work on a problem, select one part to discuss, suggest possible solutions, and so on. All of the steps do not necessarily need to occur at the same time, but the process, once begun, is carried out in steps.

A second approach is the *non-stepwise* pattern. This simply means that the activities carried out in the process of making a decision do not occur in order. Certain portions of the process are omitted or even repeated.

A third type of decision-making is the *defaulted* pattern. In this pattern the decision is actually made for the other person and occurs as a result of outside events, decisions, or a lack of decisions on the part of the partner. (See chapter 9 of **The Pillars of Marriage** for specific information on a decision-making to share in the session or to use as a reading project.)

To help the couple become specific about their present situation, you could use the following analysis. Give each person a form and ask them both to describe the decision-making process of their marriage by indicating the percentage of influence each has, for each issue. The total for each decision must be 100 percent. Upon completion, have them exchange forms and then discuss each item in your presence.

	Percentage of My Vote	Percentage of My Spouse's Vote	Who I feel is more qualified to contribute to this decision. (Write your initial or your spouse's.)
New car			
Home			
Furniture			
Your wardrobe			
Spouse's wardrobe			
Vacation spots			
Decor for the home			
Mutual friends			
Entertainment			
Church			
Child-rearing practices			
TV shows			
Home menu			
Number of children			
Where you live			
Husband's vocation			
Wife's vocation			
How money is spent			
How often to have sex			
Where to have sex			
Mealtimes			
Landscaping			
Various household tasks			

Along with developing new decision-making techniques, it is also helpful within a session to clarify and describe the couple's existing power structure. Often couples engage in an open or subtle power struggle. Power has been defined as the capacity of each person to influence one another.

One means of evaluating the structure has been

described by Duane Liftin:

Researchers in social psychology have designated at least five kinds of 'social power,' authority, or influence that human beings exercise over each other. The first is called *information power*. A person, or source, exerts this sort of 'power' over another when the information he controls influences the thinking or behavior of the recipient. *Referent power* exists when the recipient identifies with the source and desires to be like him. Thus the source influences the recipient by his example. *Coercive-reward power* exists when the recipient believes that the source can and will punish or reward his behavior. *Expert power* is the sort of influence that accrues to the source by knowing more or being able to do something better than the recipient. *Positional power* exists when the recipient accepts a relationship in which the source is permitted or obliged, because of his position, to prescribe behaviors for the recipient, and the recipient is obliged to accept this influence.[2]

Especially within the church counseling context, is it important to understand and share clearly the biblical perspective on roles, responsibilities and decision making. One of the most helpful books clarifying the biblical view concerning husband/wife roles is **Marriage as Equal Partnership** by Dr. Dwight Small (Baker Publishers). In addition, Duane Liftin's analysis of social power can be helpful in clarifying the concept of submission and authority. He says:

In examining the nature of the husband's authority over his wife as spelled out in the Bible, three crucial points emerge. First, of the five kinds of power or authority listed above, only the fifth—positional power— is designated by the New Testament as belonging to the husband; and even this type of 'power' is not uniquely the husband's, for there are areas of authority over her husband that a wife holds by virtue of her position as well (see, e.g., 1 Cor. 7:4). Second, the other four types of authority are equally available to the husband and wife alike. Although it is probably true that coercive-reward power should seldom if ever be used by either marriage partner, the Bible clearly encourages the wife to exert several of the other types of power over her husband (e.g.), the use of referent power in I Peter 3:1-4, and the use of expert power in Prov. 31) . . .[3]

There appears to be a direct relation between power and intimacy which most people do not realize. As you work with a couple, you will begin to discover the type of relationship they have developed. Four basic types can be described.

The *more or less equal* style of marriage relationship indicates a balanced power distribution. It is a complementary relationship. Both partners think of themselves as competent, and each sees the other person as competent, too. Each person has specific areas of expertise in which his or her views have greater weight than the partner, but this does not threaten the other person. They exchange different types of behaviors, and the behavior which each exchanges "fits" together. Thus they are called complementary. If one offers some advice, the other person accepts it and does not have to give advice in return.[4] Actually, it is the situation or the circumstances that influence which person assumes the leadership role. These leadership roles can be either in or outside of the traditional categories.

Another common relationship is the *dominant/submissive* type. One partner's views prevail, regardless of the circumstances or of the other person's abilities. Even in the area of thoughts, opinions, and viewpoints, we find that one person will tend to be dominated. Usually, there is very little open conflict in this type of relationship. It appears to be a complementary situation where the needs of both individuals are being met. When anger does come out, it is often expressed by the submissive person because of being overridden. There are times, though, when the dominant partner does become angry and upset because s/he feels that too much responsibility and weight is placed upon him. It is common in this type of a relationship for each to blame the other for the problem.

Some relationships are more symmetrical than complementary. Both husband and wife have the freedom to initiate action, give advice, criticize and so on, but most of their behavior is competitive. If one states that he has achieved a goal or progressed in some way, the spouse lets it be known that he, too, has attained a similar success. Each one makes it a point to let the other know of the equal status.

When conflicts in such a relationship become fairly open and consistent, the relationship is in a *warfare state*. The couple does not have an established equilibrium for the relationship because both are vying for the dominant position and exchanging the same type of behavior.

Finally, there is the *fused relationship* in which each person shares some power. But in order to have power, they each give up some of their individual identity. Separateness does not exist because it seems dangerous, and consequently there is an unhealthy type of a closeness. Sometimes individuals like this will say, "we are so close that we think alike, we feel alike, and we are completely one."

In any of these relationships we often find overlap. As you

work with couples, realize there are very few who hold to a pure position of the four mentioned here. Some of the individuals might not want to give up their position and move toward the "more or less equal" because they are receiving satisfaction. However, it is important to help them discover that there might be greater satisfaction by moving to this new level. In doing so, there is a greater possibility of developing the intimacy which could be lacking in their present method of responding to one another.[5]

The following chart indicates the relationship between power and intimacy. Using the previous description with this chart in the actual counseling session can be very enlightening for the couple.

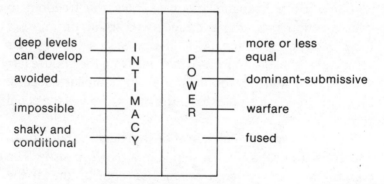

In the book **The Mirages of Marriages**, Don Jackson and William Lederer state that the failure of couples to identify, determine, and mutually assign areas of competence and responsibility, and determine who is in charge of what, is among the most destructive omissions in marriage.[6]

Efficiency and comfort in the marriage is certainly related to the degree to which both partners accept the existing balance of power. To improve an unsatisfactory condition, it is necessary to follow three steps. First, identify the areas in which each presently exercise power. Then, identify the areas in which each would ideally like to exercise power. This is followed by contracting for agreements governing power distribution. During these contracting sessions, the role of the therapist is that of mediator.[7]

The *final* step in the intervention approach involves helping the couple develop an approach to maintain these changes but also to have a degree of flexibility which will allow for continual growth.

Each couple will need to develop some type of rules to continue and protect the changes. Influence from the outside and the tendency to reverse to previous behavioral patterns (even though negative) are common sabotages to the growth of the relationship.

Each set of rules will need to be created for the uniqueness of the couple, and could include such simple items as the following:

1. Seek to end arguments and not win them.

2. Admit your own responsibility for difficulties and don't blame the other.

3. Believe that your spouse has your best interests at heart.

4. Encourage positive behavior in the other by saying "thank you" and "I appreciate that." Increase your own positive behaviors.[8]

A Behavioral Exchange Program

Another style of behavioral approach has been developed by Allan F. Rappaport and Janet E. Harrell. They describe a five-step method which is based upon reciprocal exchange and behavior modification within the marriage.

Part of the first step involves more than one counselor's participation.

The first step is a process of direct teaching and modeling which usually is unfolded in three stages.

In stage one the two counselors describe and role play a typical common marital conflict in which they can demonstrate the principles of bargaining and reciprocity. The counselors give a positive demonstration of how to negotiate demands, and then develop a concise written contract. The couple is thus able to observe a healthy model of what to do within a safe context.

In stage two the counselors bring up another hypothetical conflict. The married couple (counselees) coach the counselors this time, helping the counselors with the process. Every time the couple makes a workable and practical suggestion, the counselors give them verbal reinforcement. This, too, is safe for them, even though their involvement level is increased.

Stage three involves the married couple discussing and negotiating a hypothetical problem and developing their own contract. The counselor or minister gives assistance and positive reinforcement when appropriate. The role play experience on the part of the couple will help develop their skills and give them greater courage and confidence when they attempt to resolve the real issues.

The second step of the behavioral exchange program involves labeling undesirable behaviors in one's spouse. The husband and wife are each asked independently to write a list of three specific behaviors exhibited by their spouse which are undesirable. These should be labeled 1-3 to indicate level of undesirability. Then each is to describe, in writing, his own typical way of responding to each of the three undesirable behaviors.

The purpose of this exercise is to identify the way each person reinforces and maintains the other's undesirable behaviors.

These lists are discussed and clarified by the counselor with the couple so both are in agreement with the final list. Then the minister or counselor shares with them the concept of "vicious cycles" that exist between them. Many couples help perpetuate the very problems which they dislike within one another. Their own response actually reinforces the behavior they dislike.

The third step involves each one making a list of the specific positive or desirable behaviors which their spouse performs. Here is a sample of all three lists:

Mrs. X: Prepared Lists

I.   Undesirable Behaviors of Spouse

1. I dislike his constant complaining. He complains about everything.
2. I dislike the way he forces his ideas, wants, and desires on me. He tries to mold me and shape me to conform to his expectations.
3. I dislike the way he never compliments me without qualifications.

II.   My Reaction to These Behaviors

1. I tell him that that's the way it is and he can't do anything about it. Often, I say nothing and just keep it inside.
2. I am usually hurt by this and get angry and try to say something that will hurt him in return. I also tell him that I'm sorry that I'm not what he wants me to be.
3. I respond by usually saying nothing—just keeping it inside. Just some kind of recognition would really help.

III.   Desirable or Positive Behaviors of Spouse

1. It's nice when he gets excited about something we can both do.
2. I like it when he compliments me in front of other people.

3. I appreciate his doing the dishes.

Mr. X: Prepared Lists
  I. Undesirable Behaviors of Spouse
      1. She has no desire for sex. She laughs when kissed—shows no sexual interest at all.
      2. She walks away from me when I am talking to her. She usually tells me to shut up.
      3. She spends the little time we have together picking up things, taking showers, doing odd jobs, etc.
  II. My Reaction to These Undesirable Behaviors
      1. My first reaction was to kiss her. When I found out that this turned her off I stopped, trying not to push what obviously annoyed her.
      2. I usually get mad and say things again to make sure she understands.
      3. I usually sit there although sometimes I say something to her. It makes me feel as though her housework is more important than me.
  III. Desirable or Positive Behaviors of Spouse
      1. She is a good cook.
      2. She works uncomplainingly.
      3. Keeps house clean.
      4. Very good mother to baby.
      5. Very organized.
      6. Dependable.
      7. Thoughtful about many things.[9]

The fourth step is quite different than some would expect. This entails keeping a week-long record of the number of times undesirable behavior number three occurs by their spouse. This is not done to blame or react to their spouse, but to help each partner to become aware of his own reinforcing response to the behavior. In the presence of the counselor, the couple then negotiates a contract to eliminate undesirable behaviors and replaces them with desirable ones.

They begin with the least threatening behavior because it will be easier to work out a mutual agreement with an easier problem. This should help the couple to proceed to the other more serious behaviors which need to be eliminated.

The couple should be advised against moving too fast. Only one behavior per week should be attempted. Each time a person performs a desirable behavior it needs to be positively recognized or reinforced by the partner.

The final step is simply sharing with the couple the need for flexibility and change. As they continue their married life together, each of them will change and mature. Thus their agreements will become outmoded and need to be restructured.

There are numerous benefits to the behavior exchange approach.

1. It teaches couples how to negotiate on their own so they will be able to continue using negotiation throughout their relationship.

2. It encourages couples to eliminate undesirable behaviors on a reciprocal basis and replace them with positive behaviors which in turn build the marriage.

3. This approach places emphasis upon a behavioral analysis of the marriage.

4. It will help to determine the unmotivated person if he or she refuses to bargain in order to build the marriage.

5. It teaches the couple to negotiate their own contracts with one another.

Naturally there are some cautions to be observed. This approach will not work if one or both are unable or unwilling to compromise or bargain. Another problem involves couples who try to move too rapidly, thus sabotaging their efforts. The minister or counselor needs to be aware of and believe in the social exchange theory and operant learning principles underlying this approach. Finally, couples must be consistent in keeping daily behavioral records of their progress in this approach.[10]

Positive Reinforcement

Married couples seek satisfaction and the fulfillment of needs in their relationship. Unfortunately, many go about attaining this in the wrong way. They pay too much attention to problems and to areas which are not going so well, while they tend to take for granted and fail to reinforce positive responses from their spouse.

In marriage positive reinforcement is a must. A reinforcement or reinforcer is anything that increases the probability of that behavior's being repeated. If a wife bakes her husband's favorite cake and he responds with a threefold increase of positive comments and behaviors (and perhaps flowers the next night), this may cause her to bake this cake more often. If the frequency of what she does increases, then we know that his behavior is increasing her behavior. If her behavior stays the same, his response could still be reinforcing since it is sustaining her frequency of baking cakes. If she decreases what she is doing, then what he is doing has no reinforcing value.

An example of this would be a husband who comes home from work and his wife greets him at the door with a hug and kiss and a fresh cup of coffee. If he then takes time to converse with her (which he doesn't usually do), chances are good that she will repeat this behavior if conversing with him is important to her.

Not only can reinforcement be used to increase the type of behavior one desires, but it can be used to change another's behavior. This can be done by stating specifically what one wants from the partner and then reinforcing this new behavior whenever it occurs. This involves *not* focusing on what it is that one doesn't like, but pointing to the behaviors which one would like to occur more often. Even the smallest changes on the other's part must be reinforced. This means that close attention needs to be paid in order to observe any slight changes. The reinforcement, such as "Thank you" or "I appreciate that," should occur immediately after the new behavior. The sooner one reinforces, the more effect it has.

It is also possible to change undesirable behavior with these principles. This is done by always expressing the desired behavior in positive terms. A spouse should be told what his partner wants him to do, not what isn't wanted. The undesirable behavior should then be ignored because paying attention to it just reinforces its occurrence. Only the positive behavior should be reinforced.

It is not uncommon for couples to work out an actual written contract concerning their positive behaviors. As you work with a couple concerning their specific conflicts and problems, you will need to describe this process in detail for the couple. If, for example, a husband and wife are concerned over the issue of the husband's coming home on time, the following procedures should be followed by the wife. This may need to be written out so she can remember the steps.

1.   I want my husband to arrive home at night when he says he will.

2.   I will stop reinforcing (verbally and nonverbally) his arriving home late.

3.   I will positively reinforce his coming home when he says he will.

A simple example of negotiation and reinforcement can be seen in the distribution of time in recreational and social activities. It could be that expectations prior to the marriage may be affecting the present relationship. Regardless of the couple's own values or beliefs, it is helpful to share with them the following points concerning the use of time.

1.   Each person needs his or her own individual recreation, either by themselves or with separate friends.

2.   Each couple needs recreational time with each other.

3.   Every couple needs recreational time with other couples.

4.   Every couple needs recreational time with their children.

Each person will have a different need level for solitude and togetherness, and these needs will change as a couple travels through the developmental phases of their own lives and the marriage. The amount of time one desired in recreation last year may be different five years from now, and this amount of time for each of the four mentioned areas will need to be negotiated during the counseling sessions. Possessive and insecure individuals have difficulty allowing their partners enough "space". Through attempts to keep their spouses close and available, the insecure partners tend to push their mates farther away. Individuals also want to be believed when they share with their partner where they have been or where they are going for their recreation.

Here is how one couple developed an agreement. The husband wanted to be able to stop off at the gym and work out once a week. One Friday a month he went out to dinner with his office staff, but whenever he mentioned to his wife the night before that he was going to do this, he felt and heard resistance from her. His reason for going to the gym was to unwind and relax and work off some of his tensions and frustrations, but his wife couldn't see why he couldn't come home to relax and unwind. Thus each time the husband expressed this desire, they quarrelled. Harsh words and hurt feelings resulted.

In the counseling session as he explained his need for this time away, she realized that this actually had a beneficial quality to it. She not only could see its value and was accepting, but she also agreed to the counselor's suggestion that whenever he would tell her he would be out, she would respond by saying "Thanks for letting me know. Have a good time." This example is a characteristic of a healthy relationship.

A building positive approach variation is an activity called "Pleases," which is similar to the "Caring Days" model described in an earlier chapter. This approach will take some creative work on the part of the counselor, for he provides the couple with a list of 100 ways in which one spouse can please the other. This can include comments or actions or even nonverbal responses. As each person looks at the list of "pleases," he can select the ones to which he would respond, and/or suggest his own special "pleases."

Daily each person keeps track of the various "pleases" they observe on the part of their partner. Then they share their lists with one another and discuss both their feelings and desires for more or variations of the "pleases". By doing this, each person is forced to notice and concentrate upon the positive aspects of their marriage which have probably been taken for granted. Each now has a better idea of what pleases the other and both can concentrate their efforts in this direction. It is also helpful to find out how each acknowledged the pleases to determine if they are being adequately reinforced.

Contract or Covenant Therapy

There are a number of counselors and pastors who use a written treatment contract. This is often referred to as contract therapy. This process is similar to the negotiations of a labor contractor, for in a real sense the minister/counselor becomes an active negotiator. The goal of this approach is similar to others: to attain a more fulfilling and harmonious marital pattern. The negotiator role involves assisting each party to obtain what they want. Such behavior agreements occur in three categories: privilege, performance, and penalty.

A privilege is any behavior which one partner wants but is not able to experience at the present time. It could also be a behavior he or she feels should be continued but has a negative response to it, or it could be some kind of behavior change in their spouse. By building upon privileges, behavioral contracts provide for the exchange of positive responses from spouses. Most contracts are written to describe specifically the responsibilities each must meet in order to receive the privileges.

Performance is what the person is willing to exchange for the privilege.

Penalty is a secondary behavior agreement to be completed when a partner failed to fulfill their performance following a privilege. This category is not used all that much anymore because of its negative quality.

Some counselors and ministers may prefer to describe the contract approach as "covenant therapy." Such wording has the advantage of emphasizing the gracious and personal rather than the "legal" or explicit aspects of the agreements. The use of the word "covenant" may therefore be less threatening to the counselor couple. Dr. Donald

Tweedie described his preference for the covenant terminology:

Some three years ago I had started to use the term *covenant* as an alternative synonym for a contract. I liked the flavor of it and noted that it drew less resistance. I thought it best just to use it as an alternative since *contract* was the identifying nomenclature and change would be resisted. When I subsequently discovered that I had difficulty remembering what Kareem Abdul-Jabbar used to be called, I decided that change is quite easily accepted.

I was amazed at the differential of the two words. A theoretical dissertation in pastoral care was written, discriminating the "two procedures" that I considered identical! The author decided covenant was the best method, and I was inclined to agree. Covenant therapy was deemed to be more "Godlike," gracious, and personal.

There is an etymological advantage also. Covenant therapy assumes that all divine and human relationships and interactions may be expressed as facets of a covenant, an interpersonal agreement. Most covenants are implicit and covert; others, as in the case of legal covenants, usually called contracts, are explicit and overt.

Most personal covenants change over time, and the parties may not be aware of the changes. The covenant of marriage is often an implicit agreement to perpetuate the pleasure of courtship, cemented by sexual privilege. It is rarely designed to cover the exigencies related to the less present problems of "life together." Family covenants, like topsy, usually just grow.

Every human interaction may be specified as a

covenant relationship, and every change, as a covenantal modification. Every affirming of relationship is a covenant renewal. Covenanting is a way of life. Most people in distress desire better covenants with the important people in their lives. The following brief account will indicate the typical pattern of covenant therapy.

The couple requested therapy for a very conflicted and unsatisfactory marriage. The husband had been having an affair over a period of several months with his secretary and had finally left home for a brief time to live with this girl. The wife was acutely depressed and very discouraged about the prospect of the marriage surviving. The husband expressed his love and concern for their three children as a ground for his returning home. In addition to this third-party problem, the couple presented a variety of conflict areas, especially with reference to their religious behavior. Both were from a Roman Catholic communion, and the wife felt unable to be active in church attendance inasmuch as she felt estranged from the church by her regular use of oral contraceptives.

In spite of a moderate amount of reluctance to use behavior rather than feelings as the focus of therapy, they rather quickly became involved. There was also initial difficulty in getting the wife to move from general privileges such as love, concern, patience, and respect to specific instances of these attitudes in action.

The following are the series of agreements that were incorporated into the final signed covenant: (1) She requested as the first privilege that he would see that the children's seatbelts were fastened each time before they went on a family drive. She in turn agreed to make no negative comments about his driving. (2) He requested "solitude times." These became defined as the time from 7:00 to 8:00 P.M. on Mondays, Wednesdays, and Thursdays in which he could be by himself at the poolside behind their home or at a nearby golf driving range. In exchange he would participate in three weekly "talk times." They were to be from 10:00 to 10:30 P.M. on Tuesdays, Thursdays, and Sundays. (3) The wife also wanted him to open the car door for her and to help her with her wrap when they would be out in public. In return he joined the company bowling league, with the proviso that she could accompany him when she wished. (4) The husband requested that she would not again mention the affair in which he had been involved or the name of the girl. For this privilege, he would take her out to dinner weekly. She would decide whether alone or with the children. (5) He also requested that she would accompany him and the children to church regularly. His performance was to assist in several specified household tasks.

After four sessions, the wife's depression lifted, and both spouses became hopeful and helpful in the covenanting. The defensive aspect of agreement changed to mutual cooperation. The above were the provisions of the finalized covenant. They were seen for a total of ten sessions. Subsequent follow-ups of three months, one year, and two years report a high level of enjoyment and satisfaction in the marriage.

Covenant therapy is a process whereby the relationship of two or more persons which has become pathological and/or nonfunctional is treated through attaining and experiencing an explicit, mutually agreed upon, and satisfactory relational covenant, mediated through the services of a third person.

Covenant therapy involves both the attainment and the experiencing of a better covenant. The former is obtained through agreements of privilege-performance, the latter through validation in life of whether these agreements work. The covenant must be explicit so that each party understands precisely what he offers, what he expects, what the consideration for the offer is in precise detail. These dyads of privilege and performance change the system of behavior and stimulate positive attitude changes, which in turn bring about health and satisfaction to the marital relationship. Covenant therapy, as developed to this point, is radically conjoint, radically behavioral, and based upon a radically biblical model of man.[11]

NOTES

All materials quoted are used by permission.

1. Alan S. Gurman & David G. Rice, **Couples in Conflict,** (Jason Aronson, Inc., New York), 1975, p. 248. From an article by Richard B. Stuart. "Behavioral Remedies for Marital Ills: A Guide to the Use of Operant-Interpersonal Techniques."

2. William F. Arndt and F. Wilbur Gingrich, **A Greek-English Lexicon of the New Testament and Other Early Christian Literature,** (Chicago: University of Chicago Press, 1957), p. 278. As quoted in "A Biblical View of the Marital Roles: Seeking a Balance," by A. Duane Liften. Bibliotheca Sacra, Dallas Theological Seminary, October-December, 1976, pp. 335-336.

3. William F. Arndt and F. Wilbur Gingrich, **A Greek-English Lexicon of the New Testament and Other Early Christian Literature,** (Chicago: University of Chicago Press, 1957), p. 278. As quoted in "A Biblical View of the Marital Roles: Seeking a Balance," by A. Duane Liften. Bibliotheca Sacra, Dallas Theological Seminary, October-December, 1976, pp. 335-336.

4. Robert Paul Liberman; Eugene Wheeler; and Nancy Sanders, adapted from "Behavioral Therapy for Marital Disharmony, and Education Approach." **Journal of Marriage and Family Counseling,** October, 1976, pp. 383-389.

5. Jerry M. Lewis, M.D., **How's Your Family,** (Brunner-Mazell, Inc., New York, 1979, pp. 21-25).

6. Don Jackson and Richard Lederer, **The Mirages of Marriage,** (New York: W.W. Norton and Co., 1968, pp. 248-249, adapted).

7. Alan S. Gurman, David G. Rice, **Couples in Conflict,** (Jason Aronson, Inc.), 1975, pp. 252. From an article by Richard B. Stuart, "Behavioral Remedies for Marital Ills: A Guide to the Use of Operant-Interpersonal Techniques."

8. Alan S. Gurman, David G. Rice, **Couples in Conflict,** (Jason Aronson, Inc.), 1975, pp. 241-257. From an article by Richard B. Stuart. "Behavioral Remedies for Marital Ills: A Guide to the Use of Operant-Interpersonal Techniques."

9. Alan S. Gurman, David G. Rice, **Couples in Conflict,** (Jason Aronson, Inc.), 1975, pp. 268-269. From "A Behavioral Exchange Model for Marital Counseling" by Alan F. Rappaport and Janet E. Harrel.

10. Alan S. Gurman & David G. Rice, **Couples in Conflict,** (Jason Aronson, Inc.) 1975, pp. 258-277. From "A Behavioral Exchange Model for Marital Counseling" by Alan F. Rappaport and Janet E. Harrel.

11. Gary R. Collins, **Make More of Your Marriage,** (Waco, Texas: Word Books, Publisher), 1976. ("A Model for Marital Therapy" by Donald Tweedie, pp. 130-132).

CHAPTER 9

The Cognitive Approach
to Marriage Counseling

Cognitive Counseling and Scripture

Because a person's thinking process or self-talk can both determine and influence his emotional and behavioral responses, an emphasis upon the couple's thought life or cognitive process goes hand-in-hand with the behavioral emphasis within marital counseling. This theory also holds that people can control what they think. There will be occasions when the inner thoughts or self-talk will be analyzed and reconstructed at the onset of the counseling process.

In most cases the approach to both marital counseling and the treatment of depression involves a behavioral emphasis. This gives a foundation for the thinking and emotional process to move toward a positive note. Then an equal concentration upon thought process can be used to reinforce the positive behaviors and enlarge them.

Numerous studies are available which help to substantiate this approach to counseling. David Pecheur has summarized these findings in his article, "Cognitive Theory/Therapy and Sanctification: A Study in Integration."

According to Pecheur, research shows plainly that the fundamental tenets of cognitive theory are supported by a solid foundation of experiments, observation, and practical experience. Research has shown that cognition has a central role in reconciling emotion and behavior, and therefore the cognitive self-statement modification approach to therapy is highly effective.

Pecheur goes on to say that while on the one hand what people say to themselves determines their behavior, evidence has convincingly demonstrated that a counselor can "significantly influence" what a client says to himself.[1]

What do we mean by cognitive counseling? What is self-talk? Cognitive counseling or therapy is a four-step process.

First, the counselee or couple is presented with the basic rationale, which is that what we think determines how we react to others and to situations. Often couples believe that the spouse's behavior or lack of behavior is what creates the difficulty. Cognitive theory states that it is what we *tell* ourselves about what is occurring which creates our feelings and our behavioral reactions. It also needs to be expressed to those in counseling that often we are not aware of our self-talk because some statements or labels have been used so much and so long that these thoughts are automatic.

What light does scripture shed upon this initial state? David Pecheur summarizes this:

The Scripture verse which most manifestly supports the theoretical framework of cognitive therapy is found in Proverbs: "For as a man thinketh in his heart, so is he" (23:7). It follows, then, that "the thoughts of the wicked are deceit" (Proverbs 12:5), "for they that are after the flesh do mind the things of the flesh; but they that are after the Spirit, the things of the Spirit" (Romans 8:5) ["Mind" is from the Greek word phroneo, meaning to think, or to be minded in a certain way (Vine, vol. 3, 1940)]. Since Scripture teaches that what we think reflects either our old nature or our new nature, it behooves us to become aware in what type of self-talk we are actually engaging.[2]

The second step in this process is for the counselee or couple to become an observer of his/her thoughts, feelings and behaviors through an increase in awareness. By paying deliberate attention and developing a new sensitivity, a person stays closely in tune with his thoughts, feelings and behaviors. When the person discovers a negative or unacceptable thought or behavior, this serves as a signal to produce positive thoughts and/or behaviors which will counter it. This assists the person in gaining a feeling of control over his/her feelings and behaviors. Many couples blame one another for their feelings and behaviors and seem to attribute to the spouse a tremendous amount of absolute control and power. But through the above process one begins to discover that the control resides within himself. If one partner has control, the other either handed it over to him or cooperated with his power tactics.

Again this point needs to be viewed in light of the scriptures. The Psalmist says "Search me, O God, and know my heart; Try me and know my anxious thought; And see if there be any hurtful way in me, And lead me in the everlasting way" (Psalm 139:23, 24). This awareness of inner thoughts and verbalization, coupled with the Word of God, helps us become aware of our thought. "For the Word of God is living and active and sharper than any two-edged sword, and piercing as far as the division of soul and spirit, of both joints and marrow, and able to judge the thoughts and intentions of the heart." (Hebrews 4:12).

Scripture also tells us that the heart of man is the center of our intellectual and volitional life (Romans 10:9-10) and our thoughts are accessible to awareness (Matthew 9:4, 15:19; Mark 7:21; Luke 2:19, 2:51, 5:22; Acts 8:21, 22). We are to direct our attention to our thoughts and notice them. In doing so, we become open to change. It is interesting to note how early in the scriptures man's thoughts were observed as being such a problem: "The Lord saw that the wickedness of man was great in the earth, and that every imagination and *all* intention of all human thinking was only evil continually" Gen. 6:5 (Amplified).

The third step in cognitive counseling is based upon the second. The observation of one's thoughts now make it possible for the person to begin to give statements and behaviors contrary to the negative thoughts and behaviors. Once again scripture is considered.

When a person becomes a Christian, God gives him a new life through the new birth (*see* John 3). He becomes a new creation (*see* 2 Corinthians 5:17) and receives a new *capacity* of mind, heart, and will. Many Christians struggle along with their previous pattern of thinking and do not avail themselves of the new freedom and discipline available to them. By activating his new mind and following the scriptural pattern for thinking, a person will have the emotional freedom he seeks. This scriptural pattern is found in several passages.

In Ephesians 4:23, Paul says to be *renewed in the spirit of your mind.* This is allowing the spirit of the mind to be controlled by the indwelling Holy Spirit. The spirit of the mind is that which gives the mind the discretion and content of its thought. The renewal here is basically an act of God's Spirit powerfully influencing man's spirit, his mental attitude, or state of mind.

Romans tells us, *Do not be conformed to this world, but be transformed by the renewal of your mind . . .* (*see* verse 12:2*)*. This passage is talking about a renovation, a complete change for the better. The word *renewal* here means *to make new from above.* Man's thoughts, imaginations, and reasonings are changed through the working of the Holy Spirit. As Dr. Bernard Ramm puts it, "The Spirit establishes the direct connection from the mind of God to the mind of the Christian."

The first step in controlling your thoughts comes from the ministry of the Holy Spirit in your life. This reflects, however, upon *your own willingness* to let the Holy Spirit work in your life and to stop trying to run your life by yourself. Renewal of the mind brings about a spiritual transformation in the life of the Christian.[3]

Christians are not to be passive in redirecting thoughts, but active. In Col. 3:12, we are instructed to choose, deliberately, a definite mindset: "And so, as those who have been chosen of God, holy and beloved, put on a heart of compassion, kindness, humility, gentleness and patience." The words *put on a heart* or *set your affection on* mean to think or set the mind on. This is similar to what is found in I Peter 1:13: "Therefore, gird your minds for action, keep sober in spirit, fix your hope completely on the grace to be brought to you at the revelation of Jesus Christ."

Peter's phrase, *gird up your minds* refers to mental exertion, putting out of the mind anything that would hinder progress in the Christian experience. Thoughts of worry, fear, lust, hate, jealousy, and unforgiveness, are to be eliminated from the mind. Nowhere in Scripture does it say we are to get rid of these thoughts *if we feel like it* or tell someone else to get rid of them. The responsibility is upon the individual. It takes effort, determination and a desire to be rid of these emotions or thoughts. When the desire is there, the ministry of the Holy Spirit is available to assist. Through the work of the Holy Spirit a person can exert his will over those thoughts that work against the Christian life.

Herman Gockel writes in *Answer to Anxiety* about this process:

> There is much more to this whole business than merely getting rid of negative or unworthy thoughts. In fact, the concept of "getting rid" is itself a sign of negative thinking. We shall succeed in this whole matter, not in the measure in which we empty our minds of sinful and degrading thoughts, but rather in the measure in which we *fill* them with thoughts that are wholesome and uplifting. The human mind can never be a vaccum. He who thinks he can improve the tenants of his soul simply by evicting those that are unworthy will find that for every unworthy tenant he evicts through the back door several more will enter through the front (see Matthew 12:43-45). It is not merely a matter of evicting. It is also a matter of screening, selecting, admitting, and cultivating those tenants that have proved themselves desirable.

This is the pattern set forth in Philippians 4:6-8 which tells us what to *stop* thinking about and what to *begin* thinking about.

Many Christians fail to bring into their minds the proper thoughts. Others hold onto the old pattern of thinking while they attempt to bring in the new pattern of thought. The result is conflict.

A third passage, 2 Corinthians 10:3-5, talks about *casting down every vain imagination and bringing every thought captive.* Imagination is the deduction of man's reason. Every thought that would be contrary to the

Christian way of life is to be eliminated. Every thought
should be brought into subjection to Jesus Christ.[4]

It is vital for each person to understand these passages
fully, as well as to discover how to apply them to his own life.
Many verses depict the fact that using God's Word will be a
stabilizing factor in our life; "Thy word I have treasured in
my heart, That I may not sin against Thee" (Ps. 119:11); "Let
the Word of Christ richly dwell within you, with all wisdom
teaching and admonishing one another with psalms and
hymns and spiritual songs, singing with thankfulness in your
hearts to God" (Col. 3:16); "And being found in appearance
as a man, He humbled Himself by becoming obedient to the
point of death, even death on a cross" (Phil. 2:8). David
Pecheur discusses this fact along with the caution that our
self-talk not become merely a rote task:

The preceding verses lucidly attest the central role of
biblical truth in preventing sin and in promoting growth in
sanctification. However . . . merely memorizing various
passages of Scripture in a rote manner does not
guarantee that positive change will take place. In fact, no
change will be the most likely outcome. In order for the
Word of God and "Spiritual self-talk" to be genuinely
implanted (internalized) within the believer's heart, there
should be an accompanying awareness of one's identity
as a child of God (John 1:12; Romans 8:15-16; Philippians
2:15; I John 3:1-2). This fundamental realization enables
the believer to view God's Word and his "Sanctified self-
talk" as accordant with and as a true reflection of his
innermost self. He, therefore, does not employ the
"Word" and his "words" as implements of defense in
order to ignore or cover up underlying sinful cognitions.
Such a use would only serve to promote deception of and
dishonesty with one's self (I John 1:8, 10). Instead, in the

process of self-exploration ... the Christian's sinful cognitions are recognized and confessed, being seen as ego-dystonic (ego-alien) and as utterly incompatible with his new divine nature (2 Peter 4:4) and his new identity (I John 3:9). And ... the Word of God and "Sanctified self-talk" are emitted and impressed (upon the Christian's psyche), being seen as ego-syntonic in that they both perfectly express the nature of his core self as well as faster growth in sanctification.[5]

The fourth step in the cognitive approach involves the permanency of the new change. What the counselee says about his new thoughts, new behaviors and new reactions from others will influence whether or not this new pattern will last. A Christian is a person who has the greatest opportunity for change to occur and to last because of the sufficiency of God's Word and the ministry of the Holy Spirit in a person's life. Romans 8:26, "And in the same way the Spirit also helps our weakness; for we do not know how to pray as we should, but the Spirit Himself intercedes for us with groanings too deep for words;" A Christian is responsible for change but has a relationship and interaction with God. Many whom we see in our counseling are highly resistant to God's working in their life. Yet, if they are at least willing to put God's Word into practice (which is a behavioral and attitudinal change), their will comes to the place of being willing to do God's Will.

When the person or couple makes that decision to do God's Will and to have it expressed in their married life, God responds to work with them. He does not force His Will upon them, but desires them to take the first step. In his letter to the Phillippians, Paul expressed God's response:

"Therefore, my dear ones, as you have always obeyed (my suggestions), so now, not only (with the enthusiasm

you would show) in my presence but much more because
I am absent, work out—cultivate, carry out to the goal
and fully complete—your own salvation with reverence
and awe and trembling (self-distrust, that is, with serious
caution, tenderness of conscience, watchfulness against
temptation; timidly shrinking from whatever might offend
God and discredit the name of Christ). (Not in your own
strength) for it is God Who is all the while effectually at
work in you—energizing and creating in you the power
and desire—both to will and to work for His good
pleasure and satisfaction and delight." (Phil. 2:12-13,
Amplified).

For many people, bringing about the necessary changes
may be a slow process. Our patience, encouragement and
belief that it can occur will assist them. Often the process
involves altering the patterns of a person's thinking.

The Process of Altering Thought Life

What are the specific steps involved in altering messages
or thought life? We frequently use the phrase *self-talk* as we
discuss a person's thought life. Often people spend years
cultivating negative or maladaptive thought patterns. They
develop false premises and assumptions which then create
inappropriate emotional responses.

In the process of assisting in the analysis of self-talk,
several steps are followed. First, a person must be aware of
what he is thinking. This means learning to identify the
messages or self-talk one makes about situations or other
individuals.

Then the thoughts or self-talk must be evaluated or
challenged in light of evidence and facts. In doing this it is
possible to discover whether these thoughts are accurate or

not.

Then one needs to learn how to counter or challenge the inaccurate self-talk. In doing this a person will learn to substitute accurate thoughts and judgments for inaccurate ones.

Here is an example of this sequence of analyzing self-talk:

A couple attended a party together. Shortly after they arrived, the husband began ignoring his wife and talking extensively with other women and men. That was the event. Then she began to think, "He really doesn't want to be here with me. Something is wrong with me. I know I'm not as good a conversationalist as the others. Maybe he's losing interest in me."

Perhaps this sounds extreme, but it isn't. To one degree or another, most people make some irrational thoughts. Her emotional response to her thoughts included withdrawing, rejection, depression and more irrational thinking.

The next step is to counter or challenge the negative self-talk. She could ask herself, "Now, just where is the evidence that he doesn't want to be with me? Who says he is bored with me or that he is embarrassed to be with me? This doesn't mean there is anything wrong with me. Where are all of the facts for my questions?"

The final step is answering all of these questions that have been asked. "There isn't any reason or basis for him to be bored with me. We spent the last three evenings together. He tells me he loves me. He also said that there are many business contacts here. He believes that I can take care of myself socially."

In marriage counseling this process of challenging self-talk is aided by clarification of personal behavior by the spouse. (For additional information concerning the basis for the cognitive approach evaluated by a Biblical perspective, see "Effective Counseling and Psychotherapy: an Integrative View of Research" by Keith J. Edwards). **Journal of Psychology and Theology**, Spring 1976, Vol. 4, No. 2, pp. 94-107.

Dr. Jerry Schmidt in **You Can Help Yourself** has clarified the practical use of self-talk. Scores of individuals and couples have used the following material from his book and found it to be beneficial. Many have read this section week after week for reinforcement and clarification:

Rian McMullin and Bill Casey, have identified five methods to prove or disprove something. They are:
1. Use your senses (seeing, hearing, tasting, touching, smelling).
2. Ask an authority.
3. Find out what most people think.
4. Use your reasoning and logic.
5. Use your own experience.

The really important point is that while one method is good for some problems, that same method might be ridiculous for another. Let's return to a previous example to illustrate how some of these five methods could be used to challenge your negative self-talk.

Negative Thought:

"I'm just plain stupid." (Person who couldn't get car started) In order to put this thought on trial you might use your own reasoning and logic by asking some of the following questions:

What rational basis do I have for telling myself that I'm stupid? I can usually figure things out. How can one event in which I don't know something or can't figure something out make me draw the conclusion that I'm stupid?

You might also find out what most people think by asking these questions:

Where is the evidence that people think I am a complete idiot? Can I read other people's minds to know what they are thinking? Who has ever told me that I'm just plain stupid? What, in fact, do people say regarding my intelligence? Why wouldn't people think I'm simply another fallible human being like everyone else?

Or you could use your own experience by asking and answering:

What does my experience tell me about whether I'm an idiot or not? I succeeded in learning how to enclose my patio last year. I graduated from high school, and I succeeded in passing several college courses. That proves that I'm not stupid about some things and that I can learn about things that I don't know about.

Finally, you could ask an authority:

What have my teachers told me about my abilities? My professors? What kind of report did my boss turn in on me? She said I was one of her better employees in terms of getting the job done and doing it right. Who says that I should be able to do everything right the first time I try?

Let's look at another example and utilize again some of these methods for examining evidence.

Negative Thought:

"My boss is a horrible person. I am always being criticized and insulted by him. He makes me angry every day." (Employee who is criticized by boss.)

Use your reasoning and logic:

What rational basis do I have for telling myself that my boss is a horrible person? Isn't he just a fallible human being who does things I don't like? Doesn't practically everyone do things that someone doesn't like?

Use your own experience:

Am I always being criticized and insulted? To say that I am always being insulted means that every second I am being met with critical remarks. That's silly. My experience tells me that only occasionally are critical remarks directed toward me.

Countering:

Putting your thoughts on trial and examining the evidence leads to a process called countering. When you "counter" an irrational, self-defeating thought you fight it with your reason. By asking some of the questions in the previous section you will discover counters that you can use on a daily basis to counteract irrational thoughts. Here are some examples of irrational thoughts and counters:

Irrational thought: "Since my boss criticized me that means I'm no good."

Counter: "My boss criticizes everybody!" (finding out what most people think)

Counter: "That's the first time he's criticized me in over a week." (Using my experience)

Irrational thought: "She looks like a very interesting person, but she probably wouldn't be interested in me."

Counter: "How do I know? I haven't asked her!" (using my experience)

Counter: "What can I lose by trying to meet her?" (using logic)

Irrational thought: "I'd better not disagree with

what they are saying, because then they might not like me."
Counter: "If they don't know what I think they'll never have a chance to decide whether or not they like me."
Counter: "That puts me in a horrible position, where I can only agree!"
Irrational thought: "Healthy people don't get anxious or upset."
Counter: "In my view, John F. Kennedy was a very healthy person, and he certainly got upset and anxious at times."
Counter: "The Gospels certainly describe Jesus as feeling anxious and upset from time to time. If he wasn't healthy, who was?"

Counters should be statements of reality. In other words, if your irrational thought is, "I am inferior in every way," a poor counter would be 'No I'm not, I'm superior in every way." A good counter will usually come from one of the five methods described earlier for putting your thoughts on trial. A realistic counter might come from simply asking other people for feedback about your ability. From this process you might come up with a counter such as, "everyone I asked stated that I was good at several things."

Counters should be personally believable. Your counter could include everything from a scripture passage to a simple "baloney!" The important point here is that you really "buy into" the counters you use. For example, don't just pick a Bible verse because someone else in authority says it's the right one. Find one that speaks directly to you, both personally and emotionally.

Countering can either be done during a difficult

situation or as part of what we'll call a rehearsal exercise. Let's talk about the use of counters in real-life situations first. You are about to call an old friend. You give yourself some irrational thoughts like, "I'd like to call my friend, but if she hasn't called me by now, she probably doesn't want to talk to me." Then you remind yourself to counter and begin to actively think to yourself, "That's ridiculous! If I want to talk to her, it's my responsibility to call her!" The result is that you call your friend, she is delighted that you did and you end up setting a luncheon date.

The counters that you use on the spot should be as active and persuasive as possible. Shout them out in your head! Scream internally at those self-defeating thoughts! Use several arguments for each irrational thought.

All the counters used in this chapter are arguments with thoughts, not emotions. That's why a counter such as, "No, I'm not sad" is a poor one. That kind of argument only hides feelings and is potentially harmful. A better counter for "sadness" would be to attack the self-defeating thoughts which are leading you to escalate your sadness and make the situation worse than is warranted. Perhaps something like this would be better: "I'm sad because I failed to get the job I applied for, but that does not mean that I will never find work. I have other alternatives to interview for tomorrow."

Argue with the thought, not the feeling.[6]

Values Associated To Behaviors

As you work with the inner cognitions or thoughts of a couple, you will need to help discover the values which they attribute to behaviors. Behaviors tend to communicate something about a relationship. Sometimes this is referred to as "sender's rules" and "receiver's rules".

A sender's rule is a thought such as, "If I love and care for you, I will show it by this behavior." Or, "If I do this, it is an indication that I love you." The person on the other end, the receiver, has the thought, "If you love me, I will know it by seeing you do this behavior." Another form is, "If you do this behavior, it is an indication that you love and value me." If there is a correspondence between these value thoughts and messages and behaviors, the relationship will experience fewer problems.

Difficulties arise for couples when the receiver's rule for a value message does not correspond to the sender's rule. For purposes of illustration, let's say the wife is the receiver and the husband the sender. In this case, she does not get the value message, but not because he is purposely trying to send a message of no value. It is because their language is different.

What needs to occur (which is the job of the counselor) is the clarification of the meanings of the behaviors. Through such clarification, the husband and wife can change the behavior of the sender, the thoughts of the receiver, or both. When the couple realizes that they have been speaking a foreign language concerning an issue, and that the solution is not all that difficult and threatening, they feel relief.

One example is the case of a husband who is irritated over some of his wife's behaviors. He feels he has been slighted a number of times. One of his main complaints is that she is frequently late for appointments they have together. The question to consider is, "what does this behavior on the part of the wife mean to the husband." The husband's thoughts are, "If she really loved me, she wouldn't be late." But this is not the meaning that being late has for his wife. Although she knows he dislikes her being late, she doesn't equate promptness with her loving or caring for him. Her family simply never put a priority on being on time, and she still doesn't. Therefore, she is usually late to *all* appointments, including church, social events, picking up the children, and so on. The husband could have come from a family where lateness had a more significant meaning such as not caring. The mind-set, therefore, on the part of the husband is, "If you love me, you'll be on time." But the wife's mind-set does not correspond with her husband's.

How can couples break out of this binding pattern? There are a number of possibilities. If the wife realizes the significance of being on time, she can change her pattern and begin to be prompt. He, on the other hand, can begin to alter his thought life or value system concerning her tardiness. He can actually begin rehearsing a new set of beliefs. He will need to rehearse over and over, "her lateness does not mean that she does not love me. She has her own reasons for being late which come from her upbringing. I don't care for her being late, but that doesn't mean she doesn't care for me. I will find other indications that she loves me." Positive change can occur if either changes, but in our counseling we work toward both changing. It is also important for both to realize that their changing is not dependent upon the other person's making changes.

Another common problem is seen in the husband who attempts to demonstate his love for his family by working long hours in order to provide for them. His mind-set is, "I demonstrate my love by working hard." His wife does not see it in this way, however. Her value message is, "Why does he spend so much time at work? If he really loved me he would be here with me and the children!" She feels devalued by her lack of response to his love. It is important to ask him what his expectations are concerning a display of appreciation. Perhaps he would indicate that he expects her to be grateful that he is a faithful provider, and to thank him for his sacrifices.

She, on the other hand, does not say, "If I love you, I'll appreciate your working," but instead, "If I love you, I'll want you with me more. So I'll try to have you with me no matter what I have to do." This can include anger, complaining, nagging, crying, or other behaviors. Here again, messages are mixed and confused. There are four possible changes one might suggest:

1. *He* can cut down on how much he works.
2. *She* can change her view of his working so hard.
3. *She* can show appreciation for his sacrifice.
4. *He* can change his view of her absence of appreciation.

Any one of these changes will help the relationship.[7]

As you work with a couple, it is important to discover the following:

1. What are the behaviors your spouse performs that indicate that he or she loves you?
2. What behaviors does your spouse need to perform to indicate that he or she loves you?

One way of helping a couple with this process will be to look at page 3 of the Marital Pre-Counseling Inventory. Section A asks "Please list ten things which your spouse does which please you." Section B asks, "Please list three things you would like your spouse to do more often. Please be positive and specific."

As you proceed through this section with the couple, ask each person to share the reason these behaviors are so important to him. Also ask them to share their value message for each behavior on the part of their spouse. If they ask you what a value message is, be sure to clarify this and give them specific examples. Then, as you look at section B, ask the person, "Is your spouse aware that you would like this behavior performed more? If so, how did you make him aware of this? Can you give me an example of how you shared this?" (This may be an opportunity to demonstrate for the couple how responses can be shared in a positive manner.)

"What is the value message that you say to yourself about your spouse's performing this behavior? Could you put this into words for me?" After each person responds to the last question, ask, "Do you think your spouse believes the same as you do about this behavior? Do you think the same value message exists? What do you think he or she believes about this behavior?"

As you now work through section C, reverse the process which I have been describing. For example, as you read what each person thinks his spouse would like him to do more often, ask, "I wonder what your spouse's value message is concerning that behavior? What do you feel about this behavior and what it means to you?"

Another approach will be to ask each to indicate two or three areas of conflict where they seem to be at an impasse. Such an impasse could be possible if each has a different belief or value about the behavior. Using the same procedure, the counselor and the couple explore the conflict areas together.

Yet another approach is to ask each person to write a list of behaviors or channels which convey a love response. Ask each person to make a list starting with the heading, "I feel it is a sign of love if you:" (or, I feel that if you love me you will:)

Here is an example of one such list:

It is a sign of love if you: (or, if you love me, you will:)

1. Say, "I love you."
2. Say other things more or less synonymous with "I love you," e.g., "I'm so glad we're together," "You make me feel wonderful," etc.
3. Express your intention to stay in the relationship.
4. Make or buy me presents.
5. Show appreciation and gratitude for things I do for you.
6. Compliment me on things I did that you like, ways I am that you like.
7. Remember special occasions, such as birthday, anniversary, etc.
8. Touch me in a loving way.
9. Say things to other people that cast me in a favorable light.
10. Seem to enjoy sexual activity with me.
11. Smile, brighten up, and look happy to see me and have me around—i.e., communicate nonverbally, "I'm happy you're around."
12. Look for recreational activities for us to do together.
13. Be interested when I talk about my experiences and my feelings.
14. Disclose to me things about yourself, your experience, and your feelings.
15. Dress or attend to personal hygiene in a way that you know I like.
16. Help me to do chores and jobs.
17. Laugh at things I do or say that are meant to be funny.
18. Make up little surprises for me—leave notes for me that express positive feeling, make up poems for me, stop by unexpectedly, do things that let me know

you're thinking about me when I wasn't expecting you to be.

19. Be willing to talk about the relationship, think about ways to improve it, talk about things you can do or I can do to make either or both of us happier with the relationship.

20. Give in and sacrifice a certain fraction of the time when our wishes conflict, assuming that I'm also willing to give in and sacrifice part of the time.

21. Play and act silly with me.

In working with a couple experiencing these misinterpretations we help them understand the specific miscommunication. This involves clarifying the meaning attached to the behavior in question. At this time the counselor or pastor assumes the role of a diplomat and helps the couple realize that two different languages have been spoken. These now are being clarified so the two cultures can properly understand one another. Their channels of communication are open and the meaning of the messages can be clarified.

The next step involves clarifying the options available to each. Rather than the pastor or counselor telling them what thoughts to change at this time, it is better for them to make the decision and state specifically ways in which they would like to change either their thoughts or behaviors or both.

A common resistance and problem which you will encounter will be a new expectation. A new belief emerges: "Now that I've clarified for my spouse what my behavior (such as working long hours) means, she should just accept this condition." She; on the other hand, may believe that since she has clarified for him that working long hours does not convey love and also causes her to feel that he doesn't want to be around her, he should cut down at work. Both spouses should be asked how they can change their *own* thoughts and behaviors, not how the other can change.

From here we assist the couple in learning how to develop new thought patterns and how to visualize new positive behaviors which they can each perform toward the other. This needs to be done prior to an actual situation occurring for two reasons. Often when the problem situation arises, the emotion accompanying it is so strong that it is not possible at that moment to develop new constructive patterns of response. Clear thinking is shut down because of the physiological changes. Secondly, by having visualized and rehearsed new behavioral and thought responses in advance, a person then has a new plan to put into effect and thus can begin the process of positive change. To be sure that new behavior and thought responses are working, review what occurred during the week concerning thoughts and events when couples return for their next session.

Another potential problem which could be shared verbally for the couple prior to its occurrence concerns purposely continuing the now-clarified problem. How can this be handled? One way is to say something like, "Occasionally when couples clarify their thoughts and the meaning of behaviors to each other, one or both may try to use this clarification in a negative manner. For example, if you (husband) become angry at your wife, you may decide not to express your anger directly, but instead continue to work long hours even though you know that this upsets your wife and she feels devalued. You cannot say that you didn't know what this means to her. You do know, and are now choosing to use this knowledge for your anger. If you (the wife), however, become able to tolerate his long hours and accept that you are not devalued because of it, then his attempt to use his long hours to express anger is not really being successful."

Using the couple's own situation and illustrating how we can sometimes misuse new information may stop a problem from occurring before it ever has a chance to start. Continuing to be late after knowing both how it affects the other and what it means to the other person can definitely be an act of hostility if one chooses to use it in that way.[8]

Marital counseling, then, is designed to allow the couple to mature spiritually in both their thought life and behaviors. Such spiritual maturity will bring greater stability to their emotional life as well as to their marriage.

NOTES
All materials quoted are used by permission.

1. David Pecheur, "Cognitive Theory/Therapy and Sanctification: A Study in Integration" **Journal of Psychology and Theology,** Fall, 1978, 6 (4), 239-253, p. 246.

2. David Pecheur, "Cognitive Theory/Therapy and Sanctification: A Study in Integration" **Journal of Psychology and Theology,** Fall, 1978, 6 (4). 239-253, p. 248.

3. H. Norman Wright, **The Christian Use of Emotional Power** (New Jersey: Old Tappan, New Jersey), 1974, pp. 39-40.

4. H. Norman Wright, **The Christian Use of Emotional Power** (New Jersey: Old Tappan, New Jersey), 1974, pp. 43, 44.

5. David Pecheur, "Cognitive Theory/Therapy and Sanctification: A Study in Integration" **Journal of Psychology and Theology,** Fall, 1978, 6 (4). 239-253, p. 250.

6. Jerry Schmidt, **You Can Help Yourself,** (Irvine, CA: Harvest House), 1978, pp. 89-94.

7. Joseph Strayhorn, M.D., "Social-Exchange Theory: Cognitive Restructuring in Marital Therapy" **Family Process,** Vol. 17, December, 1978, p. 446.

8. Joseph Strayhorn, M.D., "Social-Exchange Theory: Cognitive Restructuring in Marital Therapy" **Family Process,** Vol. 17, December, 1978, pp. 437-448.

CHAPTER 10

The Structure of the Counseling Session

Factors Which Determine Structure

The structure of a counseling session is determined by several factors. Some counselors choose to respond to the couple's feelings and/or the content of their shared thoughts, with no distinct pre-planned strategy. Others see the counseling—or therapy—as a progression that varies according to the couple's problems and ability to use help. Consequently, various approaches are used. If one is following a strict behavioral approach to counseling, there will be a definite structure that will be followed in each session. Here is an example from a behavioral therapist:

. . . each session has an agenda, and each agenda bears a direct relationship to a clearly specified treatment goal. Clients are seldom unclear as to why a therapist structures a particular session the way she/he does. From session to session, there is continuity, coherence, progression, and predictability. The structure follows from the theoretical model as well as from the use of a behavioral technology; in addition, it serendipitously fosters confidence and credibility. The marital therapist must often struggle to maintain the structure and direction provided by the treatment program. Couples often attempt to alter the agenda. The therapist can and must resist couple's efforts to control or redirect the content of a therapy session. The most difficult challenge to the therapist's attempts to follow-through on a pre-planned agenda is the occurrence of "crises" during the week. The couple enters the therapist's office asking him/her to referee a major fight or become involved in a dispute. Although these events can and should be discussed in the process of perusing the previous week's data, they should not assume preeminence. In the excerpt below, a couple brings an argument into the therapist's office. He deals with it in a way consistent with our beliefs:

Wife: So, John spoiled the whole weekend by acting like a creep. All my friends were uncomfortable.

Therapist: It sounds like you were not only angry but also embarrassed.

Wife: You bet I was embarrasssed.

Therapist: It's clear from your data, as well as from what you're saying now, that it was a bad day. I also notice that you bounced back rather remarkably the next day. John, how did you change your behavior on Sunday to make Helen feel better?

(Here the therapist attempts to place the negative event in proper perspective, by emphasizing the positive elements in the week rather than dwelling on the negative).[1]

Often when the Taylor-Johnson Temperament Analysis has been used, a session may open with a discussion of the traits on the TJTA, or the traits may be used to discover a discussion issue or to move into an existing one.

One couple came into counseling because of a request by

the husband who was fearful about the state of his marriage. He wanted his wife to tell him she loved him and to demonstrate her love. He was jealous and appeared to have placed her on a pedestal. The Marital Pre-counseling Inventory indicated that their sexual relationship and communication patterns were quite unsatisfactory.

The following statements and scores from the marital precounseling inventory indicate the state of their marriage:

1. Everything considered, how happy are you in your marriage?
   HIS — 25%   HERS — 5%
3. Everything considered, do you expect to become happier as time goes by?
   HIS — 75%   HERS — 5%
5. How committed are you to remain in your marriage?
   HIS — 95%   HERS — 5%
6. How committed do you think your spouse is to remain in your marriage?
   HIS — 60%   HERS — 95%

The wife also contended that the marriage needed a miracle to bring her happiness. She explained that she was tired of trying, trusting, disagreeing and becoming a nothing.

Their scores on the Taylor-Johnson Temperament Analysis were:

	His	Hers
Trait A — Nervous (vs Composed)	80%	83%
Trait B — Depressive (vs Lighthearted)	4%	91%
Trait C — Active-Social (vs Quiet)	66%	60%
Trait D — Expressive-Responsive (vs Inhibited)	77%	11%
Trait E — Sympathetic (vs Indifferent)	28%	4%
Trait F — Subjective (vs Objective)	52%	81%
Trait G — Dominant (vs Submissive)	67%	4%

Trait H — Hostile (vs Tolerant)   66%   55%
Trait I — Self-Disciplined (vs Impulsive)   99%   83%

(See the appendix for a complete description of the traits).

After having each of them predict their scores, the results of their Self-Discipline vs. Impulsive scores were shared. Carrie's score was high at 83, but Roger's was at the 99th percentile which was as high as it could go. This indicated someone who could be not just a highly self-disciplined individual, but one who could also tend to be rigid, excessively controlled, perfectionistic with high expectations for himself and others. The session proceeded with the following discussion:

Counselor: (To Carrie) Do you see any of the self-disciplined tendencies in Roger such as I have just described?

Carrie: Well, I see them very definitely, but in other areas, not at all. In fact, at home he flakes out.

Counselor: I'm not sure I understand what you mean.

Carrie: Well, I'll tell you then (she looked angrily at her husband at this point). He can be very disciplined when he wants to, but around the house he's useless. He hasn't taken care of the yard for six months. I have to do anything if it's going to get done. He doesn't even water the lawn! I have to remind him to take out the trash just like a child. For four years I've asked him to paint the spare bedroom. When we do have guests they have to stay in it and it's terrible. I've given up even asking him. I just wish . . . I wish he would . . . do . . . something. He doesn't realize just how much I want that help. He says he loves me and if he's so darn self-disciplined why don't I see it! He just doesn't want to be around the house. That's it! And he complains about me not loving him! Doesn't he realize if I saw some action on his part I wouldn't mind his caresses . . .

Roger: Well . . . she's right . . . there's not much else to say—I do what she describes—I don't perform that much around the home . . . I've been working awfully hard the past six months and now that I've slacked off I want to enjoy myself some. I guess I need to start though . . .

Counselor: If this is as she describes your situation, Roger, I'm curious as to what immobilizes you though—you appear to have the capability that she is looking for. What is it . . . anger, resistance, what?

Roger: Not anger, I don't know. I really love her. I guess I wasn't hearing how much this meant to her in terms of being an act of love . . . I guess I could tackle some of those tasks.

Counselor: I don't think she's asking for a one time accomplishment. I think she's asking for a consistent, continual approach to the tasks, and without having to remind you about them. And if you begin to change, I think you need to consider the possibility that Carrie may not initially have the trust in you that you want . . . She may feel that this is a one time action, and not believe that you're going to continue . . . (she was nodding her head at this). Why don't you and Carrie discuss the problem—your feeling and what you can do. (They continued to work together at this point).

Others take the approach of responding to the content and/or feelings as they are offered and presented, with no distinct plan in advance.

Shirley Luthman gives an example of a continuing session whereby she responds to the emotions of the counselee which were shared verbally and nonverbally. The initial statements and interventions quickly move the couple toward a positive interchange:

Note that the intervention of the counselor is aimed not at changing feelings but at enabling each spouse to express himself fully and accept the other's expression of feeling in a nonjudgmental way.

The therapist's interventions enable each of them to see the other's expression of feeling as a gift—

Husband: "Things have been pretty hectic this week; a lot has been going on."

Therapist: "You seem low to me."

Husband: "Low?"

Therapist: "Sad, somehow. Your posture is slouched, your expression is somewhat sad, your tone is low."

Husband: "Well, I am tired. I've been busy..."

Wife: "Well, Tom died Wednesday, it was sudden. You have not said much, but I'm sure it upset you."

Husband: "Oh, yes. (Aside to therapist) Tom was a good friend my age I have known for 20 years. Also, our daughter went to camp this week..."

Therapist: (Interrupting) "You shifted very quickly from Tom. You must have had lots of feelings about that. Could you respond to your wife's offer to hear your feelings?"

Husband: (glances at wife, then down) "Well, it did hit me pretty hard, it was so sudden, made me think of my own death."

Therapist: "I notice you are talking to your wife, but not looking at her."

Husband: (looks up with tears in eyes) "I don't know why I am doing this. I never cry."

Therapist to wife: "Your husband is giving you a gift of his feelings and you seem very far away—what are you feeling?"

Wife: "I have never seen him like this. It frightens

me..."

Therapist: "Could you share that with him? Would you look at each other and share that?" (They look at each other.)

Wife to Husband: "I have never seen you cry before. It frightens me like something bad is happening."

Husband: "I don't feel bad, it feels good, like a relief—like I have been holding it in a long time."

Therapist (to wife): "Could you explore further with your husband what his tears mean to you?" (To husband): "Could *you* listen and hear her words as an effort on her part to understand herself and you and not as a criticism of you?"

Husband: "I think so."

Wife: "I always want you to be strong. I guess tears mean weakness to me. Yet, I don't *really* feel that way. People should cry if they feel like it. My father could cry, but I did not respect him very much—I never felt I could depend on him."

Therapist to wife: "Maybe you made a connection there where there really isn't one."

Wife to husband: "I never thought of that. You are dependable, you have never really let me down; I am sorry if I have kept you from expressing what you really feel to me."

Husband: "I guessed I thought it was weak to cry, too—my father was a stoic, a good man but the strong, silent type."

Therapist to both: "So we have a discovery, that the expression of feeling, no matter what the feeling, is a strength rather than a weakness. It is the road to understanding and profound contact between husband and wife.[2]

Yet the way in which couples progress in therapy can vary. Another view and approach to what happens is described by Billie Ables:

Our position is that therapy is a progression, in which the use of the tasks is varied according to the couple's problems and capacity to use help. Many of the tasks that are crucial to attend to early, such as altering a blaming orientation and eliminating an argumentative style, are difficult; they are never totally mastered and then replaced by new tasks. Rather, these tasks, along with others, will need to be continuously focused on with the hope of eventual proficiency in as many tasks as possible. The therapeutic process consists of continual working and reworking with varying degrees of success; the therapist must be ever ready to reinforce forward progress but also ready to soften the discouragement of temporary failure. One hopes through this continuous process to develop a momentum that will eventually be strong enough for the couple to carry on without the help of the therapist. Expressed another way, this is to say that the couple will feel sufficiently confident with some of their increased awareness and newly learned skills to tackle their problems alone as they arise.

For couples with sufficient investment, therapeutic help, and adaptability, this kind of momentum will occur. The therapist will become aware of increased learning by changes in therapy as well as those reported at home, for example, the greater assumption of personal responsibility for problem-solving or the giving up of the expectation that the therapist can offer definitive solutions. One good indication is if the couple, when beginning a session, assume responsibility by either posing a problem for themselves or for the therapist to work on. Other evidence is a couple's willingness to begin using their new skills and awareness at home and to discuss their success or lack thereof.

As the therapist becomes aware of behavior that signals progress, he or she will also notice what therapeutic tasks must still be accomplished, that is, those more difficult for the couple to achieve; the therapist will then need to focus on these. In any event, the therapist is still well advised to use what emerges spontaneously in the session to promote whatever learning is necessary to change behaviors hampering the relationship.

Thus, each couple have their own particular patterning of problems and proceed in their own way. For some spouses, the development of trust and relinquishing belief in the therapist's total power occur early, and learning to negotiate and other tasks can proceed. For others, a workable therapeutic alliance with mutually acceptable goals and procedures for accomplishing these never develops sufficiently. Lack of trust, clinging to an infantile dependent position, or a refusal to assume any personal responsibility for change may prevail, so that therapeutic progress is meager at best. Wherever the spouses are hampered must remain the focal point until progress is achieved.[3]

It is important to consider what a couple is in need of discussing and resolving at different stages of counseling. There are many ways of introducing such topics into the counseling process. This can be done by first making a direct statement and following it with a question directed to either one or both of them:

"All married people have expectations for their spouses. How do you make your expectations known to one another?"

"Married individuals want to be attractive to each other. How do you make yourself attractive to each other?"

"Couples expect to be supported and loved by each other. How do you support and love one another?"

"All couples engage in conflicts and have their own style of handling conflict. What style of conflict resolution do you use?"

"In spite of not wanting problems in a marriage, most couples seem to perpetuate them. What do you do to keep your problems a problem?"

The following is a brief excerpt from the second session with a young married couple. The man is strong and dominant and the wife appears to be somewhat passive and weak. In reality she has a great deal of strength and power in the marriage, but she is not aware of it. This session is an illustration of the kind of questioning which may occur in order to lead a couple to understand what they are currently doing and what needs to be done to improve the relationship. Note the types and direction of the questions the counselor uses to accelerate insight and change in this second session. This approach can occur at any stage in the counseling.

Counselor: (To the wife): You know, I am hearing from you what you said earlier and now I get the feeling that you have more capability and strength than you are giving yourself credit for.

Nancy: Probably ... (in a hesitant voice)

Counselor: Maybe it is a matter that you have done this for so long that it is a pattern. You are accustomed to it. It's like an old glove and it fits so well. The new glove could be a whole lot nicer, but I'm not sure how long it is going to take me to adjust to that new glove.

Nancy: Yes, the hills ahead of me always look a lot bigger than the hills behind me. I'm trying to think of what I am scared of, and what I don't want him to do or say, and I can't. I really don't know what it is I don't want him to do. I was thinking that probably when I do feel, when I do tell him, "oh, nothing is wrong" it's apparently—what I am doing is— what I am telling him—"I am upset but don't do anything about it or don't touch me or," but in a way too I want him to pamper me at that time. But by not telling him what's wrong, it makes it harder for him to be able to pamper me, too. Whether he wants to or not. So probably if . . . (turning and talking with her husband) if you could maybe . . . I don't know, not get anymore intense than what you just were. Then, tell me that you really want me to tell you what's wrong and that maybe that telling you, you won't be able to come up with any answers but at least it will help me feel better. Because it always does. It always does when I talk about it. It always gets some of the frustration out. But if maybe we . . . I could be confident that you wouldn't . . . well, that you wouldn't go into it any deeper than—that wouldn't necessarily be true because sometimes I would want you to go into it deeper. I guess sometimes I want you to play counselor with me and you don't, and sometimes I don't want you to play counselor and you do. And I don't want to tell you, I don't want to have to tell you when is when because I feel like you should know.

Counselor: Essentially what you are saying Nancy, is, "I have certain needs and John, with all your training and all your abilities, you ought to be a great mind reader. And this time when I want you to help me you ought to know it. This time when I want you to backoff, backoff." But the problem is none of us, no matter how much training, can be mind readers.

Nancy: Not 100% of the time anyway.

Counselor: No, you see you have some needs you would really like to have fulfilled. One of the greatest ways of doing it is to say, "yes, there is something wrong but I really don't want to talk about it." Or, "yes, there is something wrong. I guess I would appreciate a few questions, but when I say enough . . . don't ask me anymore."

Nancy: Yes.

Counselor: This is a way where we might not feel comfortable with the other person's response. Our desire is to just sort of take them and shake them and get the answer out. We want it all cleared up, especially if we have a high degree of impatience. There are times when my wife is down about something and/or there is something that is bothering her and she will respond when I ask. "Is there something wrong or do you want to talk about it?" "No, I just want to work this through by myself when I am really having a depressed day." Fine, when she wants to talk she will come in and start talking. But that is much easier on me and that would be much easier on the rest of us, too, if we don't have to mind read. It would be great if we were all that sensitive to be able to pick up but 100% of the time we can't. I am wondering what it would be like if you would begin this new pattern of saying to John, "Yes, I am angry, ticked off at something" or "I am bothered and I need about an hour". Or "I need two hours to work it out."

Nancy: But by then he will be gone or we will be off somewhere, then it is forgotten. I need to write things down more often. I brought a piece of paper tonight so I could write down everything that really caught me. Because an hour later I will forget what it was that I really wanted to remember. So I think I need to exercise that with John. When there is something really important that I want to talk to him about, by the time we get around to getting together to have time to talk I forget what it was that I wanted to talk about. Then the next day about the same time I'll think of what it was, and then he is gone again and then I get frustrated.

Counselor: When you have forgotten, is it really that it has dissipated or it has been buried and filed away?

Nancy: Filed away.

Counselor: Ok, now what if you plan to talk with John about something and he has a meeting and is gone for three hours and you know that at 10:30 when he arrives home, that is the time we are going to talk about it. What goes on inside of you during that three hour time lapse?

Nancy: Depends on what I am doing. If I am busy then there are not too many things that bother me a lot. After I get done with whatever I am doing, then I just get really depressed or sad and then I am grouchy to the point where he comes home at 10:30 and says, "Is there anything wrong?" Forget it!

Counselor: So it is there eating away. You have to keep busy and mask it for awhile, but then when everything is done then you begin to feel it. What would be better, to go ahead and to begin to share it with John right at that time or maybe take fifteen minutes if he is going to leave in a half hour and talk about it. Or wait until later. Which would be healthiest for you?

Nancy: It really would vary from day to day because during the week he is gone until late evening and when he comes home part of the fault is mine because I . . . when he comes home after a long day at work he doesn't want to play counselor with me and so I don't like to bring anything up that I am upset about because he has had a full day. He doesn't need to hear somebody else's problems.

Counselor: You're saying that he doesn't want to play counselor with you. But I am wondering if he would be willing to listen to you as your husband.

Nancy: Yes, he probably would.

Counselor: Why don't we check it out?

Nancy: But then I would want him to play counselor with me.

Counselor: Why don't we check it out?

Nancy: After you come home from a long day at work and you get home and it's been 10:30 more than 9:30 lately, would you want to listen to what I have to talk about when I'm all depressed and not sure even what I want to say? Would you have enough energy and patience at that time?

John: (In a strong, firm voice with a firm expression on his face). Yes, I would be willing to, not only willing to but if I found that I didn't have the energy to do that, what would happen is that whoever I saw at 9:30 would just be out the door next week. And if 9:30 wasn't early enough, whoever I see at 8:30 would be out the door next week!

Counselor: I hear you being irritated and angry by Nancy's question.

John: (again in a strong irritated tone of voice). I guess I don't want to be . . . I'm not irritated. I don't want to be angry. I don't feel like I am angry; I am really intense. I really want to drive home to you just like I tried to Friday night, that my work is secondary and if you need me even at the moment when I have planned to work, I will cancel it!

Counselor: John, I hear a lot of frustration. It is almost like saying, "what do I have to do to get this message across to Nancy!" That, "I really mean this, I really want to be available." And that frustration, I think, is moving into anger. Some of your intensity has a mixture of anger with it.

John: (To Nancy) It may have, but I am not wanting to be angry about it, I am not wanting to sound angry. But I really am wondering what it is going to take to make that real to you.

Counselor: Do you know when it is that you sound angry?

John: I know what I do.

Counselor: A minute ago I heard anger in the voice, I saw anger in the face. Now I think a lot was tied to that frustration. In fact, your opening comment... to Nancy.

John: I won't get into my feelings tonight.

Counselor: I almost got the feeling of a parent speaking to a child. And I got the feeling, Nancy, that you were asking from a child's perspective, would this be all right?

Nancy: Daddy?

John: I feel gotten. (Smiles)

Nancy: Good.

Counselor: And that is okay.

Nancy: What I have heard you say sometimes—and it has been joking and serious both at different and at the same time—where you have said... I am trying to think of what it is and I can't...

John: If I ever have another meaningful relationship today... That went through my head.

Nancy: Yes...

John: Then I wonder how much of this grave I have built for myself.

Nancy: Yes, it kind of sunk in with me. To where you do come home and really don't... you aren't in the mood to talk about too much that is important.

John: I am in the mood, though.

Counselor: I hear an assumption that I would like to pick up on. It goes back to mind reading. It is important to check out two things: It is important to share with John, "Yes, I do want to talk about it," or, "no, I don't want to talk about it". Also, it is important to check out your assumptions. John is coming in after a bad day, a heavy day and you are assuming, "Oh, no, he really doesn't have the time to talk with me," or, "He doesn't want to talk with me." Maybe non-verbally we begin to come across this way and any time we have an assumption it is important to ask the question to verify it. If we act on assumptions, it means we've been mind reading and we might not be picking it up accurately. Also, in some way I feel you sort of want a guarantee that, "if I ask John to talk with me and to share with me that it is going to be an affirmative answer. He is going to say yes."

Nancy: I always like a yes.

Counselor: How do you handle it when the night comes, though, when John says, "I would really love to talk with you but I am just so tired I am just totally wiped out." Because if he is human, and he is, those nights can occur.

Nancy: I feel like I could say, I understand. (to John) Do

you sometimes not understand when you come to me like that?

In this particular session this brief excerpt illustrates several different events which can occur in marital counseling.

1. The counselor encouraged and affirmed Nancy. He helped her to see that she had more ability than she was giving herself credit for, and that she was a person who needed to believe more in her own abilities.

2. The counselor pointed out the struggle she would have in breaking loose from some of her own patterns.

3. The frequent problem of mind reading needed to be clarified. During the clarification statements the counselor continually and gently encouraged Nancy to consider (the thinking portion of her life) reaching out with the new behavior.

4. When people say they have forgotten about an incident or feeling, it is important to clarify whether it was really forgotten, or buried to become resurrected again with more life and energy.

5. Although the counselor kept encouraging Nancy to think of the future and consequences, he also subtly encouraged her to begin reaching out to John.

6. She was encouraged to clarify her feelings or assumptions with John even in this counseling session, with an eye to making such clarification a pattern at home.

7. The counselor felt it was important to gently confront John with his anger, since angry responses to Nancy's questions or even to her sharing could cause her to retreat. Because the counselor brought this into the open, Nancy herself may gain the courage to say to John, "I feel you are angry and I see it on your face and hear it in your tone."

This session continued and then concluded with the

couple's commitment to pay close attention to what each was doing with their feelings. In addition, both committed themselves to practice a new method of responding to one another.

Facilitating Change

In addition to knowing how to use questions as a means of leading a couple to understand their current behavior; the ability to think creatively and quickly is a necessary skill for any type of counseling. This involves discerning what a counselee is and isn't saying, determining how they are defending or resisting change, and then deciding how to proceed in order to facilitate change.

Consider what you would do with each of these situations facing you in counseling:

1.   A husband continually complains about his wife's persistant nagging. How can you redefine her behavior in a different manner which would cause the husband to reconsider what is occurring between the two of them?

2.   A wife complains about her husband's withdrawing from her. How can you redefine this behavior in a different manner which would cause the wife to view their interchange in a new light?

3.   How would you respond to a wife's question, "Don't you think my husband should stay home nights instead of going out every night of the week?"

4.   A couple complains of fighting most of the time. How can you relabel the fighting so it has a different meaning?

5.   Would you ever encourage a couple to behave in their usual way of behaving, even if it is problem behavior? If so, for what reason?

During the process of marital counseling many issues will

arise and various approaches may be used. Some of the most constructive and insightful have been suggested by Jay Haley in **Strategies of Psychotherapy**. In the following account from his chapter on marriage counseling, note the emphasis:

1. Relabeling what the couple does.
2. Emphasizing the positive aspects of their relationship.
3. Redefining the situation as different from or even opposite to the way it is perceived. This is an exceptionally helpful concept and can be used to help one or both develop a new perspective upon the other's behavior.
4. Directing a couple to behave in a certain way and encouraging them to behave in the same manner. This is a way for the counselor to take control of the couple's life.

Defining the Rules

Besides intervening in a marriage merely by being present, a marriage therapist will actively intervene by relabeling or redefining the activity of the two people with each other. In the early stages of treatment his comments and directives tend to be permissive as he encourages the couple to express themselves in a context where each will have a fair hearing. Accusations and protests are nurtured so that as much as possible is made explicit. One way of encouraging a more free discussion is to define the consultation room as a special place: a "no man's land," where the rules are different from ordinary situations. In this special place it is appropriate to bring up matters which they have on their minds but have avoided expressing. Although this framing of the therapy situation appears a mild directive, couples will often accept the idea that they can protect each other less in that room. Sometimes a therapist may forbid the couple to discuss certain topics between sessions so that only in that special place are they discussed.

As a couple express themselves, the therapist comments upon what they say. His comments tend to be the following: *Those comments which emphasize the positive side of their interaction together, and those comments which redefine the situation as different from, if not opposite to, the way they are defining it.*

An emphasis upon the positive typically occurs when the therapist redefines the couple's motives or goals. For example, if a husband is protesting his wife's constant nagging, the therapist might comment that the wife seems to be trying to reach her husband and achieve more closeness with him. If the wife protests that her husband constantly withdraws from her, the husband might be defined as one who wants to avoid discord and seeks an amiable relationship. Particularly savage maneuvers will not be minimized but may be labeled as responses to disappointment (rather than the behavior of a cad). In general, whenever it can be done, the therapist defines the couple as attempting to bring about an amiable closeness but going about it wrongly, being misunderstood, or being driven by forces beyond their control. The way the couple characterize each other may also be redefined in a positive way. If a husband is objecting to his wife as an irresponsible and disorganized person, the therapist might define these characteristics as feminine. If the husband is passive and inactive, he can be defined as stable and enduring. When the therapist relabels a spouse in a positive way, he is not only providing support, but he is making it difficult for the couple to continue their usual classification. In addition, when the therapist redefines a spouse, he is labeling himself as the one who classifies the couple. By emphasizing the positive, he does his classifying in such a way that they cannot easily oppose him.

Resolving Problems of Who Is To Set The Rules

Although the major conflicts in a marriage center in the problem of who is to tell whom what to do under what circumstances, the therapist might never discuss this conflict explicitly with the couple. If a husband says that he gets angry because his wife always gets her own way and is constantly supervising him, the therapist will not emphasize the struggle for control but will emphasize the strong feelings in the situation. Explicitly talking about the control problem can solidify it. However, specific directives given by the therapist are most effective when they are designed to resolve the struggle over who is to set the rules for the relationship.

Any comment by a therapist has directive aspects, if only to indicate "pay attention to this," but the marriage therapist often specifically directs a marital couple to behave in certain ways. These directives can be classed for convenience into two types: the suggestions that the couple behave differently, and the suggestions that they continue to behave as they have been.

A marriage therapist will direct a spouse to behave differently only in those cases where the conflict is minor or where it is likely that the spouse will behave that way anyhow and is only looking for an excuse. That is, a husband who never takes his wife out may be advised to take her out to dinner, but usually only if the husband is moving in that direction. Such a suggestion permits a couple an evening out without either spouse having to admit they wish it. Mere advice to a couple to treat each other in more reasonable ways is rarely followed or goes badly if it is followed. A couple, like an individual patient, can only be diverted into more productive directions and cannot be forced to reverse themselves. To tell a husband and wife that they should treat each other more amiably does not provide them with new information or give them an opportunity to follow the directive. More important, if a therapist directs a couple to behave differently, he has often been led into this directive by the couple and so is responding to their directive. A couple in distress have provoked many people to advise them to behave more sensibly; such advice proves only to the couple that the other person does not understand them and they continue in their distress. In general, when a therapist is provoked into giving advice the advice will be on the terms of the person doing the provoking and therefore will perpetuate the distress. For example, if a wife says to the therapist, "Don't you think my husband should stay home nights instead of going out every night of the week," if the therapist agrees he is being led down the garden path. If instead of agreeing and so offering such advice the therapist says, "I think it's important to understand what this is about," the therapist is not only encouraging understanding but making it clear that he offers advice on his own terms only, not when provoked into it. However, this does not mean that the therapist should not offer advice or directives on his own terms. The psychoanalytic approach to couples is to merely listen and such a procedure avoids being led into directives by the couple. Although there may be theoretical rationales for remaining silent, such as developing deeper layers of the intra-psychic conflicts, the main function of silence is to avoid behaving on the patient's terms. However, a therapist who remains silent also avoids taking those actions which would move a couple in the direction of a more satisfactory relationship. To be silent when provoked by the couple may be necessary; to remain silent when directives which would produce change could be given on the therapist's terms is wasting time.

A couple can be instructed to behave differently if the request is small enough so that the implications of it are not immediately apparent. For example, if a husband says he always gives in and lets his wife have her own way, he may be asked to say "no" to his wife on some issue once during the week. When this is said in the wife's presence, the groundwork is laid for the suggestion to be more easily followed. Further, the suggestion is more likely followed if a rationale is provided, such as saying that any wife should feel free to do what she pleases with confidence that her husband will say "no" to her if she goes too far. Given such a directive, the couple may at first treat the "no" lightly. However, if it is on a major issue, or if the instruction is followed for several weeks, there will be repercussions in their relationship. The more rigid the previous "agreement" that the wife will always have her own way, the greater the response in both of them if he says "no" and thereby defines the relationship differently. The fact that he is doing so under direction, and so still accepting a complementary relationship, will ease the situation. But since the message comes from him, the wife will react. Similarly, an overly responsible wife may be asked to do some small irresponsible act during the week, perhaps buy something she does not need that costs a dollar or two. If the previous agreement was that she was the responsible one and her husband the irresponsible one, a small request of this kind undermines this definition of the relationship. Even though the wife is being irresponsible under therapeutic direction, and so doing her duty by doing what the therapist says, she is still spending money for something she does not need and so behaving irresponsibly. However, in general whenever a directive is given for a husband or wife to behave differently, and so break the marital rules they have established, the request must be so small that it appears trivial.

Actually it is extremely difficult to devise a directive which is a request for marital partners to behave differently from their usual ways when their usual ways of behaving are conflictual. That is, a wife who insists she is the responsible one in the marriage is usually irresponsible at another level. For example, she may be so responsible about the budget that she is irresponsible because she is overemphasizing money at a cost to her husband and children. To ask her to do something irresponsible is not necessarily to ask something new of her. Similarly, a husband who never says "no" to his wife directly, is usually a man who is constantly saying "no" by passive resistance. To tell him to say "no" is only partly asking for different behavior. Even if one should suggest that a husband who is treating his wife coldly be more considerate of his wife this may not be a request for a change in behavior because treating her coldly may be considerate of this type of woman. In fact, if her husband treated her more amiably she might feel great demands were being placed upon her or become so overwhelmed with guilt that sudden amiable behavior on his part would actually be inconsiderate.

Often a directive can appear to be a request for different behavior when actually it is not. For example, a husband had spent some years crusading to have his wife enjoy a sexual orgasm. He had made such an issue of the matter, and become so angry and exasperated with her, that the issue had become a grim one between husband and wife. The wife was told, in the husband's presence, that one of these days she might enjoy some sexual pleasure and when she did she was to tell her husband that she did not enjoy it. If her husband insisted on her saying whether she had really not enjoyed it or was just following this directive, she should say she had really not enjoyed it. This directive had various purposes, including the purpose of introducing uncertainty into the situation and freeing the man from his over-concern about his wife's pleasure (he suffered from ejaculatio praecox). However, from what had been said, there was some indication that the wife was enjoying sex while denying it and so the directive actually was an encouragement of her usual behavior.

Encouraging a couple to behave in their usual way is paradoxically one of the most rapid ways to bring about a change. Such a directive can be calculated or it can occur as a natural result of encouraging a couple to express themselves. A wife can say that her husband should stop being so ineffectual, and the therapist might respond that perhaps he needs to behave in that way at times and they should try to understand his reasons for it. When the therapist makes such a statement, he is permitting—if not encouraging—the husband to continue to be in-effectual. Most procedures which ostensibly emphasize bringing about understanding can be seen as subtle encouragement of usual behavior. Note that this proce-dure is quite different from the way the spouse typically handles the problem: a spouse usually tells the other to stop certain behavior and the result is a continuation of it. When the therapist permits and encourages usual behavior, the person tends to discontinue it.

When a therapist "accepts" the way a couple is behaving he begins to gain some control of that behavior. He is placed immediately in the center of their problem: Who is to lay down the rules for the relationship? Although a couple cannot easily oppose the kind of relationship the therapist is prescribing if they are already interacting that way, they can still respond to the idea of someone else defining their relationship for them and this response will produce a shift. For example, if a wife is managing her husband by being self-sacrificing and labeling all her behavior as for the good of others, the husband cannot easily oppose her, even though he may not wish to be in a secondary position in a complemen-tary relationship with her. Such a woman will tend to handle the therapist in a similar way. However, if the therapist encourages her to be self-sacrificing, the woman is placed in a difficult position. She cannot manage him by this method when it is at his request. If she continues to behave that way, she is conceding that she is managed by the therapist. If she does not, then she must shift to a different type of relationship. If the therapist goes further and encourages the wife to be self-sacrificing and the husband to attempt to oppose her and fail, then the couple must shift their relationship with each other to deal with being managed by the therapist.

As an example of a typical problem, a couple can be continually fighting, and if the therapist directs them to go home and keep the peace this will doubtfully happen. However, if he directs the couple to go home and have a fight, the fight will be a different kind when it happens. This difference may reside only in the fact that they are now fighting at the direction of someone else, or the therapist may have relabeled their fighting in such a way that it is a different kind. For example, a husband might say that they fight continually because his wife constantly nags. The wife might say they fight because the husband does not understand her and never does what she asks. The therapist can relabel or redefine their fighting in a variety of ways: he might suggest that they are not fighting effectively because they are not expressing what is really on their minds, he can suggest that their fighting is a way of gaining an emotional response from each other and they both need that response, he might say that when they begin to feel closer to each other they panic and have a fight, or he can suggest they fight because inside themselves is the feeling that they do not deserve a happy marriage. With a new label upon their fighting, and directed to go home and have a fight, the couple will find their conflict redefined in such a way that it is difficult for them to continue in their usual pattern. They are particularly tempted toward more peace at home if the therapist says they *must* fight and that they must for certain reasons which they do not like. The couple can only disprove him by fighting less.

As a marriage therapist encourages a couple to behave in their usual ways he gains some control of their behavior because what occurs is being defined as occurring under his direction. At this point he can shift his direction to bring about a change. The change he brings about may be an expansion of the limits of the type of relationship of a couple, or a shift to a different type of relationship.

An example of extending the limits of a type of relationship is a classic case reported by Milton Erickson. A woman came to him and said that she and her husband were finally going to purchase a home, as they had hoped to all their married life. However, her husband was a tyrant and would not permit her any part in the choice of home or in the choice of furnishings for it. Her husband insisted that everything connected with the new home would be entirely his choice and she would have no voice in the matter. The woman was quite unhappy because of this extreme version of a complementary relationship. Erickson told the woman that he wished to see her husband. When the old gentleman came in, Erickson emphasized the fact that a husband should be absolute boss in the home. The husband fully agreed with him. Both of them also enjoyed a full agreement that the man of the house should have complete say in the choice of a house to buy and the choice of furnishings for it. After a period of discussion, Erickson shifted to talking about the type of man who was *really* the boss in the house. When the old gentleman expressed a curiosity about what type of man was really the boss, Erickson indicated that the real boss was the type of man who was so fully in charge that he could allow his underlings a say in minor matters. Such a boss kept full control of everything, but he could *permit* certain decisions to be made by those beneath him. Using this line of approach, Erickson persuaded the tyrannical old gentleman to lay out 20 plans of houses and

20 plans of house furnishings. Then the husband permitted his wife to choose among *his* plans. She chose a house she liked and the furnishings she liked. In this way the husband was still fully in charge of all aspects of the house purchase, but the wife could choose what she wanted. The limits of a complementary relationship were extended to satisfy both partners' needs.

Accepting what a couple offers, or encouraging them to behave in their usual ways and later suggesting a change can also provoke a shift in the type of relationship. For example, a wife was protesting that her husband avoided her, and that he would leave the dinner table when the family was eating to sit in the living room alone and later make himself some dinner. Although the husband at first indicated he did not know why he behaved this way, he also indicated that his wife spent the time at the dinner table nagging the kids and nagging at him. At the first suggestion that she was behaving in this way at the table, the wife said that she had to correct the children at the table because he never did. The husband said that when he attempted to, she interrupted, and it was not worth a battle.

The wife was instructed to correct the children at the table during the coming week, and to observe the effect of this upon her husband. Her husband was instructed to observe the way his wife dealt with the children, and if he strongly disagreed with it he was to get up and leave the table. Actually the instruction was merely to continue to behave as they had been.[4]

Just as the couple must learn to accept one another's differences, the counselor must also accept each couple's uniqueness and at the same time be aware of his own expectations concerning what they do and what they say.

Their growth and progress is essentially their choice and responsibility as they evaluate their lives and alternatives.

Any of the techniques and approaches suggested are for the purpose of helping the couple unravel their conflicted relationship in order to move toward a marital relationship which is healthy and growing. The use of any approach, style, or technique of marriage counseling must not be simply borrowed from someone else, but instead integrated into our own language and personality framework. Taping your sessions whenever possible and relistening to them will help you to refine and modify your techniques. Such refinement will occur as you give thought to the material suggested in this text and as you continue to work with couples.

NOTES

All materials quoted are used by permission.

1. Neil S. Jacobson and Gayla Margolin, **Marital Therapy,** (Brunner & Mazel, Inc.), 1979, p. 132.

2. **Family Therapy,** Vol. 1; No. 1, Summer 1972, Libra Publishers, N.Y.: Shirley Luthman, The Growth Model in Marital Therapy, pp. 70, 71.

3. Billie Ables, **Therapy for Couples,** (Jossey-Bass Publishers, San Francisco), 1977, pp. 240-241.

4. Jay Haley, **Strategies for Psychotherapy,** (Grune & Stratton, New York), 1973, pp. 139-140; 141-144.

CHAPTER 11

Helping Couples Resolve Conflict Problems

Conflict is a normal part of marriage, but most couples have not been taught a healthy pattern of handling it. The word *conflict* actually means "to strike together." Webster defines it as a "clash, competition, or mutual interference of opposing or incompatible forces or qualities (as ideas, interests, wills)."[1]

Many marriages are characterized by strife and bickering rather than peace and harmony. Couples who have developed harmony are not those who are identical in thinking, behavior, and attitudes—they are not carbon copies of each other. They are the couples who have learned to take their differences through the process of acceptance, understanding and, eventually, complementation. Differing from another person is very natural and normal and adds an edge of excitement to a relationship.

Because each person is unique and because what each brings to the marriage is unique, conflict will emerge. In fact, there will be numerous conflicts throughout the life of the marriage.[2]

For many couples, the normal day-to-day conflicts are not resolved, and so they escalate into ongoing feuds. The intensity of anger and frustration within the marital relationship varies greatly. For some, individual therapy may be necessary to overcome the life-long accumulation of hurt and inappropriate patterns of response.

When couples begin sharing about their difficulty, they will use words and phrases which must be defined. For example, "We fight constantly." "We have so many conflicts." "He abuses me and the children," and such words need clarification. What do they mean by "constantly"—every minute they are together? What kind of abuse? What is a fight?

Conflict Patterns

Often as you begin working with couples who experience typical marital conflicts, it is helpful first to identify their fight or conflictual pattern. We do this by actually showing a visualized presentation of these patterns. The following diagram is shared with the couple on a flip chart, chalk board (or whatever you feel comfortable in using) as you describe the various styles. Your description should be free from the negative or positive value of each style. Such value judgments can be drawn from the couple or shared with them after they have identified their style.

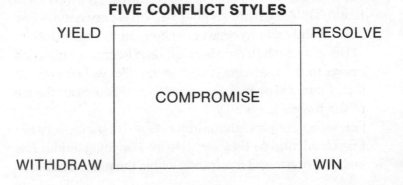

FIVE CONFLICT STYLES

YIELD   RESOLVE

COMPROMISE

WITHDRAW   WIN

The counselor begins by explaining that most people use one of five basic styles or methods of dealing with marital conflict.

The first way is to withdraw. People who tend to see conflict as inevitable and who think they can do little to control it, may not even bother to try. They may withdraw physically by removing themselves from the room or from the environment. Other times they may withdraw psychologically by ignoring the other person, by refusing to speak, or by insulating themselves so carefully that what is said or suggested has no penetrating power. This is the least helpful style of handling conflicts.

Winning is another alternative. If one's self-concept is threatened or if he feels strongly that he must look after his own interests, then winning may be that person's choice. Winning is a way of counter-attacking when one's position of authority is threatened.

People employ many different tactics in order to win. Since married couples are so well aware of each other's areas of vulnerability and hurt, they often use these areas to coerce the other person into giving in to their own demands. "Winners" may attack self-esteem or pride in order to win. They may store up grudges and use them at the appropriate time in order to take care of a conflict. They may cash in old emotions and hurts at an opportune moment. Winning becomes the goal regardless of the cost, and although the goal may be achieved, it is sometimes at the expense of the relationship.

A third approach people use in handling conflict is yielding. We often see yield signs on the highway; they are placed there for our own protection. When people yield in a conflict, they also protect themselves. They do not want to risk a confrontation, so they give in to get along with their partners.

We all use this approach from time to time, but yielding sometimes becomes a regular pattern. Consistent yielding may create feelings of martyrdom or eventually may create guilt in the spouse.

Another method of dealing with conflict is compromise, or "giving a little to get a little." One spouse has discovered that backing off on some of his ideas or demands helps the other give a little. This approach involves concessions on both sides and has been called the "horse trading" technique. Yet such concessions can leave one or both spouses dissatisfied with the results. Sometimes the bargaining involved means that some values are compromised. There may be a feeling of uneasiness following the settlement, even though one or both spouses think, "Well, it's better than nothing." Such a situation could actually threaten the relationship.

A fifth method is called resolve. In this style of dealing with conflicts, a situation, attitude, or behavior is changed by open and direct communication. The couple is willing to spend sufficient time working on the difference so that even though some of their original wants and ideas have changed, they are satisfied with their solution. Resolve is the most desirable method.[3]

Alternatives For Resolving Conflict

After the couple had identified their conflict or "fight" pattern, the counselor can present alternatives for resolving conflict. John Strong suggests nine guidelines for handling disagreements:

1. **Recognize conflict issues.** To be aware of issues that cause conflict is not to be "looking for a fight." But if

disagreements do arise, each partner can accept them as opportunities to develop self-understanding and understanding of one another. Consequently, the period of resolving conflict can be a time of growth. The attitude of the couple—whether pessimistic or optimistic—will influence and determine the outcome!

2. **Listen carefully to the other person.** Proverbs 18:13 says that it is "folly and shame" to one who gives an answer before he hears, and James 1:19 reminds us that "it is best to listen much, speak little, and not become angry." (TLB) Whenever one person listens to another, he discovers that the second person begins to take him seriously and to listen, too. Each spouse must hear and understand any changes the other desires.

Here is how one marriage counselor describes this problem of listening and how he helps couples in counseling:

...Most people are really very poor listeners. They "hear" with preconceived prejudices; they generally twist and misinterpret much that is said to them and often only hear what they want to. It seems to me, therefore, that an essential part of therapy—particularly when one is working with two people as in a marriage, a parent-child relationship, or some form of partnership—is to aid individuals to say clearly what they mean and to learn to listen openly in order to hear accurately what the other person is attempting to say.

I ask couples seen in joint therapy sessions, to use the "feedback" technique repeatedly to facilitate understanding each other and to get their messages across.

"We're going to try an experiment," I told the Rogers. "Obviously, the two of you aren't getting anywhere the way you're going at talking, and I have found a method that really proves helpful to people. I imagine that most of the talking at home between the two of you is just like you were doing here a minute ago, right?"

Both people nodded vigorously. "Oh, yes," Mary said. "Why even last night..." her eyes started to fill with tears, and I could tell we were in for another angry tirade.

"Hold it," I said firmly. "Continuing to blame each other for faults and shortcomings is, as we've discussed before, the opposite of rationally accepting the things other people say and do, even when what they do is admittedly poor. We don't have to *like* what people do, but we do have to accept what they do and say because that's reality. Then we can go ahead and try to change some of the ways that other people act, to see if we can get the world to be more the way we'd like it. But the way the two of you are trying to change each other doesn't seem to me to be bringing you the kinds of results that you both have repeatedly told me you want. So let's try something new, OK?"

I went on then to outline the ground rules for the "feedback" technique. First, one spouse could say anything he or she wanted—bring up a problem, "bitch" about something, etc. I instructed them to try to keep it fairly brief; during the time one person was talking the other was not allowed to interrupt or say anything. When the first person had had his say, then the other person was to say back to him the gist of what had been communicated. He did not have to use exactly the same words or terms, but what was important was to try to say back the *meaning* of what the first person had said. The original speaker was then either to agree (yes, that was what he had been trying to say) or disagree (no, that was not quite what he really had meant, or even that was *definitely* not the correct interpretation). If the second person did not "feed back" what had been said to the satisfaction of the first person, then the first party was instructed to repeat his message.[4]

One variation of the "feedback technique" as a method of developing listening skills is the use of a communication game. It is called the Revolving Discussion Sequence, or RDS. RDS is non-competitive and is designed to help the couple arrive at a compromise in which no one wins at the expense of the other. The game is played with simple rules, described here by John Lavender:

One of you makes a statement. Before the other person can reply, he or she must restate, to the first person's satisfaction, what the first person said. When you have established a clear understanding that what the first person said is what the second person heard, the second person must find a way to agree with that. If there is total agreement, you don't have a problem. However, you may not agree entirely with what your mate said, so you reply in a manner such as this 'I can agree there's considerable truth in what you say.' Or, you may grudgingly admit, 'There's a grain of truth there.' If you don't agree at all, you simply agree that this is how your mate thinks and affirm his or her right to that opinion.

After the statement, restatement and agreement, the second person is free to make his or her statement. Again, before the mate can reply, he or she must restate, to the satisfaction of the second person, what that person said and find a way to agree with it. This process is continued until the matter is resolved.

So the rules are simple: statement, restatement and agreement . . . statement, restatement and agreement.[5]

By emphasizing listening and understanding, the counselor helps the couple learn to replace insults and accusations with positive statements.

3. **Select the most appropriate time.** "How wonderful it is to be able to say the right thing at the right time!" (Proverbs 15:23, TLB). If one or both spouses are hungry, fatigued, or emotionally upset; or if there is a limited time available, perhaps because of an appointment or work schedule, problem solving should be delayed. The couple should agree to a definite time, rather than saying *later*. This is because "later" may have a different meaning for each person.

The time selected should allow for the greatest understanding and cooperative effort. Both parties should know what the subject or issue is and understand when it will be discussed. In this way, each one can practice what he wants to say and how he wants to say it. There is also opportunity to think about one's feelings and needs.

4. **Communicate in such a way to make it easy for your partner to respond.** In a conflict it is most helpful for both partners to share what they want by *making statements of preference, not necessity.* If one partner feels unloved by the spouse, one way to communicate that need is to *initiate loving behavior toward the spouse.*

. . . Often when we feel that others do not love us, we may believe that we are not worth loving. If you begin to perform loving acts your spouse might act more loving toward you, but if not, that's all right. Your act of love can fulfill some of your own needs and is also a demonstration of Christ's love toward another person. Remember that real marital love is an unconditional commitment to an imperfect person.

Another way to communicate so that the spouse can respond more easily is to *make "I" statements rather than "you" statements,* and to share present feelings rather than past thoughts or feelings. The Minnesota Couples Communication Program has suggested four skills for expressing self-awareness:

a. *Speaking for self:*

Husband: "I'd like to go out tonight."

Wife: "I would too. I'd like to eat out at a nice restaurant. How about you?"

Husband: "I think that's a good idea. I'd like to go to..."

The *under-responsible* person doesn't speak for himself, doesn't let others know what he wants or feels (or tries not to, anyway). He says things in indirect ways, often making sweeping generalizations about what "everyone" thinks or feels:

"Some wives would be angry at your staying out all night."

"Other guys expect their wives to look good when they go out together."

This type of person is trying to avoid being candid about his own thoughts, feelings, and intentions. Often he is put in the position of denying his own thoughts, feelings, and intentions, almost as if he were a non-person.

Wife: "Some wives would be angry at your staying out all night."

Husband: "You mad or something?"

Wife: "Oh no, I'm not. But some wives would be."

Another type of person, the *over-responsible* person, also leaves out the "I." But his problem is trying to speak for the other person instead of for himself. So he says what the other person thinks or feels or intends. To do this, he usually sends "you messages":

"You don't like that kind of TV program."

"You're pretty tired tonight, aren't you?"

"You want to go on a fishing trip this year, don't you?"

When you presume to speak for someone else, you proclaim that you are an expert on what he thinks, feels, or intends. You tell him that you *know* what is going on in his mind—maybe even better than he does. But can you really?

A close variation of speaking for yourself is what is called the "I message." It is very helpful in resolving conflicts. "I messages" are messages that identify where the speaker is and thus are more oriented to the speaker than to the listener. The speaker may want to modify the behavior of another person, to change a situation, or simply identify his position on feeling. An "I message" is distinguished from a "you message" in that the speaker claims the problem as his own, for example, instead of saying, "*You* make me so mad," an "I message" would be "*I* feel very angry when you do that."

An "I message" consists of three parts: the feeling, the situation, and how it affects the sender. It is a statement of fact rather than an evaluation and, therefore, is less likely to lower the other person's self-esteem. It is also less likely to provoke resistance, anger, or resentment and is, therefore, less likely to hurt the relationship. The "I message" is risky because it may reveal the humanness of the speaker and the listener may use this vulnerability against the speaker. But it helps a person to get in closer touch with his own feelings and needs. It models honesty and openness.

b. **Documenting with descriptive behavioral data. Documenting is describing:**

"I *think* you're elated. I see a smile on your face, and your voice sounds lyrical to me."

Documenting is an important skill. First, it increases your own understanding of yourself. It gives you a better idea of *how* you arrived at your own thoughts, feelings, and intentions. And at the same time, it gives the other person a much clearer idea of *what* you are responding to.

c. **Making feeling statements.** When you make a feeling statement, you don't know how the other person will respond. So, feeling statements are risky.

Wife: "I feel sick to my stomach when I see you bow and scrape to your boss."

There are four main ways to describe feelings verbally:

(I) Identify or name the feeling. "I feel angry"; "I feel sad"; "I feel good about you."

(II) Use similies and metaphors. We do not always have enough labels to describe our emotions, so we sometimes invent what we call similies and metaphors to describe feelings. "I felt squelched"; "I felt like a cool breeze going through the air."

(III) Report the type of action your feelings urge you to do. "I feel like hugging you"; "I wish I could hit you."

(IV) Use figures of speech, such as, "The sun is smiling on me today"; "I feel like a dark cloud is following me around today."

d. **Making intention statements** is a way of expressing your immediate goals or desires in a situation. These statements provide a different kind of self-information to the other person—an overview of what you are willing to do.

Wife: "I *want* very much to end this argument."

Husband: "I didn't know that. I thought you were too mad to stop."[6]

Often couples experience conflict over how one spouse

handles the other's feelings. Denial of a person's feelings is commonly expressed with statements like, "You shouldn't feel that way" or "that's all in your head. Don't let it bother you." Whether to have or not to have feelings cannot be legislated, however. And what is unimportant to one partner may be very important to another. When a wife tells her husband that he shouldn't feel a certain way, we might suggest, "You know, feelings are hard to legislate for another person. Could we just accept the fact that your husband has those feelings, and talk about what he could do that you would prefer more?"

5. **Define the conflict issue or problem specifically.** It often helps to have the couple put their feelings into writing, because although it is time-consuming, writing helps a person understand how a problem relates to unfulfilled needs. It helps him see the relationship between his view of the conflict and the basic psychological need that may have authored it. In defining the issue, one must consider both his own and his partner's behavior, as well as the environment. It is often beneficial for a person to ask the following questions of himself when trying to clarify the problem:

How do *you* define the problem? How do you think the other person defines the problem? In your opinion, what behaviors contribute to the conflict? What behaviors do you think the other person sees as contributing to the conflict? What are the issues of agreement and disagreement in this conflict? The more narrowly the conflict is defined, the easier conflict resolution will be.

As couples fight or disagree, they tend to lump together feeling or intentions and behaviors. It is common to find that when a negative feeling is provoked in a person, he blames the other for purposely doing the behavior which created the response. "You come home late on purpose just to make me angry." "You didn't go to the store like I asked just to get back at me." Feelings distort one's evaluation of another person's behavior. Here we need to focus upon the person's assumptions and beliefs concerning behavior, and help him learn how to challenge his own beliefs.

6. ***Identify your own contribution to the problem.*** In trying to resolve conflicts, the couple is basically saying to each other, "*We* have a problem." The way in which they approach one another and the words they use will be important in this step. When one person accepts some responsibility for a problem, the other senses a spirit of cooperation. Often this helps him to be more open to the discussion. John Strong suggests some practical steps in opening the discussion:

Choose one word that best indicates what you want to talk about.

State the word or subject that you want to talk about in one complete sentence. Be precise and specific. Try not to blame, ridicule, or attack your partner, and do not overload him with too much information all at once.

Take responsibility for the problem, and tell your partner the reason that you are bringing this matter up for discussion. For example, "I have a problem. I have something that is a little difficult for me to talk about, but our relationship is very important to me, and by talking about it I feel that we will have a better relationship. I feel that _____ is the problem, and this is what I am contributing to it: ... I would like to hear what you think and how you feel about it." Any statement similar to this is a very healthy way of expressing yourself and approaching what otherwise might be an explosive confrontation.

If your partner approaches you in this manner, respond by saying, "Thank you for telling me. If I understand what you feel, the problem is _____

_____ . I can agree that you feel this way." Restate the problem to make sure you have correctly understood your partner.

The conflict may be the result of a specific behavior of the other person. Take, for example, a husband who does not pick up after himself. His wife approaches him with a typical response: "Time after time I've asked you to pick up your things. Good grief! You couldn't be this sloppy at work or you wouldn't keep your job. I'm sick of this. I'm not picking up one more item around here after you. What kind of an example are you giving to the children?"

Contrast that to the wife who selects a proper time and approaches her husband by saying, "Dear, I have a problem, and I feel that I need to talk to you about it, as it does involve our relationship. Perhaps I have not shared my real feelings with you, but I am bothered by our differences in neatness around the house. I would feel better toward you and less resentful if I felt you were helping by picking up your clothes in the morning and putting your work away from the night before. If this were done, I would feel better and actually have more time . . . How do you feel about it?"[7]

Of course, the statements in that example are only suggestions. The couple must choose their own words. They should be encouraged to be explicit when sharing not only their spouse's undesirable behaviors but also their own behaviors that the spouse probably finds unacceptable.

7. **Identify alternatives.** After the couple has identified their individual contributions to the problem, the next

step is to find a solution that would be advantageous to both. Each person should think of as many solutions as possible, with behavioral changes on both parts. Posing a number of alternatives promotes flexibility and eliminates the "either-or" solution. All proposed alternatives should meet the needs of each spouse.

8. **Decide on a mutually acceptable solution.** The couple should identify and evaluate each alternate solution. In evaluating, they should consider the steps in bringing the solution about and the possible outcome of each alternative. They should ask themselves what each person will have to change if a given alternative is chosen, and how the change will affect the marriage and the behavior of each spouse.

Sometimes one spouse will like an alternative the other finds unacceptable. In such a situation, they should discuss the reasons for their preference. Sharing in this way can prevent feelings of rejection.

9. **Implement new behaviors.** Couples should be encouraged to concentrate individually on their own behavior changes, not on the changes the spouse is making. After the changes have occurred, the couple should evaluate the effect upon the relationship?[8]

It is important to allow the couple an opportunity to attempt to resolve conflicts during a counseling session. The following is an example of one such incident in which both partners had strong feelings about household tasks and their own areas of the home. Notice how numerous factors—each person's room, wanting to do things together, lack of trust because of the past, double messages, hearing only a portion of what the other said—contribute to the conflict. Quite a bit of arguing occurred during this session:

Heather: Do you think that there is any way that we can work a schedule or a plan—basic plan—for when things will get done?

Kurt: Sure, if we work on it together. I am . . . I feel like I work on it by myself. You know how to do as many things as I know how to do.

Heather: No, I don't! (definite)

Kurt: Yes, you do! (definite) And it is safe to say that you don't because then there is no pressure on you to do it. But you *do* know how to do it, you know even though it feels like you don't know how to do it! A lot of the things that I am doing, I am doing for the first time myself. So I have got just as much experience or inexperience as you do, and a lot of that stuff is not necessarily important for you to wait on me to do it—if it *is* so important that it get done right away.

Heather: We will have to talk about that . . . Now? (This was stated in such a way to indicate, "let's talk about it at home." The counselor non-verbally encouraged her to go on.)

Counselor: You don't want to talk about it now?

Heather: Well, I can paint in the bedroom. I can do that painting you asked me to do, but what I plan for the kitchen . . . is not something that I could have done if we were going to paint just what was there. But if you are going to rebuild the kitchen, I can't do that. I *don't want* to do that. What are you thinking that I can do?

Kurt: Is it that you can't do it or you don't want to do it or both?

Heather: Both.

Kurt: I am interested in talking . . .

Heather: I *don't want* to do the kitchen! I will paint, I will finish the kitchen and I'll do all the painting. But if that is not what you want, then I feel like you need to take charge of that.

Kurt: Well like, there are other projects though.

Heather: Like? (This was said with some defensiveness).

Kurt: The den.

Heather: What in the den? (defensive question)

Kurt: The organization of things in the den fully.

Heather: I feel like we need our Friday nights that we scheduled and they haven't happened. I need you there. (All during this discussion Heather was stronger in her argument with Kurt than ever before).

Kurt: Why?

Heather: When I do that.

Kurt: Why?

Heather: Because everything that is on the bed right now, I can't label those files. They are in files. I put everything in stacks in files. I can't label them. I don't know what they are. I need you there to help me answer questions that I have. Because if I was just going to . . . I can do part of it, but I can't do all of it.

Kurt: How about the fireplace?

Heather: Fireplace. Sanding the fireplace?

Kurt: Yes.

Heather: Doesn't that have to be done with a machine?

Kurt: No.

Heather: I guess I feel stubborn on some of those things

because those are things that you want done and I don't
want to do it.

Kurt: You don't want them done?

Heather: I don't like doing it myself.

Kurt: Neither do I.

Heather: Well, I will do what I can to do what I can! (This
was stated quite emphatically).

Kurt: I don't want you to have to feel that you have to do
any of it on your own, but I would like us to be able to talk
about it with you doing more or considering doing more
than I feel like you have been open to. I want to talk about it.
In other words, I am not expecting you to do everything that
is not done, but I would like to talk about it with the
consideration that you are capable and able to do more.
Just by virtue of the fact that you're a woman and you have
never done things, doesn't mean that you can't learn or
make mistakes that I make in the process of doing them in
order to do something. I started out the closet. The one
header I put up I had to tear back down and had to do some
additional plastering because of the mistake I made. So I
guess you are going to do it perfect or that you are going to
do it right, but it is going to be good enough. I mean you are
going to learn from it; I'll be happy with it. I will be happy with
it just because you do it. You put effort into doing something different because that is more important to me than
what the finished product turns out like.

Heather: I guess I feel like we would want different
things. I think we just need time working on it together on
things like that. That would help me to do what I need to do.

Kurt: Ok.

Counselor to Heather: The whole issue of what you have been talking about comes down to that doesn't it? Doing it together.

Heather: Yes. I think so. I just have a hard time when we schedule time to do things, and we are just too tired or not in the mood or something comes up. Do you think that would work? Having time to work on things together?

Kurt: Yes. I don't think that it isn't something that we haven't been doing. My perception is that a lot of things that aren't getting done are things that are looked as if I am the one to do them. You have talked a lot about my desk top not being completed, and I have shared with you several times I like the way it is. I don't have the difficulty with the incompletedness because it doesn't feel incomplete to me. You do . . . you are just as capable of doing it as I am, I feel like. The reason why I don't is because it is not a high priority for me. It has little, no, or little significance. It becomes a priority for me probably the more that it becomes talked about, or I get talked at about it, or possibly yelled at. Not yelled, but at first—but pressured to do it. You know. I would just rather not have that pressure. If it is that important to you and if you think I am being inconsiderate of you in some way, I would be happy to hear that. But I don't see how those kind of things are inconsiderations for you.

The counselor let them continue on for awhile before bringing them back to an analysis of the communication process. He wanted especially to come back to the last comment, which contained a double message.

Giving double or mixed messages—messages with both positive and negative information—is common to couples in conflict. It is important to encourage couples to share positive comments in such a way that they do not lead to quarrels or hassles.

One wife shared with her husband how much she appreciated him taking the children to their sports practice on Saturdays. As she continued, she mentioned that she had been doing this for years with no help or assistance, but now finally she had help. The minister could see a change in the husband's non-verbal responses when she mentioned the last part. The husband was quick to point out in a raised voice that on a few occasions he had taken the children.

This situation is an example of giving a mixed message of both positive and negative. Here the wife should be asked if she heard what she had said, which part her husband had responded to, and if she could see that she had communicated her positive statement in such a way that she literally diminished its significance. Whenever a compliment and a criticism concerning a major issue are stated together, the criticism is what is heard.

Here is how the counselor addressed the question of double messages with Heather and Kurt:

Counselor: Heather, what are you feeling about the last ten minutes of conversation of communication that has come between the two of you. What are your feelings?

Heather: A little bit of frustration.

Counselor: Your foot was saying that.

Heather: Almost like it . . . I don't know if this will do any good. (Stated in a discouraged manner). The whole conversation. I guess it just needs to be dealt with issue by issue and closet door by cupboard door. And figure out what we are going to do and if we do that, then that will be really good. I guess I would use the word *if,* because I don't have the confidence that it will necessarily happen. But there is a chance of it, but I am not real confident that it will happen.

Counselor: I hear you saying that you have a lack of trust.

Heather: Well we just, maybe ... in both of us because we have set times aside before and said, "ok, Friday night we are going to do this or Saturday morning," and it just never quite works out. So I don't know if we both maybe don't have our priorities right and let other things interfere when maybe the other things really aren't important as getting something done.

Counselor: I wonder how this affects the way that you are going to behave and respond now toward Kurt with the, "Yeah, Heather, we talked about it but I am not sure it is going to occur."

Heather: I am sure that affects it.

Counselor: What kind of an edge does that put on your response to Heather?

Heather: What kind of an edge like right now? or when ...

Counselor: Or in the next few days. It is almost a lingering thought or fear that is back there and I am wondering how that affects you.

Heather: I would be kind of thinking inside, "Oh yeah, yeah, I have heard that before."

Counselor: How does that limit you then, in the way in which you respond to Kurt?

Heather: Less sensitive probably.

Counselor: What else?

Heather: More critical, and if his intentions are sincere I might not be as accepting.

Counselor: I would guess there would be a general restraining and holding back of giving yourself to him. I think giving yourself to him unreservedly is very, very important for him. What would you like, then, for Kurt to do to assist you in believing him more?

Heather: Working with me to follow through on goals that are set. When we have an appointment to do something, to go ahead and do it instead of letting something else interfere. Whether it is just the fact that we don't feel like it, sometimes we have to do some things that we don't feel like—me and both of us. Maybe if we have just a couple successes.

Counselor: What kind of success would you like to have this week?

Heather: Just talking through things, putting it on paper. Paper is important to me. Putting it on paper. That would be success if we could get it on paper.

Kurt: Get what on paper?

Heather: A plan for repairs. A plan for anything. I would settle for anything.

Counselor: I am not sure I understand what anything is?

Heather: Goals, goals of any kind. Either for repairs in the house or the chapter in the book that we read on setting goals, short term/long term. Those are the two major things. That would encompass a lot.

Counselor: Ok. How did you feel about the process of communication that went on from Kurt toward you?

Heather: I felt accused. Is that what you mean?

Counselor: Well, I am not sure if that is what I mean. I am asking what you were feeling. That was one feeling, that you felt accused. What else did you feel?

Heather: I need that word list in front of me.

Counselor: You're doing fine.

Heather: What did I feel? I don't know what words...

Counselor: Let me ask some questions about the first part of it. Did you feel affirmed by Kurt?

Heather: No.

Counselor: At any point?

Heather: No. I don't think so.

Counselor: The reason that I asked. (To Kurt) I think I heard you affirming Heather in the sense that I heard you sharing with her the belief that "you can do a lot of those tasks." How? Maybe it was mixed up in the whole message.

Heather: I felt like that was an accusation.

Counselor: It wasn't coming through, but underlying that there was the belief that, "You have got as much capability as I do." And so there is the belief that you are a woman. You can do things. You can paint. You can fix several items. So that was one part of it. I think the message was clouded. That was one item. One concern that I had, Kurt, in the messages that you were giving to Heather, was a phrase: "I would like to know if you considered that inconsiderate of me. I don't consider it inconsiderate."

Heather: What's that?

Counselor: That is what you said to Heather. It was like, "Tell me if I am being inconsiderate by"—I think it was not fixing the doors on the cupboards. That part of it would be a positive comment, but then you followed it right up with your belief, "I don't feel that that is inconsiderate, but if you feel that it is, tell me." I think dropping off that last value judgement on your part.

Kurt: Did I say that?

Counselor: Yes, and that would not free Heather up to go ahead and say, "Well yes, I really do." It is like there would be a tension, because "if I do feel it, and I know that you don't think it *is* inconsiderate, then maybe I might hold back." I think from your previous discussion you want Heather to be very open with you and to share with you and to really develop an intimacy in the communication. I point that out so that you can hear yourself a little more. In fact, it would be good sometimes to hear that portion on the tape, because you would be able to pick up on it. It is like a double message, and Heather might feel in a bind. I think it is good, your asking Heather to be specific. I think that one of the issues that came up was territoriality. You each have different territories, and I began wondering if the desk top was your territory and the kitchen cupboards are your territory, Heather. We each have some importance attached to them.

The discussion continued with an agreement to develop some time-related plans to implement during the week.

Conflict and Abusiveness

Many couples will come into counseling with typical day-to-day conflicts such as those detailed above. But there will be a number whose conflicts have mushroomed out of control and have moved into the painful realm of abusiveness.

The enormity of the problem of spouse abuse has gradually gained recognition over the past several years.

As Representative Mikulski (D., Md.) introduced her 1978 Family Violence and Treatment Act, she gave the following representative figures: Approximately one fourth of all murders in the United States occur within the family, and half of these are spousal killings. One fourth of American couples engage in an episode of violence during the course of their relationship, 16% of American couples report an abusive episode each year, and 10% experience extreme admitted physical abuse. Steinmetz estimated that out of the total married population of 47 million couples, 3.3 million wives and over a quarter million husbands are subjected to severe beatings from their spouses. While husbands are more likely to commit violent actions that require physical strength, husbands and wives are relatively comparable in terms of committing violence with objects and committing homicides. Contrary to early notions, marital violence is not selective; it occurs in all social classes and is perpetrated by persons who may otherwise be exemplary citizens.[9]

Many Christian couples have learned to hide any signs of conflict or abuse because of their fear, but they do abuse one another emotionally and physically. When a couple such as this sits in your office, there is an approach which helps the couple to refrain from destructive expressions of anger and helps them eliminate the level of anger arousal. Gayla Margolin has suggested that couples initially need an orientation toward the relationship which can help them accept responsibility for their anger and behaviors. Three principles are involved.

First, abusiveness is a *learned behavioral response*. It is neither a disease nor a personality defect. All people are capable of and have the potential for violence. Excessive anger is not inherited. A thought such as this helps couples realize that they are responsible for doing something about their behaviors.

Second, abusiveness is a *mutual* problem. It is easy to believe that one partner is the victim (the "good guy") and the other the victimizer (the "bad guy"), but such labels only tend to accentuate the problem. As you work with couples where extensive anger outbursts or even violence occurs, be careful of siding with the victim. In some cases victims elicit sympathy and thus continue to get away with their own aggression, which is probably passive in nature. Passive aggression can take many forms and can be very irritating and frustrating to those at whom it is directed.

Forgetting is a common form of aggression. Agreeing to do something and then proceeding to forget is the usual format. In some cases the forgetting can be selective, and usually what is forgotten is what is important to others. Eventually people may not ask him to do things anymore. This form of behavior is one way of saying "no" or "I don't want to."

Misunderstanding is another manifestation of this problem. Statements like, "Oh, I thought you said . . . " or, "I thought you meant . . . " are frequent and innocently stated.

Procrastination is a form indicated by, "we'll get it done soon" or, "don't worry" or, "don't be so impatient." Keeping others waiting or forcing others to remind them of the time is a frequent occurrence. Here, too, the procrastination can be selective in terms of who is kept waiting and when. A variation of the procrastination is the latecomer. He is a classic expression of hostility. Arriving late for meetings or appointments becomes his means of expressing anger towards the person or the event. A person like this has usually developed a repertoire of excuses.

As you discuss the relationship, therefore, you may

discover that both have contributed to the increase of anger. The physically abusive spouse usually receives most of the blame, and yet the other is often abusive in more subtle ways. This can mean that each could be both the abuser *and* the victim.

After carefully analyzing the relationship, a question such as "Had you ever considered the possibility that each of you is an abuser and a victim?" may lead to a discussion which develops new insights. By discussing the situation in this way the couple may see that their abusiveness is a mutual problem. The purpose is not to relieve them of responsibility, but to help them to accept it mutually.

Third, one of the main reasons that abusiveness occurs is the *lack of good problem-solving skills*. Abusiveness is a desperate negative attempt to change the marriage. Thus decreasing violence is not the answer; teaching problem-solving skills can help.[10]

An Anger Reduction Approach

There are numerous approaches to take in assisting abusive or angry spouses. Here is a practical seven step program which can be diagrammed on a flip chart and explained in detail to the couple or to an individual:

1. **Identify the cues that contribute to the anger.** Assessing the couple's communication pattern to discover how and when they express anger to one another is the first step. We are looking for what brings about the anger and what keeps it going. The purpose is to discover the causes and not to lay blame on either partner. Even responses that continue to feed the difficulty are part of this problem. Each partner must learn to recognize the early signs of anger, especially his own.

Dr. Margolin suggests the use of a behavioral diary. Each spouse records four items whenever anger occurs:

a) the circumstances surrounding the anger (i.e., who was present, where did it occur, what triggered it);

b) the specific behaviors that the spouse emitted;

c) reactions to those behaviors; and

d) the manner in which the conflict was eventually resolved. It is best that spouses record this information immediately after the occurrence of an angry episode while the details are still easily recalled.[11]

2. **Establish ground rules for "fair fight" rules.** (See the chapter on communication for information on ground rules.) Each partner makes a firm commitment to follow through in keeping these rules.

3. **Develop a plan of action for interrupting the conflict pattern.** This plan should involve immediate action to disengage from the conflict and also a way to face and handle the problem at a later time. Interrupting the conflict is an application of Nehemiah 5:6-7: "I (Nehemiah) was very angry when I heard their cry and these words. I thought it over, then rebuked the nobles and officials."

Even the neutral expression of the phrase, "I'm getting angry," "I'm losing control," "We're starting to fight," "I'm going to write out my feelings," is a positive step. Upon hearing this statement, the other could share a developed phrase like, "Thank you for telling me. What is it that I could do that would help right now?"

A commitment from both partners not to yell or raise the voice and not to act out the anger is essential. This step is called *suspending the anger*. It is a positive move if couples agree to return to the issue at a less conflictual time. Most people are not used to taking the time to admit, scrutinize, and then handle their anger. These steps and procedures should be practiced and rehearsed via role play in your presence.

The interruption period can be an opportune time for the person to focus upon the cause of his anger. In counseling, it is important to teach counselees how to discover the cause, so in the future they will be able to respond with less anger. Anger stems from three basic causes.

One cause is *hurt.* When a person experiences hurt such as rejection, criticism, or physical or emotional pain, the normal response is anger. A counterattack occurs. Another cause is *fear.* A person who senses he is in a vulnerable position and doesn't like feeling vulnerable will counter with anger. A third cause is *frustration.* Frustration occurs in many forms. Usually it is an indication that one's needs and/or expectations are being blocked. A person wants something and being thwarted elevates the anger.

One way to help a person identify the causes of his anger is to introduce him to the concept of a STOP! THINK! Card. On one side of a 3 x 5 card the word *Stop!* is written. The other side contains the following three questions: "Am I experiencing hurt over something right now? Am I in some way afraid? Am I frustrated over a need or expectation?" The minute one begins to experience anger, he is to take out the card, read the word *Stop!* twice (out loud if possible), and then turn the card over, read and respond to the three questions. Another advantage to the card is that reading it is a beneficial delaying tactic to control the anger.

David Mace has offered two other positive suggestions for the control of anger.

Renounce your anger as inappropriate. This does not mean you do not have a right to be angry. In an appropriate situation, your anger could be a life-saver. Anger enables us to assert ourselves in situations where we should. Anger exposes anti-social behavior in others. Anger gets wrongs righted. In a loving marriage, however, these measures are not necessary. My wife is not my enemy. She is my best friend; and it does not help either of us if I treat her as an enemy. So I say, "I'm angry with you. But I don't want to be angry with you. I don't like myself in this condition. I don't want to want to strike you. I'd rather want to stroke you." This renouncing of anger on one side prevents the uprush of retaliatory anger on the other side, and the resulting tendency to drift into what I call the "artillery duel." If I present my state of anger against my wife as a problem I have, she is not motivated to respond angrily. This is like the use of Style 4 in the Minnesota Couples Communication Program. Instead of a challenge to fight, it is an invitation to negotiate.

Ask your partner for help. This... step is the clincher. Without it, not much progress can be made. The anger may die down, but that is not enough. Both partners need to find out just *why* one got mad with the other. If they do not, it could happen again, and again, and again. A request for help is not likely to be turned down. It is in your partner's best interests to find out what is going on, and correct it, if a loving relationship is going to be maintained. When the request for help is accepted too, the stimulus that caused the anger is usually completely neutralized, and the negative emotion dissolves away. Then the work can begin right away if possible, or at some agreed future time. The whole situation can thus be calmly examined, and some solution found. In fact, conflicts between married people are not really destructive. Rightly used, they provide valuable clues that show us the growing edges of our relationship—the points at which we need to work together to make it richer and deeper.[12]

4. **De-cue the Victim.** If one partner has certain behavior that tends to provoke violence from the other, this behavior should be eliminated so the first partner doesn't have any reason to retaliate. Minor or even defensive behaviors can be a trigger. Leaving clothes on the floor, a hair dryer on the sink in the bathroom, bringing up the past, banging pots and pans are triggers which are easy to change. If a partner's cowering elicits abusiveness, he or she can leave the room before the abuse occurs. In determining the cues it may be important to talk through some of these episodes to discover specific triggers and then to seek alternatives.

5. **Change faulty thinking patterns which effect the relationship.** Here again the problem of expectations and assumptions arises. The faulty beliefs will need to be both exposed and challenged. Some common themes are:

"You won't love me if I tell you how I really feel."

"You won't love me if I disagree with you."

"It's better just to hide how I feel."

"It's better just to fake it and go along with what he wants."

"Even if I do speak up, you'll win anyway."

"He should know what I need."

"All anger is wrong so I'm not going to express any."

"I'm not going to lower myself and get angry like he does."

An educational approach to anger and disagreement can help a couple to develop a more realistic belief system with regard to conflict. The counselor should share a balanced Biblical perspective as well as the normality of anger. **An Answer to Anger** and chapters ten and eleven of **The Pillars of Marriage** by H. Norman Wright can be used with the couple as an additional resource. Analyzing and challenging assumptions and eliminating mind-reading will also be necessary at this time.

6. **Develop problem-solving skills.** To alter a couple's previous pattern, they must develop new communication skills and a definite plan for making decisions and solving problems. They will also need to clarify their expectations and come to an understanding of need fulfillment. Specific guidelines would include the following points:

    a. Use neutral language without "gunpowder" words.
    b. Use positive statements rather than vindictive ones.
    c. Demonstrate positive behaviors toward one another.
    d. Have a joint discussion of new rules the couple would like for their relationship.
    e. Follow steps to improve the overall tone of the marriage.[13]

7. **Redirect the focus** from "who is right or wrong?" to what are the behaviors involved and how do they affect the relationship?"

The Effect of Blame

Blame is a relationship crippler. It discourages healing of hurts and erects even greater walls. When marital discord occurs, each spouse needs to remove his own guilt. He therefore looks for a scapegoat rather than evaluate his own investment. If one can succeed in placing blame, then his own responsibility has been lifted. When one attacks, the other counters with an attack. Eventually they both become proficient combaters.

It is easy to view a couple as attackers, and yet it is possible that each of them is struggling under the pain of self-criticism.

Dr. R. V. Fitzgerald described it by saying:

One blames the other because he feels a blame within himself; by ascribing the fault to the spouse, it becomes confirmed and amplified in the spouse. Unable to forgive himself for his own shortcomings or limitations, each patient finds himself unable to forgive the other; neither can help the other spouse to modify the degree of guilt they both share. The therapist, of course, must avoid judging the topics under discussion, although the couple repeatedly offer him implicit, tacit, or even open invitations to do just that. Comments are to be directed at the process.

In this type of situation, I have found several kinds of intervention helpful:

1. Pointing out how they keep tossing a big black ball of blame back and forth as though it were in a game of "catch."

2. Asking what would be accomplished if I could, with scientific precision, weigh the exact amount of blame and assign, for example, three ounces to one and three and a half ounces to the other.

3. Explaining the essential difference between guilt and responsibility and illustrating this by saying, for instance, "Whatever happens in this room among the three of us is like an equation, a times b times c equals z. If we succeed, we do so together, the three of us; and the same holds true if we fail. Since I am the professional involved, I am always ready to take 40 percent of the responsibility."

4. Expressing compassionate concern about the pain they are experiencing.

5. Robbing the blame of its significance by labeling it

futile, a waste of time, oriented only to the past, and unable to help in solving present problems.

6. Suggesting the cultural basis for learning this process: Their parents may have been more interested in finding out who started a fight than in stopping it.

Intuition, tact, and his own feelings are the only guides the therapist has to fall back on in matching couple to the tactic. A certain amount of trial and error is necessary.

Doing something to stop repetitive blaming is unquestionably better than doing nothing. My main aim, however, is to emphasize the importance of dealing with behavior, as opposed to subject matter. It is seldom possible to get beneath the blaming process until the process itself has been modified or interrupted.[14]

Most husbands and wives do not need to refine their skills any more in blaming. To allow this to continue is to court destruction.

There are several practical steps which can be taken:

1. Suggest to the couple that instead of blaming the other each of them could share their own inner hurt and feelings rather than attacking the other. This is usually where the blame is coming from.

2. When couples have calmed down sufficiently enough to share complaints in a constructive manner, then some of the principles of communication or conflict resolution could be discussed.

3. Sometimes difficult but necessary is distinguishing between the person and his negative behaviors. This eliminates labeling the person as "bad" or "destructive."

4. When one suggests that the spouse intentionally behaves in a negative manner, you could pose the question, "How would you respond if you knew that what happened was unintentional?" The person's original statement indi-

cates that he is more of an expert on the person than he really is. In a sense this follows Jay Haley's approach of redefining, which was discussed earlier.

5. Often it helps a couple to identify ways in which they are similar and ways in which they are different. Differentness is just another way of responding and by itself is not necessarily bad. But in their interaction, for some reason, differentness has become a problem because of the couple's resistance to and inability to deal with or accept the differences. Is there any possibility of viewing these differences as complementary? Can the differences be used in any way?

There are five basic approaches which couples choose in dealing with the area of differentness, and these can be explored and evaluated. One approach is the *surrender* of one partner to the other. *Subversion* is another. Subversion uses manipulation and other underhanded means of resolving the conflict. A third is *open warfare*. All three increase pain and dissatisfaction. *Negotiation* can lessen the pain and bring some satisfaction, but acceptance, adjustment, and self-change can produce individual and marital growth and satisfaction.

This last approach involves the application of Ephesians 4:2 to the marriage. "Living as becomes you—with complete lowliness of mind (humility) and meekness (unselfishness, gentleness, kindness), with patience, bearing with one another and making allowances because you love one another" (Amplified). The latter portion of this passage (making allowances) involves the *acceptance of individual differences*. The acknowledgement and utilization of these differences can be a powerful source for the marriage if somehow the couple will grasp this fact.

But what happens when there is a deadlock and neither

wants to change? When such a deadlock does occur, which is easier to break: behavior, belief, or attitudinal patterns? It is easier for one partner to accept his spouse's beliefs and feelings when they don't involve behavior or actions. If the deadlock has to do with behavior, possible alternatives with their ensuing consequences can be explored. In some cases one will be willing to "give" in the deadlocked area if the spouse is willing to "give" in another.

Rebuilding a couple's communication style and conflict pattern in counseling frequently enables them to handle their other areas of strain, since they now have an improved vehicle of sharing and problem solving. Time is involved in teaching and reinforcing these new approaches, but couples will gain hope as they see their negative lifestyles changing.

NOTES

All materials quoted are used by permission.

1. Webster's **Third New International Dictionary**, G. & C. Meriam Company, Publishers, 1976.

2. H. Norman Wright, **The Pillars of Marriage**, Regal Books, Ventura, Calif., 1979, p. 133.

3. Adapted from **The Pillars of Marriage** by H. Norman Wright, Regal Books, Ventura, Calif., 1979, pp. 146-151.

4. **Handbook of Marriage Counseling, Second Edition,** Edited by Benard Jr. and Constance Callahanard, Science and Behavior Books Inc., Palo Alto, Calif., 1976, (article "Feedback Techniques in Marriage Counseling", John Williams, p. 382).

5. John Allan Lavender, **Your Marriage Needs Three Love Affairs,** Denver, Co. Accent Books, 1978), pp. 118, 119.

6. **Minnesota Couples Communication Program Hand-**

book, (Minneapolis, Minnesota Couples Communication Program, 1972), pp. 23, 31.

7. H. Norman Wright, **Communication and Conflict Resolution in Marriage,** (David C. Cook Publishers, Elgin, Ill.), 1977, p. 12.

8. Adapted from John Strong, "A Marital Conflict Resolution Model Redefining Conflict to Achieve Intimacy", **Journal of Marriage and Family Counseling,** (July, 1975), pp. 269-276.

9. Gayla Margolin, "Conjoint Marital Therapy to Enhance Anger Management and Reduce Spouse Abuse", **The American Journal of Family Therapy,** Vol. 7, No. 2, (Summer 1979), p. 13.

10. Gayla Margolin, pp. 14, 15. Adapted.

11. Gayla Margolin, p. 17.

12. David R. Mace, "Marital Intimacy and the Deadly Love-Anger Cycle", **Journal of Marriage and Family Counseling,** (April, 1976), p. 136.

13. Gayla Margolin, pp. 18-20.

14. Fitzgerald, M.D., R.V., **Conjoint Marital Therapy,** (Jason Aronson Publishers, New York), 1973, pp. 48, 49.

CHAPTER 12

Communication Problems and Principles

Communication Patterns

When difficulties occur in a marriage, communication is usually involved. It may be the actual problem, or it may be the holding tank into which other problems spill. There are numerous types of communication patterns which are counter-productive in the marital relationship, and there are factors which hinder communication.

One problem has been labeled a *repertoire deficit*. This usually occurs because of the way in which an individual learned his original style of communication. A person who never learned to allow others to talk probably dominates the conversation with his spouse. Lack of a model of expressing emotions or feelings creates an inexpressive person. Some may be so limited in either education or life experience that their range of topics is narrow.

Another problem is that of *referent conditions*. In this situation the quarreling will be about one area of the marriage while the conflict stems from another area altogether. An example might be the couple who quarrels about child-rearing when the actual conflict is in the area of finances. Sometimes one partner chooses not to discuss a certain topic because disagreeing is too painful. Many couples choose this communication pattern, quarreling less frequently the longer they are married. It is not that they communicate more on a greater variety of topics; they have simply learned what *not* to talk about.

Another communication inhibition is labeled *setting events*. These are conditions present within a person which affect the way in which he communicates. A man who has not had sexual relations with his wife for some time may be grouchy. Experiencing anger at work may affect the conversation at home. If one or both are physically exhausted and then engage in a serious discussion or conflict issue, a serious disagreement could occur. Sickness is another factor which will affect the process.

Structural deficits involve the absence of conditions which would create positive communication. Some couples may not communicate much because of their schedules or lack of time.

Partner interaction difficulties are varied. If one partner shares in a pessimistic, negative manner and the spouse responds in a way that is pleasing, that positive reinforcement will occasion this response again. If nagging works, why shouldn't a person continue to nag? Whenever there is continual negative criticism, there can be an immediate negative counterattack which serves to reinforce the initial statements. On the other hand, if a partner fails to reinforce the positive reponses of his spouse, the likelihood of the partner responding positively is lessened.

Dysfunctional communication can take many forms. Edwin Thomas analyzed them in detail. The following descriptions are of a few of the common forms which may be brought to you as complaints. It is often helpful to describe, both verbally and visually, complaints such as these. Such description assists the couple in identifying their own problems and lets them know that they are not isolated.

In *content avoidance,* an interactant clearly and openly averts the opportunity to talk about a given subject or subjects. The topic may be clear, as indicated by a speaker asking questions about it or by what the previous speaker has said, it may be implicit or, in some cases, may be an assigned topic used for purposes of practitioner assessment. An example for the husband:

W: What happened at the doctor's office today?

H: Nothing.

W: You mean to say he told you nothing about your health?

H: I don't wish to talk about it. [*And, in fact, he does not discuss the topic further.*]

Content shifting is defined as an interactant prematurely introducing a different topic from what is currently being discussed. The example again involves the husband:

W: What happened at the doctor's office today?

H: I've been wondering how Joe did in school today? Did he get his test back in mathematics?

In *underresponsiveness,* an interactant says too little in relation to what a previous question or comment appears to call for. (This applies to speeches as distinguished from undertalk, to be presented later.) This next example involves a woman who has been having pains in her legs, has suspected phlebitis, and has a heart condition and arthritis.

H: What happened at the doctor's office today?

W: Not much. He looked at my leg and ankle.

H: Is that all?

W: He took my blood pressure.

Quibbling involves an interactant endeavoring to clarify or dispute a tangential and irrelevant detail. In the example following, both get involved in the quibbling.

W: What happened at the doctor's office today?

H: I didn't go to the doctor's office today.

W: You did too.

H: No, I went yesterday.

W: I thought it was today.

H: No.

W: Are you sure?

H: Positive.

A *detached utterance* consists of an interactant talking on a subject whose relationship to the immediate focus of the discussion is not clear. The talk may involve irrelevant examples, ideas, or hypothetical situations. In the example below the italicized part for the husband is illustrative.

W: What happened at the doctor's office today?

H: Yes, I went to the doctor today. He said my blood pressure was a little high. *I had a good lunch, turkey and stuffing. Gravy was not too good, though.* My heart is okay. Says I'm too fat. Need more exercise.

Topic content persistence consists of an interactant speaking excessively on a given topic. The following example presumes lengthy prior discussion of the football game by the husband, with the wife already having indicated that she was familiar with the game and was finished with the subject.

H: That was some pass to Jones in the end zone. He was wide open. No one around. What a play!

W: Yes, I saw it, you know?

H: The pass was overthrown slightly but that guy

Jones got it anyway. Good hands—and he runs fast. A very crucial play.

W: *(Silence.)*

H: It was fourth down, too, just fifteen seconds left before the half... [Etc., etc.]

Overresponsiveness involves an interactant speaking too long, with what is said going beyond what is called for in response to the partner's talk. (Overresponsiveness relates to speeches of the speaker in response to what is requested or suggested by the others whereas over-talk, to be given later, applies to speaking to more than one's partner, or others, in the interaction, considering the entire period of verbal interchange.) The example below involves overresponsiveness of the husband. [This example and several of the others here are revisions of examples of verbal categories suggested by Robert Hodnefield and Harriet Fusfeld.]

H: Well, it's halfway down the first block, on the left side; I think the drive is on the right, with a walk made out of bricks. Yes, it's painted dark green and has a mailbox in front with their name on it.

W: Are there other green houses on the street?

H: No, just that one.

W: Oh, that's all I needed to know.

In general, content is handled well when the speaker avoids excessive negative talk, expression of opinion, disagreement, and pedantry while also engaging in a goodly amount of acknowledgment and positive talk so as to sustain a reasonable level of verbal behavior of the partner. Details involving each of these are given below.

In *negative talk surfeit* an interactant expresses excessively frequent or lengthy negative evaluations of others, events, or other aspects of his surroundings. When these negative evaluations are applied to the behavior of others with whom he is interacting, they are referred to as *faulting;* when these negative evaluations are not tied directly to the behavior of others, they are referred to as *pessimistic talk.* Negative talk surfeit may take the form of sarcasm, recrimination, nagging, and bad-name calling. In their analysis of marital fighting, George R. Bach and Peter Wyden (1969) used colorful expressions to depict different forms of verbal abuse and negative talk in marital fights. Thus, they speak of gunnysacking, scapegoating, the Virginia Woolf (a ritualized exchange of insults), and the Vesuvius outburst (a kind of verbal tantrum in which there is great venting of emotion, but which is nonfunctional). Readers may be interested to know, incidentally, that the "ragiolic" is a person who engages in a chronic, one-way, growling rage.

An example of faulting by both partners:

H: I do think you have not been a very good mother to our children.

W: Well, you haven't been a good father; and you're not much of a husband, either.

H: You should talk; you're a lousy housekeeper—you leave things all over, don't clean up, leave the house dirty.

W: I'm sick of you. You're just a loser. Hear that, a loser!

An example of pessimistic talk by the husband:

W: We seem to be getting along fairly well now, what with you having a steady job and now that we have some savings again.

H: I am worried about expenses, though, money for our health and money for our old age.

W: But we have some insurance for those things, don't we?

H: Yes, but I still worry. My health may go bad, even though it's okay now, I guess. I worry about everything—how dull things are, no fun, the children.

In *positive talk deficit,* an interactant fails to compliment or say nice things about the other as a person or about what the other says or does. An example of positive talk deficit for the husband:

W: I guess I'm not the world's best housekeeper, but I would like to have a compliment occasionally.

H: You know how I feel about the way you do things.

W: No, how do you feel about that?

H: You do your job like you're supposed to and like other women do.

W: But how is that as it applies to me?

H: Oh, I don't know.

Acknowledgment deficit is failing to admit or give credit when the other is correct in a statement or failing to express recognition of the other's point of view or assertion. An example for the wife:

H: I like you, yet I sometimes have strong negative feelings. I guess I'm confused and I'm not sure what to do about it.

W: *(Silence.)*

H: What I'm trying to say is that I have mixed feelings about you that I finally realized I have. This is very important for me because it upsets me a lot and I don't know what to do about it.

W: So that's how you feel about it?

H: I'm not sure I think clearly but I know that my feelings are mixed. It's a very uncomfortable situation and I wish that I could get this over to you so that you understood.

W: Are you sure that's your point of view?

Opinion deficit is failure to express a preference or an opinion regarding referents when the discussion seems to call for some evaluation.

H: Let's take a vacation in Mexico.

W: So?

H: It would be fun. We could eat Mexican food, go hear the bands, and travel around the countryside.

W: What else could we do?

H: We could go to the bullfight, take special sight-seeing trips, and take some tours to out-of-the-way places. What do you think?

W: I don't know what to think.

The lack of opinion on a given subject at a given moment is not particularly indicative of an opinion deficit but the repeated failure to express an opinion on different subjects or the same subject for a long period of time would be indicative of lack of opinion.[1]

Other common problems will include the following:

— *Overtalk*. One interactant tends to dominate the interaction excessively in sheer verbal output. Likely measures: (a) total time spent in mere vocalization, regardless of content; (b) number of words uttered.

— *Undertalk*. (Not necessarily a reciprocal to Overtalk.) An interactant fails to contribute much talk despite opportunities to do so (e.g., as during periods of mutual silence or when asked to respond).

— *Fast talk*. An interactant speaks too rapidly, especially if noticed or reacted to in some discernible way by the partner.

— *Slow talk*. An interactant speaks too slowly, especially if noticed or reacted to in some discernible way by the partner.

— *Loud talk*. An interactant speaks too loudly,

especially if noticed or reacted to in some discernible way by the partner.

— *Quiet talk.* An interactant speaks near or at the point of inaudibility, especially if noticed or reacted to in some discernible way by the partner.

— *Dysfluent talk.* An interactant tends to display an excess of dysfluencies in his speech (e.g., stuttering, hesitations).

— *Affective talk.* This covers a variety of "emotional" behaviors during talk that require specification, such as crying and intense intonation.

— *Verbal obtrusions* An interactant too frequently emits utterances that occur during and after the onset of speech by the other. These remain as obtrusions only as long as they do not produce an immediate and apparently premature cessation of speech by the other. When the other stops speaking abruptly upon occurrences of an obtrusion, this constitutes an *interruption.*

— *Abusive talk.* An interactant tends to engage in too frequent or too lengthy verbal criticisms of the other and in a derogatory, nonconstructive manner.

—*Countercomplaining.* An interactant responds to a complaint with a complaint about the other, such that the initial complaint is not dealt with on its own terms.

— *Poor referent specification.* An interactant fails to speak in concise, concrete, and specific terms about a referent; his speech tends to be over-general and abstract.

— *Temporal remoteness.* An interactant tends to dwell excessively on referents in the fairly distant past or future, especially when these referents are tied only tenuously, if at all, to current referents.

— *Excessive question asking.* An interactant asks too many questions.

— *Dogmatic assertion.* An interactant tends to express opinions or points of view in a categorical, unqualified, "black or white" manner.

— *Overgeneralization.* An interactant engages in excessive stereotypic categorization of a referent as being invariably of the same type. (Look for key words like "always," "never," "every time.")

— *Presumptive attribution.* An interactant assigns to the other non-obvious meanings, motives, feelings, especially when these inferred factors are negatively valued. ("Mind-reading," "second-guessing.")

— *Excessive compliance.* An interactant overuses agreement responses, to the detriment of voicing constructive disagreements, suggestions, or qualifications in response to the partner.[2]

One miscommunication problem is a constant issue for discussion and improvement within the counseling experience. It is the reluctance of one spouse to share deep inner feelings. In the following session, which occurred about two months into the counseling experience, this issue of the husband's reluctance to share his feelings and hurt arose. This had been intimated at during earlier sessions by the husband and directly brought out by his wife, but the proper time for dealing with it hadn't yet occurred. The husband had generally mentioned the topic of fear and hurt at the conclusion of the previous session. The session began after some preliminary remarks:

Counselor: Pam, how can you and I help Tom become more vulnerable toward you?

Pam: I don't know. By helping him trust the relationship

more . . . I don't know.

Counselor: I wonder if in some way Tom needs to learn to trust himself some more. I wonder if he isn't struggling with that.

Pam: That is possible.

Counselor: I don't know. I am just thinking out loud like you are, too. You know him a lot better than I do. You live with him.

Pam: Do I know you? (to her husband)

Counselor: What are the times that he really opens up and reaches out to you?

Pam: After we have had a good time, after we have had a real enjoyable day.

Counselor: You can tell the difference when he is a little bit reserved or when he really is fully open and honest.

Pam: I am not sure that it is linked to any incident. I don't know that it is really linked to anything specific.

Counselor: You seem to be saying this sort of comes and goes.

Pam: Yes, it seems like.

Counselor: (To Tom) How do you feel about what we are talking about?

Tom: Mixed . . . I am not even sure what the mixture is. I don't know how I feel about it. I don't feel bad about it; I don't feel good about it. Kind of reserved.

Counselor: It sounds like you feel puzzled about your-self.

Tom: Yes.

Counselor: Tell me what puzzles you.

Tom: Oh, a lot of things. Some of my thinking, some of

my emotional makeup, my beliefs about myself, and things like self-esteem. Sometimes I am very confident of myself and my directions, my goals and what I want. Other times I am highly speculative of that am I living a fantasy or some kind of thing like that! I am puzzled by a lot of it. I feel like I am sometimes changing so rapidly that I surprise myself. I mean I turn around and there is something else changed and that scares me. Sometimes it goes so fast I don't know. Yes. I am puzzled a lot. I don't know how to answer the question because of my puzzledness.

Counselor: I hear you and see you being much more vulnerable now in counseling than at first, just even saying what you said about yourself. You present yourself so many times as being confident, having everything under control. But now we are both seeing the inner workings of you and accepting you just as much.

Tom: Good. (with an expression of relief) I feel like that is always a confusing issue—whether or not I am showing myself and whether people will just begin looking at you with clear eyesight. I don't know which one is the answer. I am glad that it is being perceived.

Counselor: Last week and this week you are showing more. You're letting down some of your defenses and allowing other people to come in. I am wondering what it is going to take for you to lower the wall on a more consistent steady basis in you.

Tom: That is a good question. (Pause) I don't know.

Counselor: Is your fear outer-directed or is it inner-directed?

Tom: I would say more fear of the inward.

Counselor: Tell me more about that inward fear.

Tom: I really can't. I mean, I feel like I could tell you why it doesn't feel like it is the *outward* one. But I don't feel like I can describe the inward one. I just know that. I have a concept that people don't make you anything or really can't do anything to hurt you. It is all in how you are going to react. You stand to be hurt, which is kind of an answer—"a no" to the outward one and "a yes" to the inward one. But I don't understand the inward one. That, well, and that is what is scary about it because I really don't understand it. I just know that I have a strong belief that says, "Nobody can do anything really to hurt me". I mean, I can choose to be hurt by any actions anyone does, but I am not sure I can be hurt by them. It is a matter of choosing to respond differently to different things. It is a matter of my choosing to respond to certain ways, and maybe that is protection from getting hurt from the outside.

Counselor: Do you believe that too, Pam?

Pam: What is that?

Counselor: That you cannot be hurt from the outside.

Pam: It is a choice that you make, I think. I think that you can be hurt from the outside, but you have the choice of not allowing that to happen.

Counselor: Are there times when things you have done or said really penetrated and Tom has experienced hurt because of it?

Pam: Yes, I guess so.

Counselor: It is a strange kind of concept; it is an accurate concept that we are hurt by our interpretation of things. But on the other hand it is a good defense because then it is like saying, "I am in control." And we don't like to be out of control. But perhaps in the husband/wife relationship what vulnerability means, "I am so willing to take away the controls that, yes, something that you can say or do in and of itself can hurt: it can penetrate."

(At this point Tom guided the discussion away from the main issue. When the opportunity arose, the counselor tied the conversation back into the couple's relationship:)

Counselor: What about this segment of your life? Because, if it carries over, is there a fear of being judged? It seems that is keeping you from being open and vulnerable.

Tom: Yes. I think so.

Counselor: Who is judging you in your relationship with Pam?

Tom: She is, or I have a fear that she is. My fear keeps her from doing it and I end up doing it.

Counselor: You say you have a fear that she does; I hear uncertainty that she really does.

Tom: Because I am living off of what felt like judgment before I mean, I don't let that . . . me become vulnerable long enough to be judged by her any more.

Counselor: So what occurred before has crippled you?

Tom: Yes.

Counselor: Do you always want to be crippled?

Tom: What a question! No!

Counselor: But it is safe to be a cripple.

Tom: Yes.

Counselor: And if we start . . .

Tom: You also *feel* like a cripple, though.

Counselor: You get a lot further when you fall down and you get back up. Would you tell Pam about your fear of judgment. Talk with her about it.

Tom (To Pam): Sometimes I think I am afraid—I wasn't aware of this before we came in, so it wasn't like something we could have just picked up on, started talking about. Unless you would have asked the specific questions Norm (counselor) asked.

Pam: I don't know the right questions to ask.

Tom: I won't argue that with you one way or the other, but sometimes I am afraid of sharing with you in detail some of my thoughts, fears, or even some of the things that I have said or done. I feel like you are going to go ahead and be hurt by it, or you will get defensive by it and you won't even tell me you are that way. You will walk off with conclusions made and you will close up and I won't know how to get in. There will be a lapse of time that will occur, and then you will tell me about it, and I will feel really bad because it was so much time. And I will know that all the time that transpired you were hurt by it, you were maybe angry with me, or frustrated with me or disappointed with me. But you didn't talk about it in all the time, and I am going to feel like it was a judgment on me. I am sorry for not working at it really hard, I'm trying to express this to you differently, so that we could talk about it or deal with it. And I think I want that to change.

Pam: I'm glad that you want it to change; I would like for it to change, too. I think one thing that might have started you feeling like this was, I think, that my feeling was that I think I was jealous that you were having a meaningful experience with the people you work with, and that I felt like we weren't having the discussions that we had at one time. I wasn't satisfied with just hearing about them, and I would think "well, why can't we talk like that!" Anyway I was jealous and I didn't know for sure what I needed to do to experience those kind of things with you.

Tom: I guess every time I go to share with you about work, to me that is the opportunity for that experience in sharing to be a meaningful experience for us. When you react in a negative way, I know it is not true, but I tend to generalize and think that. You don't want a meaningful experience with me because it is really a matter of feeling open and vulnerable to you when I do share. Especially when I share why it was meaningful.

Pam: How do you want me to respond to that when you do share with me?

Tom: With your feelings—verbalizing them.

Pam: How I feel about what you did, or what you said, or what they did?

Tom: All of that.

Pam: All of it?

Tom: When you get disgusted with it or when it sounds like a bunch of garbage to you or whatever, rather than getting a sigh from you and a frustrating look and then I get to spend the next 20 minutes trying to guess what it is about. You tell me; you be responsible enough to tune into you and tell me. I really need that. When I get the look anymore, it is like it just reinforces my attitude of "why bother."

Pam: To me it doesn't seem like we have done that lately. Have you gotten looks from me when you shared...

Tom: I don't feel like I have been open lately.

Pam: Ok.

Tom: I agree it hasn't happened much, but I feel like I have really been protecting myself from letting it happen to me. It is going to take some work for me to want to venture out in that area because I . . really this feels scary.

The session continued and the couple concluded with a mutual commitment to share more of their feelings and their intentions with one another. This was a starting point for them to begin to be open and more trusting with one another.

Marital Communication Inventory

One specific and practical means of both analyzing and improving the couple's communication is the use of the Marital Communication Inventory from Family Life Publications. A sampling of the 46-question inventory is listed here.

	USUALLY	SOME-TIMES	SELDOM	NEVER
1. Do you and your husband discuss the manner in which the family income should be spent?	____	____	____	____
2. Does he discuss his work and interests with you?	____	____	____	____
3. Do you have a tendency to keep your feelings to yourself?	____	____	____	____
4. Is your husband's tone of voice irritating?	____	____	____	____
5. Does he have a tendency to say things which would be better left unsaid?	____	____	____	____
6. Are your mealtime conversations easy and pleasant?	____	____	____	____
7. Do you find it necessary to keep after him about his faults?	____	____	____	____
8. Does he seem to understand your feelings?	____	____	____	____
9. Does your husband nag you?	____	____	____	____
10. Does he listen to what you have to say?	____	____	____	____
11. Does it upset you to a great extent when your husband is angry with you?	____	____	____	____
12. Does he pay you compliments and say nice things to you?	____	____	____	____

13. Is it hard to understand your husband's feelings and attitudes?   ____ ____ ____ ____
14. Is he affectionate toward you?   ____ ____ ____ ____
15. Does he let you finish talking before responding to what you are saying?   ____ ____ ____ ____
16. Do you and your husband remain silent for long periods when you are angry with one another?[3]   ____ ____ ____ ____

The husband and wife are given separate forms. The counselor may ask them to complete and discuss the inventory at home, or he may prefer to use it in the actual session, question by question. In doing the latter, you might ask the wife and then the husband to respond to the first question. One might respond by saying "usually" and the other "seldom." Such a difference may indicate either some tension or miscommunication in the given area. Even when both respond to the question with the same answer, there still may be misinterpretation, or they may not be satisfied with the status of the question or issue.

You can ask the couple to turn to one another and discuss the question. This will give you an insight into their communication style and patterns. As you proceed through the inventory, ask the husband first for his response to question two, and then ask his wife. Helping them with their process of communication in the session may enable them to take this pattern home with them to continue their discussion. Before doing this, you may wish to share the principles of communication and conflict resolution so the couple will have them as an aid to discussion. Or you may want to wait and observe their typical style first and then gradually integrate these principles as they talk.

A scoring key and analysis comes with this form. An average score is between 100-105. Anything below 90 indicates notable communication problems. (The lowest scores I have found was one couple with a 54 and 56 and another couple with a 44 and 48). Even when couples have scores above the average, communication difficulties can exist. If one spouse has a score of 108 and the other a score of 126, the difference indicates some miscommunication even though both are above the average.

Examples of Changing Negative Patterns

Couples in distress often have oppositional or even hostile styles of expressing themselves. These approaches produce negative feelings in the partners and therefore diminish the frequency of significant or substantial conversations. This in turn reduces marital satisfaction. By altering the negative style, marital satisfaction can be improved. The counselor listens to the couple as they talk, stops them when counter-productive patterns appear, and provides them with alternatives to the way they are expressing themselves.

Frequently it is necessary for the counselor to be specific and directive in order to break problem communication patterns. In such situations the counselor stops the conversation, labels the undesirable behavior, and gives the reason for changing it. Labeling it helps the couple recognize similar patterns in the future, and explaining why provides them with a motive to change.

In an article entitled "Implementation of Behavioral Marital Therapy" twelve common problems were suggested with examples of how the counselor can intervene:

1. **Interrupting**

   Partner 1: Well, I think that the best alternative would be for you to...

   Partner 2: No, I can't go along with...

Therapist: Stop. You just interrupted Partner 1. Keep away from interruptions because they frustrate your partner and show that you're not listening well. Listen to your partner, and wait for him or her to finish.

Interruptions may occur both when a partner is actively talking and when he or she has paused for a moment. The behavior should be stopped in both instances.

2. **Deciding Who is at Fault**

   Partner 1: You shouldn't have yelled at me when I was late.

   Partner 2: Well, I wouldn't have if you had been on time.

   Therapist: Stop. You're trying to decide who's at fault. It makes people angry to be blamed, and it prevents you from working together. Don't argue about whose fault things are. Look for ways to handle the situation that will satisfy you both.

3. **Trying to Establish "The Truth"**

   Partner 1: You did not come home early, it was late!

   Partner 2: I was home on time. It was only...

   Therapist: Stop. You each have a different view of how it happened, and you probably won't change the other's memory. Arguing over the truth of specific details won't help you solve the problem, and may make you both angry.

4. **Getting Sidetracked**

   Partner 1: Like I said, you leave clothes on the floor.

   Partner 2: Well, your desk is always pretty messy, too, you know.

   Therapist: Stop. You're getting off the subject. Remember to stay on one issue at a time. Other issues may seem related, but they get you off the track.

5. **Dealing With Multifaceted Problems**

   Partner 1: Well, you leave the tub full of water, clothes

on the floor, the beds unmade, dishes in the sink.

Therapist: Stop. There are many parts to this problem. It is often confusing to deal with many aspects of a large problem at one time. It is best to choose one part to work on.

6. **"Guilting" the Other Person**

Partner 1: You just don't care about my feelings. You hurt me and you don't even care...

Therapist: Stop. When you say that, whether you mean it or not, it implies that the other person is rotten, horrible and insensitive. This may make the person feel guilty, become angry, and want to say something angry back at you. Stay away from saying guilt-producing things such as that.

7. **Making Power Moves and Giving Ultimatums**

Partner 1: You do that, and I'll leave, or I'll...

Therapist: Stop. You just gave your partner an ultimatum. Ultimatums push people into a corner because they either have to lose face by giving in, or act tough and tell you to go ahead. Either way they may become resentful, and the problem is not getting solved.

8. **Using the Words "Always" and "Never"**

Partner 1: You never come home when you say you will.

Therapist: Stop. Stay away from the words "always" and "never" because a useless argument can arise over the issue of any possible time the situation did or did not occur.

9. **Using Trait Names**

Partner 1: You're just insensitive.

Therapist: Stop. You've just called your partner a name, and that may make him or her angry. When you label your partner, you imply that he or she cannot change. Instead, tell your partner the specific behavior you dislike.

10. **Justifying**

Partner 1: I don't want to go to the mountains for our vacation. As we've discussed, I don't like heights.

Partner 2: Why not?

Partner 1: I don't know, I just...

Therapist: Stop. You're justifying why you don't like something. You don't need to justify likes and dislikes. If you don't like something, you simply don't like it, and that needs to be considered in solving your problem.

11. **Mind-reading**

Partner 1: You think I spend too much money.

Therapist: Stop. You just told your partner what he or she is thinking, as if you could read his or her mind. Trying to read the other person's mind isn't good because you could be wrong, and, even if you are right, it can make the other person angry to have you speak for him or her. If you want to know what your partner thinks, ask your partner.

12. **Giving Discrepant Verbal and Nonverbal Communications**

Partner 1: Okay, if that's what you want (sighs and rolls eyes).

Therapist: Stop. Verbally you have agreed, but your sighing and rolling of your eyes confuse the message you are sending.[4]

By repeating their interactions in more positive ways, the couple can begin to practice constructive patterns which will eventually replace destructive ones. At the same time, the counselor will reinforce the couple's positive patterns by noting the pattern, labeling it, and explaining why it is beneficial.

Positive Communication Guidelines

Sometimes a couple will have few constructive patterns. In such a case the counselor will want to teach them communication skills, and offer them a number of guidelines. Which guidelines the counselor suggests will depend upon the couple and the problems to be resolved. Here are four positive steps to enhance marital communication:

First, whenever there has been a time apart—even briefly (perhaps a few hours)—greet one another with a smile and a genuine compliment. Share a positive or interesting incident. Ask questions which will cause your spouse to think and to share more information.

Second, make use of "transition times." Periods of time between leaving work (or other stressful activities) and returning home can diffuse frustrations, fears, pressures, or problems of the day. This lessens the possibility of such factors affecting the marital communication.

Third, avoid discussing important topics that have disagreement potential when either spouse is emotionally or physically exhausted, ill, in pain, or medicated.

Fourth, consider establishing a set time each day for items which involve decision-making, problems, conflicts, or business. For this concept to succeed, the couple must commit themselves to a "no interruptions and no use of this time for other activities" rule.

Whether the couple has a set time for discussion or not, it is important for them to understand and agree to the following concepts and communication. The counselor can address the couple in this way:

1. It is best to discuss complaints, joint decisions, and disagreements during an agreed upon decision-making time.

2.   It is important to remain on a topic until each person has had an opportunity to share his thoughts or feelings.

3.   Discussions of controversial issues and problems should focus upon the present. Often counselors may give couples a specific directive not to bring up the past nor debate what may occur in the future.

4.   Specific, clear statements are more effective than generalizations and overstatements. Accuracy in description will help keep the communication progressing smoothly.

5.   When a spouse is talking, the other is to give total attention. Verbal responses showing that one is in tune with the spouse assist the process and prove that one is really listening.

6.   All mind reading and speaking for the other person must be avoided.

7.   Debating over trivia or insignificant details is to be avoided.

8.   If you have difficulty understanding what your spouse said or meant, repeat what you think he or she said and meant. Then ask, "Is this accurate?"

9.   Whenever your spouse communicates in a manner that you desire, praise and reinforce your partner for what s/he has done.

10.   Each person needs the freedom to bring up topics he enjoys or those of importance to him or her. Each person should take the initiative to bring up topics that interest the other, and to communicate in a way that pleases the other. This enhances the relationship.

11.   All labeling should be avoided. Words such as lazy, inconsiderate, stubborn, intolerant, and cruel will only create more difficulty.

12.   "Why" questions are not problem-solving ques-

tions. They are directed toward the cause rather than the solution. Questions such as, "Why did this happen?" or "Why did you do that?" usually make a person feel threatened or defensive, or will cause him to wonder if he is being criticized.

13.   It is important to understand that our messages consist of three components: content composes 7% of the message; tone of voice, 38%; non-verbal (or "body language"), 55%. These three should be consistent or there will be confusion. Frowning or scowling when giving a compliment confuses the recipient. Therefore, couples should give attention to tone of voice and non-verbal components of their communication. (Videotaping of the couple communicating during the counseling sessions will do more to enlighten a couple about these processes than any other means.)

14.   When a problem is presented, begin with something positive. The initial presentation of a problem sets the tone for further discussion. Two common difficulties with problem presentation is that the statements are general and negative. The best approach is to begin with a positive statement if possible, then make the request specific and positive. Point to the behavior that you desire from the other person. The praise is not to be invented, but genuine.

The counselor should have the couple consider what it is they want from each other when they pose a problem or lodge a complaint: Is it anger, defensiveness, resistance and continuation of the problem? Or is it openness, cooperation and a change on the part of the other person? The way one approaches a problem will determine the response.

Two examples of typical complaints—"You are not involved enough with the children" and "You are never affectionate"—might be handled in the following way: "I appreciate your evaluating your schedule so you could spend more time." "I enjoy the times you touch me. I would appreciate it if you would touch me and hold me several times a day and also let me know if you like something I'm doing." Recognition and praise of what another person has done is necessary to his sense of self worth, and it also opens the door for a person to accept a constructive suggestion.

There may be occasions when the partner responds by asking a clarifying question or even a defensive question. These need a straight, positive response:

"I spend enough time with the kids. What's the problem?"

"In the last two weeks you spent time with them on three evenings. We are saying we want more of you than that."

If a complaint was registered concerning picking up after one's self around the home, and it was defensively challenged, a specific answer is necessary: "Today you left the dishes on the table, the newspaper on the floor in the family room and a coffee cup on the good table. I would appreciate it if you would..."

In the Journal article quoted earlier, the authors suggested seven additional skills for couples to learn:

1. **Talking to Each Other**

    Because a major emphasis of behavioral marital therapy is to alter the interaction style of the couple, most of the therapy session is spent with the partners talking to each other and not to the therapist. This emphasis also helps to reduce or eliminate the tendency of many partners to draw the therapist onto "their side" against their mate.

2. **Making Eye Contact**

    Eye contact is encouraged because it can form a psychological bond which helps the partners to work together as a team. Averted eyes may indicate a distracted or uninterested partner, and this may lead to resentful feelings.

3. **Making "I" Statements**

These statements usually take the form of "I feel..." or "I think..." and take the place of statements which speak about or for the partner, starting with "you feel..." or "you think...". These statements provide direct information about the person's own feelings and encourage the partners to take responsibility for their behavior and feelings.

4. **Practicing Reflective Listening**

Reflective listening shows that the partner is listening to and understanding what the speaker is saying rather than daydreaming or planning a rebuttal. This skill is especially helpful for couples who frequently interrupt each other because it slows their pace of interaction and teaches them to listen to each other.

5. **Giving Praise**

In order to change the couple's negative reinforcement schedule to a positive one, couples should be encouraged to give positive reinforcement directly. They should be encouraged to tell each other what they like about the partner, what the partner has been doing well, and what the partner says that is helpful.

6. **Giving Head Nods**

Although they can lose effectiveness if they are overdone, head nods are a good communications skill because they are a nonverbal way of telling the speaker that his or her message is being received.

7. **Stating What One Likes or Wants**

In the problem-solving format, the therapist provides a safe situation in which partners may honestly state what they like and want. Thus, they can be encouraged to be open about their wants.[5]

In addition, any of the following books can be used as homework with couples or individuals during the process of counseling:

Communication: Key to Your Marriage by H. Norman Wright — Regal Books. Each person needs a copy to work through because of the structure of the book.

An Answer to Family Communication by Norman Wright — Harvest House. Often the couple is asked to spend 15 minutes per day reading this book out loud to one another. Then they discuss how it applies to each of them.

Family Communication by Sven Wahlroos — Macmillan. This well written book discusses numerous principles and has many practical illustrations.

The following verbatim is from the fourth session with a couple. It was about twenty minutes into the session. Earlier Kurt had been encouraging his wife to make some decisions on her own. He had told her that he would eat—and be happy with—whatever she chose to fix him for dinner. In her conversation she appeared to be quite concerned about his reactions and responses.

During the session a number of important issues were raised. As you read the verbatim, note the following:

1. A question encouraging Heather to evaluate whether she is dependent upon Kurt, and then to share her thoughts about it.
2. The labeling of Kurt's communication as a double message. This labeling was for Kurt's benefit as much as for Heather's.
3. The encouraging of Heather to discover how she really felt about her cooking. This was done by noting the hesitancy in her voice and by repeating the same

question three times.

4. The reinforcement of Heather's positive communication style whenever she makes a positive change.
5. The confrontations of Kurt's evaluative statements regarding Heather.
6. The emphasis upon Heather's becoming confident in her own self-evaluation rather than being so dependent upon Kurt.
7. Comments which emphasized each person's perception of what occurred.
8. Teaching comments. One example is the counselor's explanation of what occurs when the word "But" is used after a positive statement.
9. The emphasis upon reinforcing positive changes.
10. The counselor's refusal to accept responsibility for choosing Kurt's goal. The counselor accomplished this by asking Kurt to answer his own question.
11. How the counselor helped the counselees begin to plan and visualize new changes.
12. The encouragement of Kurt to be more open in expressing his weaknesses.
13. The confrontation of Kurt's faulty communications as well as the reinforcement of his supportive and helpful communication style.
14. The allowing of Kurt to feel somewhat frustrated in that he was able to control the situation in his usual manner.
15. A summary teaching statement at the conclusion of the session, for reinforcement.

Counselor: Heather, are you quite dependent upon Kurt's reactions and feelings?

Heather: Yes, very much. Like when he was talking about cooking—that was really a frustrating part for me because

I ... when I ... well, just cooking in general is very frustrating because he's never home for dinner. So when I do cook something it's just real frustrating. On one hand he had told me before that I need to just go ahead and fix whatever and he'll eat it, but that's not true. He won't always eat it. It won't always sound good. And it's just real frustrating.

Counselor: So it's a double message?

Heather: Yeah.

Counselor: So in other words, Kurt would say: "Whatever you fix, I'll eat." You want to have that assurance that you can depend on what he has said, and you throw together, you know—peanut butter and hash and he's going to eat it.

Heather: Yeah.

Counselor: OK.

Heather: Because he's really proficient in the kitchen and so if he doesn't like ... not that he does it on purpose or anything, but ...

Counselor: But, just sort of go in ...

Heather: ... and does his own ...

Counselor: From your perspective, and from no one else: Do you want to learn how to cook better?

Heather: I want to have people to cook for, and I think that when I have people to cook for I will have more opportunities to cook. (Hesitantly) Yeah, I'd like to cook better.

Counselor: OK. For yourself—that's your own personal wish?

Heather: (Hesitantly) Well, I like what I cook, but not necessarily ... No, I feel like I'm a good cook.

Counselor: That's what I'm looking for there, because it's almost like we're into people pleasing again—"that others would like me to cook this and this"—but if you had your own choice in this to go ahead and cook the way you do now, would this be sufficient?

Heather: You mean sufficient...

Counselor: For you.

Heather: Oh, for me, yeah, I'd have macaroni & cheese every night.

Counselor: OK. That's what I'm after. I want to comment on the process that I saw occurring between the two of you. As you started out, I liked the positive statements that you were making. You weren't asking my permission or Kurt's permission to say something—you were just coming out and stating things, which I really like to encourage you to do because you certainly have the capability of doing that. I heard you, Kurt, make the statement that you feel insecure. The statement in and of itself was a healthy admission on your part because I think you like to give people the impression that Kurt isn't insecure. That Kurt has everything under control and you're on top of everything. But then after you said it, you followed it up with the statement that you're insecure *about* Heather's role as a mother—like in a sense you have to be the one to get Heather into shape as to how she's going to be the mother. You don't want to have to instruct or correct or to lift her out of a depression. Again the whole control issue is coming through there. It just seems to have permeated everything. Is that your responsibility, to create Heather into the kind of mother that she's going to become?

Kurt: No, I don't feel like it is... but at the same time I'm not...

Counselor: Let me throw another one in. Let's say Heather is a mother and Heather becomes depressed. Would it be up to her to say, "I want some help getting out of this depression," or "Let me deal with it"—because you were saying it was your responsibility to have to coax her out of it.

Kurt: Either that or it would be her responsibility to tell me, "leave me alone."

Counselor: OK.

Kurt: ... I like where I'm at and I want to stay here awhile.

Counselor: Hmmm uh ... (affirmative)

Kurt: great ... but ...

Counselor: Which is back to the issue that we were talking about last week ... I wonder, Heather, if there aren't times when you, too, have a mixture of feelings. I think that we talked about this as well ... yes, I'd like to work this out myself, but on the other hand, coax me."

Heather: Uh huh ...

Counselor: How would it affect the relationship if you came out straight everytime and said, "Leave me alone," or "no, there's nothing wrong," or "Yes, there's something wrong" and "I'm slamming the door because I'm really irritated about what happened at work today."

Heather: I don't remember what it's about, but after the discussion last week I really didn't have any opportunity to exercise any of that until about Saturday and then I tried to be more verbal with what I was feeling—not to just ... well, I tried to be more verbal about what I was feeling, and I thought I did pretty good, and I asked Kurt about it later in the day. And he felt like I needed to bring more feelings ...

Counselor: Can I stop you right now?

Heather: Sure...

Counselor: Did you hear what you just told me?

Heather: Yeah.

Counselor: What was it?

Heather: That I thought I did good, but Kurt felt like I didn't.

Counselor: Because of... why? Because you asked Kurt later on... What did he tell you?

Heather: Why I asked him?

Counselor: You asked him—which means in a sense, didn't you put yourself into a child role?

Heather: No... I don't think so, ... because I wanted to find out how he felt. I felt like I had done good... Now I feel like a little kid... Yet I wanted to see what his reaction was to it.

Counselor: Un huh.

Heather: So I didn't feel like... I felt I did OK.

Counselor: OK.

Heather: Otherwise I would never know if I did good, or if I was back doing the same thing.

Counselor: But what if you were to be the person to make the determination of saying: "yeah, I think that I improved about 50% on that one and maybe on the next one I'll come out more. And I can be the one that makes the value judgement on how I'm doing."

Heather: I guess I wanted approval...

Counselor: So if we continue on this way where you are

making strides and progress and reaching out, but then you turn to Kurt and say, "How do you think I'm doing?" What does it do to this new relationship that we're hoping to create?

Heather: I'm not sure. But it almost seems like that's an important part.

Counselor: For you, you mean?

Heather: Yes.

Counselor: His approval?

Heather: Yes, but if I don't get his appoval—like he said...I don't remember what he said...it wasn't quite what it needed to be, but I guess when I don't get that approval then I...

Counselor: OK, I want to come back to that statement in a moment, but I want to pursue this. Could you, though, come to the place where you could say: "Well, I spent 2 minutes talking about it instead of one minute, and that's quite an improvement and I felt pretty satisfied."

Heather: That's a step in the right direction.

Counselor: Could you go ahead and be your own reinforcer for awhile?

Heather: I could try.

Counselor: Might not be as strong a reinforcer as asking Kurt, but I would like to comment on what you said because that was the first time that you had a chance to practice what we talked about last week, right?

Heather: Uh huh.

Counselor: And Kurt said—it wasn't quite up to it...

Kurt: (Defensively) I didn't say that...that's her *repre-*

sentation of what I said . . . (Firmly) That's the third assumption that I've let go tonight. I haven't let any go . . . that's why I'm holding on to these three fingers.

Counselor: Why did Heather feel it in that way?

Kurt: Heather, how come you felt it in that way?

Heather: That's what I heard.

Kurt: That's what she heard.

Counselor: What did you say, Kurt?

Kurt: I believe that she asked me,—"Kurt, did you feel like I expressed myself better this time?" Is that what you asked?

Heather: Probably. Yeah, I think so.

Kurt: And I said: "Yes you did. But the part that I really needed to hear was specifics, if you were in touch with them—like—well, just approaching me." Even coming to me and asking for feedback later on was a step . . . I was a little taken back that she did what she did. I was surprised.

Counselor: Did you reinforce the fact that Heather came to you and asked for feedback?

Kurt: No.

Counselor: The very fact that she asked for feedback can be reinforced. The very fact that it was better than it had been before could be spontaneously reinforced on your part without Heather's even having to come to you and ask, which would be your responsibility that whenever you see Heather coming out, then we reinforce it. Now, (to Heather) we wouldn't expect your first try to be perfect, but it will take quite a bit of rehearsal, practicing it, trying it. It's like any time that we get a personal compliment and we respond to that compliment: "That was good, but . . ." It's very normal for us to remember everything that was said after the word "but". And that's why Heather is remembering that. I don't think that's an assumption. It's just that she's being very normal, like the rest of us. So perhaps at another time, maybe once a week, each of you can sit down together and evaluate. What do we need to do now in order to actually increase the positive steps that we have done," which again puts it in a positive light. It's accepting the fact that—Hey, you've made progress, and you've made progress in several ways. How? What do we do for the next step to increase it? Which eliminates the "yes, . . . but" part of it.

Kurt: I guess I'm not sure what I'm going to be working on—stepping out of parenting? That's a desirable goal that I have, but is that what we've kind of talked about?

Counselor: Well, is that what you would like to work on?

Kurt: Yeah.

Counselor: How do you visualize yourself doing that?

Kurt: One of the ways is, I guess I feel inadequate—uncertain, not inadequate, is how to do that effectively.

Counselor: Kurt, could you go back and rephrase that for me, and use the word "inadequate," and make it sound that way?

Kurt: Make it sound that way?

Counselor: Well, you started to use the word inadequate, but that's uncomfortable for you.

Kurt: Yeah.

Counselor: And I'd like to see you use it in relationship to learning this new role. I think that's what you feel.

Kurt: I feel inadequate . . . I guess I don't know how to step out of the parenting role!

Counselor: I feel the admission on your part of inadequacy, feeling inferior. If that side of your life were expressed a little more, it would bring in a balance. It would bring out the humanity of you a little more, which I think would encourage Heather to open up some more.

Kurt: OK. Part of what I've heard this evening is the ongoing feedback from her that I don't do that, that I'm not vulnerable, that I don't expose my brokenness, my weakness. And I just have to say, flat out, that that's not so from my perspective! (This sentence was stated in an angry, definite manner.)

Counselor: From her perspective it is, but from your perspective it's different.

Kurt: Yeah.

Counselor: OK.

Kurt: Very much so.

Counselor: Uh huh (affirmative) How do you feel that you could...

Kurt: ...I feel inadequate as to how to do it more without becoming self-defacing.

Counselor: OK. You say you're trying, but it's not registering with Heather.

Kurt: Apparently not.

Counselor: Then how would she like it?

Kurt: How would she like...

Counselor: You to become more vulnerable?

Kurt: How would you like me to become more vulnerable? (to Heather)

Heather: I don't know...

Counselor: Could we check out Kurt's statement—his first statement: Is it true that you do not see him as being open and vulnerable and expressing his inadequacy, the times that he's inferior?

Heather: I think you do. It's the kind of thing that I'd have to go home and write a list of what I observe over the week, because I feel like you do show me the inadequacies that you feel and the fears that you have, and I'd like being the person that knows that you're not perfect. You know how we've talked about you're not perfect and some people just think that you don't do anything wrong. And I know that you do. And I'm aware of your inadequacies and the way you express them to me. Yet, at the same time, I feel something that—you know just a feeling—and I'm not sure what it is, but it feels like ... I'm not sure of the right words. I guess I still feel like you're better than I am, and that makes it hard 'cause I feel ...

Kurt: Do you think that I feel that I'm better than you are?

Heather: Not really ... mostly just what I feel and the way I make myself feel ...

Kurt: Can you help make me understand how I contribute to that?

Heather: Oh ...

Kurt: I don't feel like you're any less than I am. I look up to you in a lot of areas. I shared some of those—those are your strengths that I shared with you. Right now, I don't want to parent you and try to say—you'll get over it, you really don't see things the right way, or any of those kind of comments. I just want to know how I can help ... what I'm doing that relates to reinforcing that? 'Cause I don't want to reinforce that message. I don't want you to get that message, but I definitely don't want to reinforce it.

Heather: I'm not sure. I'd have to think about it.

Counselor: Heather, does it help you to get some time by yourself where you can sit down and write out and make some lists?

Heather: I have a hard time just sitting down and writing down lists. It'd have to be . . . like if I have an item I need to be thinking about—over a course of a day.

Counselor: Or a week even, to make some observations. Would that help?

Heather: Yeah.

Counselor: I have an observation to make. Kurt, the way in which you were speaking to Heather right now had sensitivity, care and concern in your voice, which I think really made a difference. The toughness had gone out of your voice. I guess that would be the word I would use, toughness. Sometimes just in your manner of speaking you appear strong, confident and in control. You've been married for some time, and you've just built up this automatic pattern of relating and responding to one another. So we're trying to break this and make some changes. This is going to be a slow process, and there will be times when you can't think of illustrations, can't document it, but "I've got a feeling" is just as genuine and valid. And I would think that you, Kurt, begin to back off from parenting in terms of, oh, some of the types of statements or the way in which they are said, that might cause you, Heather, to feel Kurt is being more vulnerable. Maybe he doesn't change much in what he says about when he hurts, or when he's upset or when he feels inadequate, but the whole attitude or veneer begins to change.

Heather: I think that's what it is...

Counselor: That is going to perhaps make his openness stand out more. Maybe that's it. Here's Kurt and he's got this area of vulnerability, but it's sort of overshadowed by all this strength and dominance. As he learns to relax, then the vulnerability stands out a little more and that registers with you.

Heather: I don't know... (softly)

Counselor: I don't know either. (softly)

Heather: I think that a lot of (crying)...I hate to cry because it's not just crying over this, but, you know, it's a lot of things, but I don't cry about in the meantime. That's why I dread the thought of crying because it's not just right now that I'd cry about.

Counselor: A lot of things have built up and this is the release for the week? (softly)

Heather: Sort of...

Kurt: ...and for the month...

Heather: What was I going to say...I think that in trying to, I think that the feeling that we were talking about—that I can't think of specific instances of what he does—that I think that it's a lot of the way I see things that I just...You ask Kurt if there was anything that he was afraid to reveal, and the thing that I feel worse about is just that I feel bad about myself. And I think that that affects a lot of the way I react to him, and that there's not anything necessarily that he does to make me feel that he's better than I am—just that I feel that, you know, not very hot. And so that affects and gives me the feeling that he is.

Counselor: Your feelings about yourself affect your perspective of what Kurt does.

Heather: So...

Counselor: So this will be part of what we'll be spending some time working with. Heather, as we talk tonight about responding as a child toward Kurt, are you aware of those times?

Heather: Yes.

Counselor: Is there anything that you can begin to do this week to sort of catch yourself each time that you find yourself in that position?

Heather: What I can do to catch myself?

Counselor: Uh huh.

Heather: Probably just have it be a conscious effort and being aware of it...

Counselor: Then after you're aware of it, what will you do?

Heather: Look for an alternative way to react or to respond to whatever is happening.

Counselor: Then would you put that alternative into effect?

Heather: Yeah, do it right then.

Counselor: I like the way you're responding here because you're not asking me questions or asking me permission. You're stating them as the one that's making that decision, and you're in control of it—and I think you are.

Heather: Yeah...

Counselor: How are you feeling right now?

Heather: OK.

Kurt: I keep thinking there goes an easy session and that feeling...I was feeling a moderate amount of frustration probably from not being in control.

Counselor: I guess I'll go ahead and allow you to feel that and continue that and not resolve it. I'd like to reinforce what you've decided to do about the breaking of the parenting... child-parent relationship. This is just one suggestion and you can do with it what you'd like to. Sometimes people find it helpful if they realize—"Oh! I'm responding as a child"— to verbalize that out loud and say: "I think I'm responding like a child and I'm going to change what I'm saying," and then go ahead and change it. It's not a matter of your asking anybody any permission to do it. You're in charge of it and you just go ahead and do it. No one comments on your new statement as to whether your new statement is more of an adult comment or child response because you're going to be building week after week.

Heather: It seems like saying it out loud will help prevent it from being an awkward transition—like here I'm saying this and all of a sudden I'm going to change.

Counselor: Yes. It's like thinking out loud, which is certainly OK.

Heather: Yeah...

Counselor: I think that will do it for us this evening. I'll plan to see the two of you next week at the same time.

Kurt: Great.

Heather: OK.

NOTES

All materials quoted are used by permission.

1. **Marital Communication and Decision Making:** Analysis, Assessment and Change, Edwin J. Thomas, The Free Press, New York, 1977, pp. 29-34.

2. **Couples in Conflict,** Alan S. Gurman and David G. Rice, (Jason Aronson, New York), 1975. From an article, "Modification of Problematic Marital Communication" by Robert D. Carter and Edwin J. Thomas, pp. 347, 348.

3. Family Life Publications, **Marital Communication Inventory,** Box 427, Saluda, N.C. 28773.

4. **Journal of Marital & Family Therapy,** American Association for Marriage and Family Therapy, (Upland, CA, Vol. 6, #2, April 1980), pp. 191-194. "Implementation of Behavioral Marital Therapy," by Gregory W. Lester, Ernst Beckham and Donald H. Baucom.

5. **Journal of Marital & Family Therapy,** American Association for Marriage and Family Therapy, (Upland, CA, Vol. 6, #2, April 1980), pp. 191-194. "Implementation of Behavioral Marital Therapy," by Gregory W. Lester, Ernst Beckham and Donald H. Baucom.

CHAPTER 13

Overview of the Counseling Process

Every minister and counselor will have their own unique style and approach to marriage counseling which they have developed over the years through study, thought and trial and error. Several approaches and techniques have already been presented. In this particular chapter, there are two articles which illustrate different styles of assisting couples in rebuilding their communication. The first article contains not only helpful information on rebuilding communication during the counseling process but also gives an overview of a step-by-step procedure to use with the couple during their time in counseling.

The second article by Raymond Corsini, **The Marriage Conference,** is a detailed plan for rebuilding communication at home. Some of the basic ideas can be used within the counseling sessions. Most authors and counselors would suggest using the plan or approach exactly as presented. Many have found that it is best to develop and adapt a wide repertoire of approaches and techniques in order to meet the unique needs and problems of each couple who come for assistance.

Florence Beinenfeld, Senior Marriage and Family Counselor for The Conciliation Court of the Superior

Court of Los Angeles County, shared her philosophy of marital counseling in Marriage and Family Living Magazine.

"Marriage is a golden opportunity to be closer to another person than ever, ever before. No wonder there's so much hurt and disappointment when closeness doesn't happen and husbands and wives end up feeling like strangers.

For closeness to happen two people must be honest with each other, both willing to share feelings, thoughts, and ideas, and to listen and hear the other. Closeness takes two people agreeing that it's OK to disagree, that it's OK not to feel or think alike. Two people can achieve closeness by not trying to control the other and not always having to be right or making the other wrong. And closeness takes two people willing to settle disagreements by mutual give and take and compromise instead of by power struggles.

Couples can learn how to share feelings and listen to each other. They can also learn how to settle disagreements by mutual give and take and compromise. Once couples learn these important communication skills and practice them effectively, most wouldn't want to go back to their old patterns that didn't work before.

I teach couples every day to communicate more effectively. I'm a marriage counselor. Many couples tell me that the closeness they once felt has disappeared. Years of loneliness and frustration followed. Usually, by the time I see them they have already separated, and one has already filed for divorce. Some say they're not able to talk to each other at all without an argument. Others say they don't even try to communicate anymore. In spite of the serious problems they're having, some don't really want a divorce. They wish there was another way. When both husband and wife are still willing to work on the relationship and on communication, we go to work.

Listening and Sharing

It takes about an hour and a half to clean up the barriers from the past. I give couples careful instructions. I first ask them to turn their chairs around toward each other, so they're looking at each other face-to-face. Many couples find this hard to do. They've been avoiding each other's eyes for so long, it's hard for them to reestablish eye contact. I have them begin sharing resentments from the past. I let them decide who will go first. The other one becomes the listener. I tell the listener not to interrupt even if he or she disagrees with what the other is saying. I say, "Pretend you have tape on your mouth and can't talk. Just listen and get what your husband (or wife) is saying and be with your feelings at the same time." I ask the speaker to use the words, "I resent," or "I resented," and say what they are. I tell the speaker to bring up all resentments from the past: "Even if you've said them a thousand times before, say them again. This is your chance to get it all up, out, and over with." I tell them after this I want them to let go of these resentments and not carry them around any longer, or ever bring them up again. Resentments take the longest to share because there are usually so many of them and they are hard to listen to.

I see to it that the listener listens without interrupting. I say, "Great listening and great sharing," to encourage both of them. It's not until the first speaker has completely finished sharing all his or her resentments that we switch. Just before the other begins, I caution, "Bring up your own resentments now. Don't get caught into responding to what your husband (or wife) just said or defending yourself."

I explain, "That's how your spouse feels. There's nothing to say. Feelings don't have a right or wrong. They just are. If

I'm hungry, I'm hungry. If I'm angry, I didn't ask to be angry, I just am." I also explain that feelings can change from moment to moment. When feelings are expressed freely, the anger or hurt can disappear. "It's only when feelings are bottled up that they persist and destroy relationships." I tell couples there's a big difference between feelings and actions: "It's OK to feel any way you feel. It's not OK to act out all your feelings. There's great power in being in touch with your feelings and at the same time able to control your actions. You might feel like punching someone in the nose, but you don't have to do it. That's what is called impulse control. Adults have to be fully grown up. Otherwise they go around acting like little kids."

Becoming Free to Say, "I Resent"

Terri and John were ready to split up when they decided to give marriage counseling a try. They agreed to work on communication at their second session. Terri, age 23, faced her young, handsome husband. She laughed nervously at first when she and he established eye contact, but soon her jaw tightened as she got in touch with the anger and frustration that had been there for some time. She began to speak. "I . . . resent the way you tune me out. I resent the way you don't share yourself with me. I know you have feelings, but you won't let them be there. I resent the way you won't give. I feel sorry for you. I resent your phoniness, the way you try to get attention from people and never let people know you. I resent your selfishness. I want to be part of your life."

After Terri finished, John began, "I resent the way you always have to be right and won't consider my feelings. I resent the way you try to mold me and don't accept me as I am, or consider my background. I do care for people. I resent your thinking I'm selfish. I'm a very loving person, but I hold it more inside than outside like you do. I'm less affectionate than you are. You kiss this one and that one. I'd like to be more affectionate like you want me to be, but that's the way I am. The emotions are there. I'm a very emotional person. I'm softhearted and love animals. I resent the way you don't respect my feelings. I become frustrated and uncomfortable. I'm afraid of what you'll say. I resent having to watch my actions. I resent your bringing up the past and putting me down and saying 'always' and 'never' and comparing me to your old boyfriend. I feel hurt when you do that."

Learning to Say, "I'm Sorry"

After resentments have been shared, I encourage couples to bring up all the things they feel sorry about, sad about, or wish they had done or hadn't done. I explain, apologies can clear up the air and help people begin again. It's the opposite of being defensive and having to be right all the time. If one of you can say, "I'm sorry," it gives the other space to do the same.

Some husbands and wives cry when they share regrets, and some fight hard to hold back the tears. I encourage them to let themselves experience the sadness if it's there and not push it down. I ask them to use the words, "I regret—," and say what it is.

Roy faced his wife, Nancy, and began, "I have lots of regrets, using profane language to get my point across, being impatient and short-tempered with you, and being a first-class jerk for causing you the grief I have. I regret not being able to see through your problem and help you along." Tears began streaming down his face. "I feel so ashamed. Why couldn't we have done this ourselves? I didn't realize I put you down and made you feel like a second-class citizen. I regret I didn't pick up on your problem when your mother died. I'm sorry." With that they both cried.

Beginning to Share Concerns

I ask husbands and wives to share things about which they're feeling anxious, worried, or apprehensive. I tell them, "We're still working on removing barriers from the past. Concerns may seem like they're future oriented, but they're really out of your experience with someone in the past."

Dennis looked wearily into Laura's eyes. I asked him to use the words, "I'm concerned about," and say what it was. Dennis began, I'm concerned about not being recognized as an individual. I don't feel we talk as friends. I'm concerned about being unemployed and not finding a job I like. I'm concerned about money. I'm concerned about maintaining our home and not dipping into savings. I'm concerned about the children, that they don't get spoiled. I'm concerned about your inconsistency, the way you lose your temper and self-control."

Laura had listened attentively, then she began, "I'm concerned about not communicating the way you want me to and the way it affects our sex life. I'm concerned about your being at home all the time and not looking for a job—and the way you blame it all on your age. I'm concerned about doing things the way you want me to and about your becoming impatient with me if I don't. I'm concerned that you won't change, yet you expect me to."

* * * * *

I usually do resentments, regrets, and concerns in one hour-and-a-half session. Once these have been handled, I tell couples, "Now we'll be leaving the past behind and next session be moving forward in time to the present." I ask them to think about what they want to see happen in their relationship now and let them know that's where we'll be starting next time.

Expressing Wants

It was Sandra and Arthur's third session. During their first session, Sandra told me she was shocked when her husband filed for divorce. "I knew things had been bad for a long time, but I never thought he would leave me. I realized either I was going to stop yelling at him and start meeting some of his needs or lose him. I realized I still love him and want to stay married to him."

Arthur began telling Sandra what he wants to see happen now. I asked him to say the words, "I want—," and say what it was. "I want less rejection from you. I want more economic security. I want you to stop smoking and start exercising. I want to have friends. I want to be happy and feel our son's going to be happy. I want sex. I want to feel needed and feel I play an emotional role in your life. I want to be admired."

Now it was Sandra's chance to share her "wants". She looked at Arthur intensely and began, "I want mostly tolerance for my smoking and my inability to get things done. I already have enough guilt about this. I want to be loved for how I am. I need acceptance of me now, not of what I could be or what I was. This is the main thing I want. I do want to stop smoking, but I don't want to deal with this now."

Stating "Must Haves"

I ask couples to say what each must have in their relationship and in their lives. I explain that although these may seem similar to "wants", they're much stronger. "They're bottom line things without which your relationship wouldn't work for you." I encourage couples to be honest with their spouses and tell it like it is, using the words, "I must have . . . ", then saying what it is.

Jan looked into Dan's eyes searchingly. They married three years ago, had two small children, and were seriously considering divorce when they came in to see me. Jan began, "I must have more love and affection from you, and when I get upset, I must have more understanding instead of your saying, 'Never mind, it was nothing'. And once a month I must have you take me out, just you and me, away from the kids."

Dan told Jan his "must haves", "I must be able to go sailing a few days each year and be able to do it without getting nagged, without feeling bad before I go and having it destroyed for me. I must have more understanding from you. I have to calm down and start meeting my responsibilities to you and the kids."

Making Promises

Last of all I ask couples to share what they're willing to do or give to make their relationship work. Before Chris began, I asked him to use the words, "I'm willing to . . .", and say what he was willing to do. Chris had been pressuring Brenda for months to stop the divorce proceedings, but she refused. The divorce weighed very heavily on his mind. "I'm willing to do something about my drinking, not drink at all if necessary, give it up completely. I'm willing to give of myself and do whatever I can do to make us happy. I still have a lot of responsibility at home and at work. I still won't be able to take off every time you want me to."

Brenda told Chris, "I'm willing to go to work to help us financially. It may cost a lot for sitters, but I'd be willing to do it. I'm willing to work on our marriage and work on communication to make it strong so we can stay together forever and ever. It was difficult talking to you before. I felt you were overpowering. I felt tongue whipped. Now it's easier. I still love you. I'm willing to give it a try." Brenda told Chris she'd set the divorce aside.

* * * * *

This communication process can lead to a closer relationship. I've seen it over and over again, couples ready to divorce being willing to make a new beginning together. Sometimes the communication work I do with couples leads to a smoother separation, instead, and more willingness to cooperate as parents following the separation. I tell couples, "I never know where it will lead. You don't have anything this way, so it might be worthwhile for you to experience it and see where it will lead."

All six steps can be done in writing.

Sometimes I ask husbands and wives to put all six communication steps in writing and to share this with each other just before they come in for the next session. I ask them to write a separate page or pages for each part of the process: 1) resentments from the past, 2) regrets from the past, 3) concerns, 4) what they want to see happen now, 5) what they have to have in their relationship, and 6) what they're willing to do or give to make the relationship work better. I caution couples not to argue about what the other said. That would defeat the whole purpose.

One angry wife wrote 18 pages of resentments. Her husband said he didn't realize she had so many. By the time the wife came in she said, "I got a lot off my chest, and I don't feel angry anymore."

Writing doesn't take the place of verbal communication.

Even when couples have done the assignment in writing, I have them go through all six parts verbally, without using notes and facing each other. Most couples need positive practice and experience in talking to each other and listening to each other directly.

Most couples could do this on their own.

There's no magic in what I do. I simply provide the setting and the structure. What I suggest for couples who want to try this on their own is that they set aside a couple of hours when they can be alone, and begin to take turns sharing resentments first, then regrets and concerns. The simple instructions given here are sufficient to start developing sharing and listening skills. There should be no time limit on completing each part. Later, time should be set aside for sharing wants, must haves, and what each is willing to do to make the relationship work.

This can also work between parents and children.

I remember a 15-year old girl who was so angry with her father she wouldn't spend any time with him. Her parents had divorced a few years earlier. After she was given the chance to tell her father all her resentments, some of her anger dissipated and she told him, "Maybe I will see you next weekend. This weekend I have plans." I encourage parents to listen to children and let them express feelings. If children can't tell parents how they feel, who can they tell? This doesn't mean parents have to give children their way all the time. A close relationship between parents and children is important for the children, so they'll know how to have a close relationship with a spouse someday. These skills are carried from generation to generation. **It's not too late to learn now.**

For those who didn't learn how to communicate effectively from their parents, all it takes is being real honest about your feelings, being willing to share yourself with your spouse, and being willing to listen.

I encourage couples to share everything openly with each other. I tell them, 'Suppose you have a best friend you can share everything with, a best friend who's always willing to listen and won't betray your confidence, a best friend who never puts you down for your feelings even if he or she doesn't agree with you. That's the kind of best friend I hope you'll be for each other.' "[1]

THE MARRIAGE CONFERENCE

By
RAYMOND J. CORSINI

"It does not require much in the way of knowledge of human nature to accept the idea that practically all marriages must be happy. To prove this statement, consider only the following propositions:

1. All people desire happiness.
2. It is common knowledge that if you mistreat another person that the person will be unhappy.
3. If the person you mistreat is your mate, you will make that person unhappy, and he/she, in turn, will make you unhappy.

4. If we live with a person in close intimacy for extended periods of time (as occurs in marriage) we soon learn what the other person considers good treatment and what is poor treatment.
5. The longer we live with a person, the better we get to know that person, the more we accommodate to that person, and the more we get to like that person.
6. Apart from all these considerations, there are many other reasons why married people should treat their partners properly and therefore be happy: the effects of the marital relationship on others, friends, family and of course children.

Pure logic based on these propositions, most of which will be accepted by reasonable people as true, leads to the inescapable conclusion that most, if not all marriages are happy. Stubborn facts indicate another story: approximately one-fifth of all marriages contracted end in divorce; another fifth end in other kinds of separation; and of the remaining three-fifths at least half of the marriages appear to be pure hell. How can this be in view of the six propositions and in view of the fact that in this country marriages are viewed as a very serious step to be well thought out, and are contracted usually after extended and intimate acquaintanceship?

This is a problem that has troubled many people. We know from various research studies that on a statistical basis, that data indicate that homogamy is related to happiness in marriage (Terman, 1938; Burgess and Wallin, 1953; Corsini, 1956). However, clinical investigations show that many couples who seem to be ideally mated do not succeed in finding happiness in marriage. We have some nomothetic generalizations such as couples should have similar interests, but we have no explanation for the many cases that should be happy in terms of statistical facts, but who are quite unhappy. Is there a single important underlying factor that explains many unhappy marriages?

Some time ago I became puzzled by my own reactions while doing marriage counseling. If I listened to the husband first, I could see his point of view, it made excellent sense, and I was sympathetic to him. But then when I listened to the wife, I understood and agreed with her, and I became sympathetic to her. To be understanding and sympathetic to both parties, each of whom is in conflict with the other imposes a great strain on the middle party. I tried to take the position that I was the doctor to the marriage and not to the individuals, but a marriage is an abstraction. It is the real individuals that one has to deal with. When I tried to bridge the gaps between the two, they often turned and attacked me for trying to be a peacemaker, and for trying to bring some order and rationality into the relationship—for trying to do what they hired me for!

One day I got an idea. The idea came from a common word so often used in marital problems: *misunderstanding*. "We had a misunderstanding," was the statement, and suddenly I thought I understood everything. My hypothesis, as weird and as paradoxical as the statement that many marriages are unhappy, was that in many marriages, the couples really did not communicate! Now, how foolish a proposition that is, is evident on the face of it: two people who live in close intimacy, even sharing sleeping accommodations, not communicating! And yet, the idea made sense, especially in terms of observations of couples in my office who heard but didn't listen to one another. I had listened to each intently and I had understood each, but it was evident that something had happened in the marriage in many cases in which, regardless of how loud and clear the other spoke, there was no real listening. The trick in repairing such marriages, it seemed to me, was to help couples learn effective communication.

Towards A Solution

Some twenty years before I had developed a technique in group psychotherapy that appeared to be dramatically effective in handling some problems. A patient would be given a block of uninterrupted time, say twenty minutes, to "tell all about yourself" and then when he had finished, he would turn his back to the group while they would talk about him. I had found that this uninterrupted talking about oneself tended to make the individual feel free, and he could open up with unusual frankness, and that turning his back had the effect of freeing others to talk about the "absent" person, and, most important, made the person who was being talked about extremely alert to what was being said. (Corsini, 1953). I wondered whether something of the sort might not be effective in helping people in trouble in their marriage to communicate better.

It so happened that at the time of this thinking a new couple came to consult with me. It was a classic case. The husband was cold and distant. The wife was angry and wild. They had ceased any normal marital relationships, except for quarreling. They had four children, ranging from six to sixteen. They were contemplating divorce. When one would speak, the other would assume an attitude of indifference or anger. They shouted one another down. And yet, when I saw them individually, as usual, they seemed very nice, quite reasonable, quite persuasive, and it seemed, as it often does, a tragedy that the family should be broken up. We met for a number of sessions and it seemed as though there were no hope that relationships could be improved. Out of desperation, I suggested the technique, which I have labeled, *The Marriage Conference,* which will be soon described. The results were dramatic. Between the time I suggested this technique and the time I saw them again, this couple had had four sessions of the Marriage Conference. When they returned they were smiling and evidently happy with each other, and the three of us had a very good session. I continued seeing this couple for several more weeks and then kept in touch with them for over a year. They both insisted that it was the technique that had made the difference, that it was this that had brought them together, and that they would make the Marriage Conference a permanent part of their marriage.

Being rather cynical and suspicious of miracles, I probed this couple intently about the change, but they kept insisting they had finally broken through to each other, finally understood each other, and thanked me extravagantly for bringing them together. Naturally, at the first opportunity I prescribed the Marriage Conference again. To my surprise both individuals rejected the idea out of hand, saying things such as, "We didn't come here to play games," "we are not interested in gimmicks," "we want to get to the root of the problem," and "we communicate all right — perhaps too much," and "no, thank you, we are not interested in this Marriage Conference." This couple dissolved their marriage eventually.

Intrigued by the first success, and the second adamant refusal, I began explaining and prescribing the technique to couples that came to see me, and soon a very clear pattern appeared. Almost every case that employed the method exactly as prescribed succeeded in the sense that the marriage continued and in the sense that they both were happy with their conferences with me. In almost every case where the couple did not accept the notion, or where they started the Marriage Conference but didn't keep it up for the prescribed four sessions, or where they made variations of any kind, the marriage failed!

Now, the writer is not so naive as to think for one moment that the high rate of success of those who employ the Marriage Conference is due exclusively to the use of this technique, but it is still possible that some of the success is due to this method. In the two years since the method was discovered, I have employed it on approximately forty couples, and have made some minor changes in it. Since there may be something worth exploring in this technique, I would like to make it available to other marriage counselors. I shall give below two sets of instructions, one for the marriage counselor, and the other for couples.

Instructions for the Marriage Counselor

1. In using this technique, regardless of your orientation, you must take a strong and positive stand in the manner of a physician giving a prescription. If you can take this position: "You have consulted with me. I want you to use this method in your own home, and to use it precisely as prescribed, and if you (a) don't want to use it, or (b) don't use it after you agree to, then please find yourself another marriage counselor," so much the better. That is, you have to be convinced this technique is likely to work for the couple and you must insist that it be used exactly as prescribed.

2. In explaining the method, add this argument: "I want you both to cooperate with me, and I want you to feel that you have done everything possible to improve matters. The marriage conference is done by you two

alone—and it costs you nothing." This economic argument is often impressive.

3. It is most important that the counselor insist that the instructions be followed to the letter. Emphasize to the couple that you will make a point-by-point check to make certain that both did precisely what was called for in the instructions. Absolute rigidity and insistence is needed here.

4. To emphasize this point the counselor may say something to this effect: "If you make any variations at all, it means you are not really serious. I want you to use this method just as it is given to you."

5. If after the couple has been instructed what to do, and when they return, inform the counselor that for some reason or other they did not do what they were told to do, I would suggest that the counselor inform them that they must start again, and this time follow instructions. I would suggest telling the couple that you will not counsel them unless they do what you tell them to do. The counselor must be adamant that this technique be used exactly as prescribed.

Instructions in Using the Marriage Conference

1. These instructions are to be agreed to by both the husband and the wife in every respect otherwise this technique should not be used. There must be no variations at all. Any violations of the procedures must be reported to the counselor. The counselor may then require you to begin all over again.

2. At the soonest possible time, go to a calendar and set up four one-hour appointments with each other. Agree on the place, the day and the hour. Select, if possible, a

place where there will be no visual or sound distractions; and a time that is mutually convenient, where you will be reasonably alert, unfatigued and in as good mental and physical condition as possible. Have no more than one conference a day. Try not to have conferences on adjacent days. Ideally, a conference every two or three days is best.

3. Each person is to go to the agreed-on place at the time appointed without notifying the other. Just go to your appointed place at the appointed time. Be exact with respect to time. This conference appointment should have precedence over every other event, except dire emergencies. Treat it precisely as if you had an appointment to have X-ray treatment for suspected cancer. You have no responsibility for reminding the other to be present. His/her absence will be an indication that the other is not serious about improving the marriage.

4. If the other person does not appear, act as though he or she were there. You are to stay in the appointed place for the agreed upon hour and you will act precisely as if the other were present. If your mate does show up late make no acknowledgement. Keep on doing whatever you were in the process of doing.

5. The wife always starts first in the first session by doing whatever she wants. Usually she will talk, she may want to be silent. She has the floor for precisely thirty minutes.

6. Now, comes the first hard part. The husband during the first thirty minutes of the first session does nothing, except perhaps look at a clock that should be in the line of sight of both parties. He is not to say anything, of course, but also, he must not make any noises or

exclamations or gestures, or grimaces. He is to be absolutely silent and motionless.

7. If the husband does anything at all to distract the wife, she is to get up and leave the room in silence. Likewise, when it is the husband's turn, and the wife makes any remark of any sort, or if she should make faces, etc., the husband is to get up and leave the room in silence.

8. Should this happen, it should be reported to the marriage counselor who will suggest probably that you start over again and may suggest some means to prevent distraction by one of the couple or the other.

9. If everything goes well, and if the husband listens in absolute silence without any distraction, at the half hour, the wife stops talking (if she has been talking) and the husband begins.

10. Now, the wife listens in absolute silence, and the husband talks, or does whatever he wants. Even if he should talk for only five minutes, both remain in the room, and the wife keeps absolute silence, for thirty minutes. They cannot agree to end the session, but must remain there, perhaps just looking at each other in silence until the exact minute of the end of the hour.

11. Now comes what is the most important part of the instructions. The husband and wife are not to discuss anything between sessions that was taken up during the session. To repeat and to emphasize this simple point: there must be no discussion whatever—not a word—between them in the interval between the appointed sessions about anything taken up during the session. It would be best between sessions to avoid any argumentative topics, but anything taken up between sessions that was mentioned during the session is cause for canceling the whole set of conferences. Should either

bring up any element of any topic discussed, the other should leave the scene immediately and refuse to discuss the topic. Please keep in mind this is the most important element of the Marriage Conference.

12. At the next session, as usual, the husband and wife meet at the appointed place at the appointed time, and this time it is the husband who starts first. The same instructions apply. The husband says or does whatever he wants, for the first thirty minutes, and the wife looks and listens. If either one feels that the one who is looking and listening is disturbing, he can ask at any time for the other to turn his/her back. At the end of the thirty minutes the husband shuts up, and now the wife has thirty minutes for herself.

13. The next two sessions continue as before, with the wife starting off on the third session, and the husband having the second thirty minutes; and the husband beginning with the first thirty minutes at the fourth session, so that after four sessions, each has had four opportunities to speak without any interruption or distraction for thirty minutes.

Discussion

I shall ask myself some questions and give myself some answers about this technique, hoping that in this way I may be able to respond to questions that may be in the mind of the reader.

What is the theoretical rationale of the Marriage Conference?

I have already stated that I believe that in many marriages things come to such a pass that real communication no longer exists. Each knows the other's arguments and does not really listen to them. Often, one or both are so hurt, that they don't want to listen to the other, and are waiting for the other to stop talking so that he/she can get in with counter-arguments. Complete silence is seen as a sign of acceptance. Following the orders strictly is seen as a sign of acquiescence, evidence of good will, and indication of love.

The person who is gagged (and some people may actually gag themselves if they feel they are unable to keep quiet otherwise) and who is unable to do anything else, such as knit, or read, is forced to listen. This forced listening under these restricting conditions may actually lead the person to understand the other, to finally get empathy, and feel with the other. We are trying to do two things: (a) get the couple to submit to the discipline of the counselor, so that both become his children as it were, and (b) force each to listen intently to the other.

Why not permit some interaction by the passive partner, such as saying "Uh-uh" or nodding or smiling, etc.?

In cases where the Marriage Conference is used, any reaction, no matter how apparently innocuous, may be seen by the other party as hostile and offensive. Any stimulus emitted by the passive party, auditory or visual, can be interpreted by the active one as a hostile gesture or sound. In one of my unsuccessful cases, a sneeze was interpreted by the wife as evidence of lack of interest. Both theory and experience indicate the notion of complete silence and passivity is best. In some cases, even rolling of the eyes, or looking in a glazed manner, etc., can be disturbing. The important thing then is for the passive partner to be as inconspicuous and as neutral as possible.

Do you really believe that lack of communication is the real problem in most problem marriages?

Not really. Often, there is too much communication, but it is the quality of communication that is important. We hear things like this often, "I told him a thousand times..." or "he keeps telling me..." So, there is communication in the intellectual sense. What is missing is empathic communication, or real understanding in the emotional sense, a lack of comprehension of the person himself.

Why all the rigidity of rules? Why all the insistence that things be done just so?

I have found that it is best that the counselor be exceedingly firm, so that both parties feel that they are in competent hands. If the counselor gives evidence that he knows what he is doing, and if he is insistent that things go just as he prescribes, then both will feel confidence in him and will surrender themselves to his demands. This in turn means they will tend to do exactly what is involved in the instructions, which cooperation with each other (and with the counselor) can be the turning point in the marriage. We are looking for a breakthrough.

Why the insistence that there be no discussion of disputed or argumentative matters between sessions?

There are several good reasons. First, and perhaps foremost, this leads to a respite from the bickering and arguments that are so frequently found in couples that come to a marriage counselor. It is like letting a wound heal. Second, during this respite period both tend to be very active internally, doing a great deal of self-arguing and thinking, planning on rebuttals, considering the other's argument, and otherwise ruminating and meditating. Third, the very fact that each is aware that the other is following orders tends to make each one sympathetic to the other, in that this compliance is evidence of good will. So each is doing a lot of thinking and self-communicating in a peaceful state of relationship.

Suppose a couple reports it is unable to find time to meet for the marriage conference?

One can do a number of things. First, you can offer them your office, charging them your usual rates, while you are outside of the room. Second, you can regard this as evidence that they don't mean business, and discharge them as patients. Third, you can help them try to find time.

Won't you lose patients by such an intransigent attitude?

No. What brings clients and patients to any professional person is his success. If he takes the reasonable attitude that those who come to him have to follow his advice or leave him, patients are much more likely to stay with him than if he takes a weak attitude. I have found that when I try to discharge patients for this reason, they are incredulous, and usually decide to follow my orders.

Can a non-directive therapist employ such a technique?

I don't see why not. He can say to them that he believes that each should be the other's therapist, as it were, and that this rather simple and restrictive technique may help them help themselves, and if they will not employ the method in the spirit of a working hypothesis, that he feels that he cannot handle them.

What about your rule that a person should stay in the room alone by himself/herself if the other doesn't show up?

Several good reasons for this. First, if the other does not show up, the solitary one will spend time thinking about the marriage. So, the time is well spent. Second, if the other comes in late and sees that his/her mate is waiting patiently, this will affect that person favorably in terms of attitude. Say a husband comes in ten minutes late and sees and hears his wife talking to herself. This can affect him deeply, and may be the crisis point in changing his attitude.

What are the philosophical implications of the marriage conference?

The basic one is that couples ought to learn how to settle their problems by themselves, and that before neither one really listened to the other. The alert and responsible marriage counselor may find that by using this method the couple can experience a breakthrough which he then can exploit and lead them to more useful patterns of living.

Is the conference to be only four sessions?

No. I have found that some couples use the conferences as a regular part of their marriage, meeting routinely in this manner once a week. Others employ it from time to time. I may prescribe it for two, four, six more times if it seems indicated.

Summary and Conclusions

The Marriage Conference is a technique that depends on the autochthonous creativity of the couple. It is highly structured and rigidly controlled to permit one person unlimited freedom of communication while the other is forced to listen. It seems to be quite useful in some situations. When and with whom to apply it is up to the discretion of a marriage counselor. Whether it is in its final stage of perfection is unknown. The writer suggests that whoever uses it, tries it first in its present form, and that variations should be attendant upon experience with it in this orthodox manner.

As stated earlier, when couples "buy" the concept and use it, the rate of success is high, whatever be the reason. I suspect this rate of success is dependent on the degree of confidence expressed by the counselor in the probable efficiency of the method.

I do not wish to give case histories, but I have found this method successful with some cases that I had thought would be unsuccessful. Since we cannot replicate individual cases, we can only come to probable conclusions on the basis of judgment. My judgment is that this method should be in the ammamentarium of marriage counselors for those cases where it may appear to apply as either the method of choice or as an auxiliary technique.

Perhaps the strongest argument that I have for its employment is my belief that any real improvement in any marriage must be attributable by the couple themselves to themself."[2]

References

Burgess, E.W. & Wallin, P. *Predicting Success and Failure in Marriage*. New York: Prentice-Hall, 1939.

Corsini, R.J. "The Behind-the-Back Technique in Group Psychotherapy." *Group Psychotherapy*, 1953, pp. 6, 102-109.

Corsini, R.J. "Understanding and Similarity in Marriage." *Journal of Abnormal and Social Psychology*, 1956, pp. 52, 327-332.

Terman, L.M. *Psychological Factors in Marital Happiness*. New York: McGraw-Hill, 1938.

NOTES

All materials quoted are used by permission.

1. Used by permission of Marriage and Family Living Magazine and the author. **"New Hope for Troubled Marriages"** by Florence Beinenfeld, pp. 6, 8, 9. October, 1980.

2. Raymond J. Corsini, Ph.D., Senior Counselor, Family Education Center of Hawaii, Honolulu, Hawaii. Used by permission of the author.

CHAPTER 14

Sexual Concerns

The frequency of sexual difficulties within marriage is probably more extensive than most people realize. Masters and Johnson of the Reproductive Biology Research Foundation in St. Louis estimate that at least fifty percent of all married couples have some difficulties which are sexual in nature.[1] These problems range from minor difficulties which require information or minimal help to those which can bring marital disaster if not properly treated. Such difficulties could either be the basic problem within the marriage, or they could be symptomatic of other problems.

As you work with a couple, one or both may complain about their sexual relationship. In some cases this difficulty is not immediately shared but is hidden behind or in the midst of other complaints. As the individual or couple becomes more comfortable with the minister they may express the sexual conflict or frustration. Or there may be appropriate openings for a question to be asked about the sexual relationship.

Each couple who seeks counseling will have their own set of beliefs and feelings concerning the sexual relationship. If this part of the relationship is in pain then both the attitudes and behaviors should be explored. Attitudes will range from a negative attitude toward sex in general on the part of one to a belief by the other that sex should be provided on demand.

It is essential for a couple to develop a continual, growing satisfaction with their sex life as it contributes to the overall happiness of the marriage. If one or both are dissatisfied, this feeling can begin to erode the overall satisfaction level of the marriage.

A simplistic approach to problems in this area is insufficient. Telling a couple to go home and "make love" or requesting a wife to be "submissive" to her husband does not remedy the problem.

Dr. William Carrington described a simple overview of the discussion of sexual difficulties.

In any counseling with partners in sexual difficulties the counselor will generally attempt to gain some knowledge of the total background of the situation by getting some idea of the sexual history of the partners. Much of this may come out spontaneously in the stories that each of them give, but the counselor can add to this by some well designed questions when there is an opening for them. He can keep his own mental processes in an orderly sequence by working back from the present to the past. The general history of the present marriage and the sexual attitudes and methods, the number of children and of miscarriages if any, and the feelings of each about them may come first. Then the history of any previous marriages, the conduct of the courtship and engagement period and of any previous love affairs may be discussed, and an opportunity given for an account of anything that may have been a cause of deep regret or disillusionment. Then the attitude of parents and siblings and playmates at school, and the way in which the early introduction to sex was conducted may be reviewed, together with the emotional attitudes of the client to the various manifestations of sex.

The progressively frank discussion of these emotionally charged elements of the situation in the calm accepting atmosphere of counseling will often prove to be an entirely new experience for the client, and it will do much to overcome many of his bewilderments and fears and to bring a growing release from his emotional conflicts and tensions. Even when there are deeply repressed elements, which need psychotherapy if they are to be adequately dealt with, the experience of counseling will provide an important part of the therapy, and may even help the clients to a point at which they can go on developing themselves without specialist help. Much will obviously depend on how naturally and comfortably the counselor is able to handle the sexual aspects of the clients' narratives, and counselors need to be at ease in their own personalities in this field if they are to be adequate for the work.

Finally in this discussion of the sexual relationship it might be suggested that at its best human sexual intercourse can be regarded as a complete abandoned self-offering of each to the other as an expression of outgoing unselfish love, a reenactment together of the partners' "one-flesh-ness" in the marriage relationship, through which it can be progressively deepened and the partners brought to an ever closer union. If it can be accepted in this way there will be less desire to demand and more willingness to offer. There will also be more regular personal attention to the quality of love which the regular sexual intercourse seeks to express, and in this way the partners will be much more likely to grow together to greater maturity in their total relationship.[2]

Sexuality and The Minister

For the minister involved in marital counseling an understanding and knowledge of the intricacies of sexual functioning and dysfunctioning is essential. This is not to say, however, that a minister would be involved in the treatment of some of the more serious dysfunctions. Recognizing what they are and having a basic awareness of some of the various treatments will aid in making a proper referral.

More and more states are moving now to develop standards and training for those engaged in sex therapy. Thus it is important to know one's own limitation and expertise as well as the laws of the state in which your ministry occurs.

It is important for a counselor to be open and specific in discussion of sexual matters. Such an ability will help the couple to become more open and specific as they develop the freedom to share.

Nevertheless, ministers and counselors often experience some of their greatest threat and inner conflict when a couple begins to share their struggles with sexuality. Sometimes it is because the sharing of sexual conflicts induces similar feelings on the part of the minister. Or perhaps the attractiveness of a counselee may affect the minister's thoughts or desires. The denial of our own sexuality as a person and the fact that a counselee would be attracted to us and/or us to them will only serve to make us more vulnerable and threatened.

In order to defend against this threat, a counselor may try to limit what topics may be discussed within the session, or he may read into a counselee's behavior or verbal sharing and interpret to them something of a sexual nature or even describe it as a sexual advance.

If a woman counselee is responding in a seductive manner, she could be a person who learned early in life that behaving in a seductive manner increases the likelihood of positive responses from males. In a sense she has learned to disguise her real needs and to express them sexually.

Need for affection and approval have often been couched in sexual expression. Naturally, the question is, how do we deal with such behavior?

A thorough awareness and understanding of sex and its meaning is one support. Creating a healthy and open sexual relationship within one's own marriage is another. Both can help us deal with our own potential threat.

As we become aware of what the counselee is doing, it is important to become neither defensive and contained nor overly solicitous. In other words, proceed as we have been.

Sometimes nonverbals (such as sitting closer or dressing provocatively), facial expressions, or verbal cues such as positive comments about our care, looks, or compassion are designed to gain a positive response. The statement, "Your wife is very fortunate to be married to a caring person like you," can be treated as any other compliment without either denying what was said or asking for an elaboration. (A woman counselor will experience the same approaches from a male counselee).

Often, asking the person what his/her specific needs are and how these are usually manifested can help the counselee begin to understand what s/he is doing. Eventually the seductive behavior will be discussed along with its underlying meaning. When this is done in a nonjudgmental or nonthreatening manner, this will be acceptable and each person—counselee and counselor alike—will feel less threatened.

Causes of Sexual Dysfunction

Some sexual difficulties occur over time and could develop because of other marital problems. Or the sexual problem could be there at the onset of the marriage because of negative attitudes or experiences or severe personal problems. The initial lack of sex or the gradual withdrawal of sex throughout the marriage will create negative relations. Often couples learn to use sex as a means of attack or inflicting hurt. Excuses for not participating, making the experience unpleasant, hurting one's partner, or making caustic comments are typical patterns.

Often the physical components of sexual problems are considered to be the source of the difficulty, but sexual dysfunctions can have either emotional or physical causes, or both. What occurs in the sexual organs comes from physical stimuli and mental images from the brain and nervous system. The most important organ of the body for sex is the brain, not the penis or vagina.

When the term *sexual dysfunction* is used, it means a malfunctioning of the sexual response system. Specific causes of sexual problems can generally be grouped into four main categories.

Emotional: A person's feeling or emotions can control the actual physical response. Sex can be blocked because of worry, fear, anger, or hatred. On the other hand, feelings of love, worth, and affection can enhance the response. Feelings and attitudes are very much involved in this physical act.

Intellectual: Even in an era when sex is so openly discussed, ignorance abounds. Most do not want to admit their lack of knowledge when everyone is supposedly so enlightened. The ignorance can involve a lack of understanding of sexual response, anatomy, male/female uniqueness, or love-making techniques. Also involved in this category is a lack of knowing what is both pleasing and necessary to the other for proper stimulation.

Psychological: Negative attitudes about any phase of sex can inhibit a healthy sexual response. Fear of being hurt, becoming pregnant, or being unable to perform, along with depression, stress, guilt, or disgust are just a few of the common blockages. Past experiences, early childhood training, or a negative environment could be the contributing factors. Negative feelings or a break in the relationship will inhibit a physical giving of one's self to another.

Some suggest that anxiety is the common denominator of all sexual dysfunctions. The origins and intensity of this anxiety vary. It could be a result of childhood conflict or related to situational performance fears. If anxiety occurs during the sexual act itself, the results will be the same as a long-standing anxiety problem.[3]

Physical: A number of physical causes can impair sexual activity. Illnesses such as hepatitis, diabetes, multiple sclerosis, malnutrition, vitamin deficiencies, heart or lung diseases could all decrease sexual desire.

One common cause is that of drugs. Alcohol has two basic effects. It releases inhibitions, but it also acts as a sedative which lessens the sensations and responses. Alcohol is a major reason for impotence in males. Numerous other drugs in small doses may increase sexual appetite and response, but in larger doses these can have an opposite effect. An example of this would be barbiturates.

Common Sexual Problems

Hypoactive sexual desire is considered to be the most common of all of the sexual dysfunctions. One specialist, Dr. Helen Singler Kaplan, reported that 40 percent of individuals who seek help for sexual problems at the Marriage Council of Philadelphia were suffering from inhibited sexual desire. What surprises many is the fact that there is a significant number of men who have a low sexual drive.[4]

Response to a lack of sexual drive varies. If there is no pressure from a spouse, a marriage may go on for years with little or no sexual activity. Other couples may feel miserable to the extent that their entire outlook on life is influenced. The partner's reactions may vary as well. They may accept it or feel a personal rejection. They might begin to believe that they are the cause because of being unattractive. This problem may then become the focal point of the marriage.

Many conflicts will center around differences in sexual preferences. These could include frequency, the place sexual activity occurs, position, or type of sex play. These difficulties could be used as a means of punishing, controlling or manipulating the partner, or they could be present because of attitudes. It is important to clarify attitudes and feelings when dealing with these issues.

Sometimes sexual dysfunction occurs with the husband. *Premature ejaculation* can be described as an inability to control ejaculation for a sufficient length of time during intercourse to satisfy his wife at least fifty percent of their times of sexual intercourse. He ejaculates before he wishes to do so. This could occur before entering the vagina or immediately upon entering.

Impotence is a condition whereby a man is unable to achieve an erection. *Primary impotence* means erection does not occur at all, whereas *secondary impotence* means erection has occurred some of the time.

Ejaculatory incompetence is a difficulty in which the man becomes excited and has normal intercourse but cannot reach orgasm.

Sometimes the dysfunction occurs with the wife. For many years the term *frigid* was used to describe a woman who could not have an orgasm, was "cold", unresponsive or didn't enjoy sex. Frigid, today, is used to describe a woman who finds the sex act distasteful or even offensive. A woman who does not achieve orgasm is termed *nonorgasmic* or *preorgasmic*. She may become aroused to a certain point but cannot achieve orgasm.

Dyspareunia or painful intercourse may be slight or severe. It is a common complaint which gynecologists hear.

Vaginismus is a condition in which the muscles of the vagina constrict involuntarily. Vaginismus either prevents the male from entering or makes intercourse too painful to continue.

Whenever any of the above difficulties occur, the counselor should ask the couple if they have sought medical help. This is usually the first step. In most cases the woman would see a gynecologist and the man a urologist.

There are three helpful resources which can be used with an individual or couple. The book, **Intended for Pleasure** by Dr. Ed and Gaye Wheat (Revell) and the tape series, **Sex Problems and Sex Technique in Marriage** by Ed Wheat have been helpful as a beginning step.[5] Another tape series which discusses in detail the various problems mentioned earlier is **Overcoming Sexual Inadequacy** by Dr. Steven Niger, who is a sex therapist. The material presented on the tapes is the specific information Dr. Niger presents to a couple in counseling.[6] (See the footnote page for details on acquiring these tapes).

Many of the couples who share some type of sexual difficulty will be helped by your counsel and information resources, but when the problems have been longer in duration, or more serious, or when there has been no response to your counsel and resources, a referral to a sex therapist may be in order.

Affairs

On the basis of a survey of 100 marriage counselors across the country, former President of the American Association of Marriage and Family Counselors, Dr. Frederick G. Humphey, stated that nearly half of the cases brought to marriage counselors involve adultery. It is difficult to know for certain the incidence of adultery in the population, whether with Christian or non-Christian couples. Morton Hunt describes the situation bluntly:

Many people cheat—some a little, some a lot; most who don't would like to but are afraid; neither the actual nor the would-be cheaters admit the truth or defend their views except to a few confidants; and practically all of them teach their children the accepted traditional code though they know they neither believe in it themselves nor expect that their children will do so when they grow up.[7]

One study by Cummings indicated there were two significant aspects to every affair. These were the deprivations at home and the attractions away from home.[8] (It may be well to point out that many people have non-sexual, non-personal affairs. They have affairs with their jobs, their hobbies, their drive for further schooling, their churches. In essence something else is receiving the care and attention that rightfully belongs to the marriage, and the marital relationship is hurting because of it.) As you counsel with those who are involved with another person, it may be helpful to determine both the deprivations and the distractions.

Causes:

Why do people—many of whom have either a strong Christian conviction against adultery or a high sense of morality—move into affairs? There are any number of reasons.

During the mid-life phase affairs are common occurrences. For many men the desire to resolve their fleeting youth and masculinity, coupled with a sense of stagnation in their own marriage, helps to set the stage for this occurrence. For women many of the same reasons propel them to another man. An affair can be used as a means of dealing with one's sense of discontent. Dwight Small describes the process:

The affair may be a welcome diversion, a momentary tranquilizing of a burdensome, anxious situation either in his career or at home. Here's a nice break from hard reality. After all the tough years of keeping his nose to the grindstone—and for what?—isn't it time for a little reward in terms of romantic affirmation? Subconsciously, too, it may be the rather compelling need of the middle years to prove one's attractiveness at a time when confirmation from other quarters has largely dried up. Soon it will be too late; it is now or never!

What comes into such a man's life as a fresh, new event is bound to be stimulating, especially when it is secretive and furtive, risky enough to confirm his boldness and daring. There is a curious new freedom he's experiencing, perfectly understandable inasmuch as there is no past as yet to regret, no future as yet to dread, and no present sufficiently established to doubt. For the time being at least there exists no need, as in marriage, to work out compromises between opposing sets of interests. The reawakening of passion seems all but beyond belief, while the new zest for living is ample proof that the capacities of one's youth have only lain dormant, waiting for the person who could waken them to life...

He also discovers another ability that he would hardly attempt to demonstrate at home—flirtation. No wonder he's excited, suddenly having all those long-buried talents released—nothing so appealing and challenging has happened in years. A new business venture is dull by comparison. What further justification is needed beside the reawakening of love that is taking place?

Now, of course, this is a most pitiable condition. Deception is paramount. To our momentarily reinvigorated friends it seems there is no tomorrow—no price to pay; but there is. To temporarily ignore this fact is to succumb to a will-o-the-wisp. The new affection is likely no more than a regressive need for self-affirmation.[9]

In numerous cases a person will engage in an affair with someone at work, perhaps with a secretary or with another employee. Reasons for this vary. One person may be using the affair for a new sense of power or control at work. Or perhaps the person has a feeling of pity or sympathy for the other man or woman. Sometimes it's a matter of enjoying the other person's company. Dwight Small describes some other reasons for it:

After years of counseling those involved in extramarital love affairs, I'm persuaded that many men and women find themselves in a grip of passion, with which reason cannot compete. Still others do not understand what's happening to them, locating the cause outside themselves. Of course, any romantic involvement is an exciting, pleasurable interlude in a life grown dull and monotonous with routine and familiarity. Perhaps there has been a failure to find success and adequate rewards in one's career. Perhaps there are fewer rewards in marriage—the marriage one has long since ceased nurturing. The affair is a tempting compensation for the love that's lost its luster. Perhaps a man doesn't recognize a compelling need to restore a slipping self-image and the temptation to satisfy that need through the flattering attention of a younger woman—a woman who at the time may be tempted to participate in a romantically stellar performance involving herself and an admired man.[10]

Another reason may be that the wife has become so overly responsible as a wife and mother that her children's trials and triumphs have begun to take precedent over maintaining her appearance or tending to her husband's needs. Often both he and she receive the leftovers. Often when the husband leaves in the morning his wife is rushing to get the children ready and to school on time, and her attention is taken there. Or she herself is struggling to get to work on time. Sometimes it's both! Then at the end of the day she may be tired, harrassed and involved with the children. But at work the husband sees others who are "put together" psychologically and physically, and he doesn't have to see them or deal with them in the mundane activities of home.

Other reasons include poor sexual adjustment in marriage, finding the new person to be a challenge, being "in love" or infatuated, having an unaffectionate partner, having a marriage which never progressed, or getting revenge. This list could continue.[11]

Three basic patterns occur when a person chooses to terminate the affair. Some men (or women) decide that this lifestyle is not what they want. They settle down with their wives (or husbands) to build much better marriages than they ever had before.

Another pattern occurs when the man returns to his wife (or the reverse) but she will not forgive him. The problems which were there before have no resolution. The security of the marriage is not established and in the future it will probably break apart again, perhaps for good.

The third pattern is that the involved spouse likes the new partner better than the current mate and divorces.

Even though the majority of people I have seen involved in affairs are committed Christians and know what the Word of God says about adultery, appealing to this knowledge does not usually cause them to stop the involvement. Appeals to family, mother, church, or even job security also have negligible effects.

Those involved will give many reasons for continuing, "I don't want to hurt the other person." "He (or she) meets my needs so much better than my spouse." "I've led him (her) to the Lord and we've developed a close and growing spiritual relationship." "I've become a father to her children and can't leave them."

The disengagement process is difficult, but for the non-affair spouse to have a chance for the involved spouse to become interested and in love with him again, the affair needs to be broken immediately and completely. To be successful, it cannot be ended slowly or piecemeal.

Often the person replies with, "But that will hurt her!" I usually respond with, "That's true, but that's just part of the risk of an affair. Everyone gets hurt, and your spouse has already been hurt. Unfortunately people don't consider this in advance. Your spouse is at a distinct disadvantage as long as you continue the affair. That which is new, exciting and doesn't have much of the daily mundane aspects of marriage attached to it usually takes precedent over the spouse. So for her (or him) to have a chance—and if you are at all serious about your marriage—the affair needs to come to a halt now. It's your choice."

I have heard many excuses and reasons for not responding immediately, but I simply continue to express this point of view. Their being uncomfortable at this point should not affect our position.

No matter what we say, the person will probably not disengage from his/her affair until he becomes uncomfortable with it or so dissatisfied and stressful that he begins to reconsider.

In cases where an affair is occurring (or often where couples are discouraged with their marriage) you will hear the excuse, "I don't love him anymore and I can't fall in love again," or "I don't think I ever loved her to begin with," or "I'm not sure it's worth trying." The best approach that I have found to deal with these various excuses and to bring about a change in attitude is to use a resource, Dr. Wheat's series of tapes, "Love Life." Many couples have found positive change occurring as a result of these tapes. (See footnote #5 for details.)

Effects

The usual effect of an affair upon a marriage is a sense of disturbance. In most cases the partner not involved in an affair becomes aware of some new intrusion into their relationship which furthers the strain that is already there. Some probing, questioning and an increasing air of suspicion now enters the relationship. The secrecy and deception which accompany most affairs can heighten the sense of romantic excitement but it can also create a greater sense of tension, guilt and pressure.

How might the offended person respond to an affair? Some of the common mistakes or responses a wife may make if she discovers the affair or is told of it and its continuance are the following (I usually share these typical responses with the wife either to help eliminate them or to prevent them):

1. She rails and denounces him, verbally attacks and pushes him even further away. Anger will be natural, but if it continues on and on and there are no positive overtones toward him, then he finds greater justification for what he is doing.

2. She tells as many others as possible. This may include his family, people at his work, and the children. This creates further alienation for the couple.

3. She will ask his family, closest friend or even his pastor to talk to him and straighten him out.

4. Some wives either increase their sexual involvement with their husband in an attempt to win him back, or they eliminate sex entirely. For each couple, sex has a different meaning. Both the meaning and purpose of the decreased or increased activity must be explored and analyzed before a decision can be made concerning what *might* be best at this time.

5. She may see the other woman just to see what she looks like, to plead with her, or to verbally or physically attack her. If the woman is at her husband's work and the wife marches in to view the other person, this usually creates greater strain.

6. She may begin to campaign at home to make him suffer, or she may tell him to leave. Ordering a spouse to leave takes the responsibility away from him and may give

him the excuse he has been looking for all the time.

An affair is a breach of trust. It is often hard to regain trust when the affair is discovered, and some marriages are never the same. The offended spouse may never forgive. He or she may find it difficult to have intercourse afterwards because of the thought of the spouse in bed with another person. Sometimes the guilty person becomes sexually unresponsive.

The violated trust is replaced by anger, rage, resentment, distrust, fear, doubt, cynicism and indifference. Since a commitment was broken, the sense of loyalty is shattered. One's sense of self-esteem is also lowered. As one woman said, "If he had chosen a younger attractive woman I could understand it. But why her? She's older than I am! What does he find so distasteful about me?"

The offended person needs to work through his/her feelings just like in any other crisis event.

Throughout any type of marital crisis, but especially during an affair the book, **How to Cope with Conflict Crisis and Change** by Lloyd Ahlem (Regal Books) has been especially helpful. In most crises and with the affair there is a sense of loss. The loss could be the relationship itself, one's sense of identity, one's values, etc. But, whenever there is a loss, there are fairly predictable stages that a person will go through as they proceed through the change in crisis sequence. As the counselee becomes aware of the normality of this process they are much better able to deal with what is happening to them emotionally, in the relationship and in addition they can experience a greater degree of hope regardless of the outcome.

If a man thirty or over is the one involved in the affair, must reading immediately for the wife is **Men in Mid-Life Crisis** by Jim Conway and **You and Your Husband's**

Mid-Life Crisis by Sally Conway (Cook Publisher). Sally Conway's advice to the offended wife is sane and practical.

If the affair is continuing, the offended spouse's own possible contribution to this can be explored and changes can be made. But no matter how loving and responsive the offended spouse becomes, there is no guarantee of what the partner will do.

What About Confession?

Should the offended person be told? It is difficult to offer a blanket statement for every situation concerning whether to tell, how, when and what the results will be. Ask fifteen counselors or fifteen ministers, and you will find little agreement.

Many fear that confessing the affair may make things worse because there are no guarantees as to how the offended person will respond. Some people have said, "If my spouse ever has an affair I don't want to know about it. I don't need that information to weigh upon me. My spouse would relieve his (her) guilt by doing that, and he/she could walk away feeling OK. But what do I do with my anger, resentment and feeling of being betrayed?"

In fact some husbands or wives have been heard to tell their spouses, "If you ever have an affair don't ever tell me about it. I don't want to have to get over that kind of hurt."

Many say that an affair should be shared only if the partner has the capability of working through the hurt and anger. Some fear the sharing as being potentially destructive. In some cases it seems the criteria on the part of the person involved and the counselor for sharing is a guarantee that there will be no adverse reaction.

Marriage specialist Billie Ables has said,

   . . . we can think of several instances where we thought opening up with some information (for example, with regard to extramarital affairs) would have been detrimental to the relationship and destructive to the progress already made. This is not to say that we condone the behavior, but rather put emphasis on what the consequences might be. Ultimately, we hope to help a spouse having an affair to understand the motivation to tell or not to tell. The motivation may be to alleviate guilt, to punish the partner, or in the case of not telling, to spare the self the possibility of retaliation. In some cases, the information is used to encourage the partner to behave likewise, so that the spouse's own behavior is justified. On occasion, we have agreed that to tell would be harmful. We have had more than one spouse emphasize that they would rather have not found out. But we have also tried to help a spouse having an affair see what price must be paid if the behavior were discovered. We do not feel that trust is an issue to be taken lightly; many marriages have foundered when a spouse felt that he or she could no longer trust the mate.[12]

The meaning assigned to the affair by both partners is another factor to consider. If the marriage was sound and strong, the affair could have a less negative effect because of the strength. On the other hand, the affair could have a more negative effect because there seemed to be little rhyme or reason for its occurrence. If a husband or wife believe that an affair means their husband or wife no longer loves them, they will respond differently than if they believe the affair is a sexual involvement which will soon be over. Love, trust, and commitment can occur again, but it will take a great deal of work.

Even though each person involved in an affair will make up his own mind, my counsel is to confess to God and to one's spouse, realizing there is no guarantee of acceptance, forgiveness, or restoration from the offended spouse. If the affair is not confessed, and if it is discovered in the years to come, the negative effect could be even more upsetting. The one involved could spend years in fear that the discovery may occur.

The individual may have to incur wrath, suspicion and various comments for weeks or months after the confession. Just because one has been honest and confessed does not mean instant reconciliation will occur. I have found it helpful to ask the person how he expects his partner to respond when he confesses. I also ask, "what if he (or she) does_____ or ...?" "What if it takes several months?" "How will you respond if some evening your partner asks some questions which imply suspiciousness on her/his part?" "Are you aware that it will take time for your partner to move from one stage of remembering to another?"

Stage one remembering involves emotional involvement with the event. Stage two is remembering that the affair occurred, but there is no emotion left. It's like saying, "Yes, that happened. I know it did, but it no longer affects me. It's a fact of history, yet has no emotional significance or effect. It's there, but we are progressing onward at this time, and I am not hindered nor is our relationship hurt by that event." This is, in a sense, forgetting. The fact remains, but it no longer entangles the person in its tentacles of control. The person involved needs awareness and encouragement during the confession and reconciliation period.

The problem confronted here does not merely involve a person's feelings, fear of hurt, or a guarantee that everything will be all right if the affair is confessed. The issue is a Theological/Biblical matter. Confusion appears to be present concerning whether confession of sin should be only to

God or to the offended party as well. Consider John Stott's perspective, offered in his book, **Confess Your Sins**.

Some zealous believers, in their anxiety to be open and honest, go too far in this matter. To say "I'm sorry I was rude to you" or "I'm sorry I showed off in front of you" is right; but not "I'm afraid I've had jealous thoughts about you all day". Such a confession does not help; it only embarrasses. If the sin remains secret in the mind and does not erupt into words or deeds, it must be confessed to God alone. It is true that, according to the teaching of Jesus, "whosoever looketh on a woman to lust after her hath committed adultery with her already in his heart" (Mt. 5:28); but this is adultery *in the sight of God* and is to be confessed to Him, not to her. The rule is always that secret sins must be confessed secretly (to God), and private sins must be confessed privately (to the injured party).

Perhaps a word of caution may be written here. All sins, whether of thought, word, or deed, must be confessed to God, because He sees them all "O Lord, Thou hast searched me, and known me. Thou knowest my down-sitting and mine uprising, Thou understandest my *thought* afar off. Thou compassest my path and my lying down, and art acquainted with all my *ways*. For there is not a *word* in my tongue, but, lo, O Lord, Thou knowest it altogether" (Ps. 139:1-4). But we need to remember that men do not share the omniscience of God. They hear our words and see our works; they cannot read our hidden thoughts. It is, therefore, social sins of word and deed which we must confess to our fellow-men, not the sinful thoughts we may have harboured about them.[13]

Perhaps a guideline to follow would be to wait to confess

until the couple has worked sufficiently upon the marriage so that it has been stabilized enough to handle the admission. The counselor's presence when the confession does occur may be necessary for some couples to ease the process. In many cases the spouse has already had suspicions that this has occurred, and it is not as much of a shock as expected.

In one session as a husband was talking about the marriage, his wife said, "There appears to be something that you are still uncomfortable about. Is there something that you need to share with me?" He proceeded to tell her, and during the remainder of that session they began to work through the confession, hurt, and forgiveness.

Once the partner has stopped the affair and has asked for forgiveness, the couple will need to spend much time in counseling and in building a new relationship. The concept that forgiveness is a process and not instantaneous must be explored as well.

Forgiveness is not pretending. One cannot ignore the fact that an event occurred. Wishing it never happened will not make it go away. What has been done is done, and becoming a martyr and pretending ignorance of the event does not help the relationship. In fact, the lack of confrontation and reconciliation may encourage the other person to continue or repeat the same act or behavior.

Forgiveness is not a feeling. It is not a soothing, comforting, overwhelming emotional response that erases the fact from one's memory forever. It is a clear and logical action that does not bring up the past offenses and hurts but takes each day a step at a time. Gradually there will be a bit less anger and resentment and a bit more forgiveness until eventually there is a wholeness once again.

Sexual transgressions will occur. But as with other sins,

God's grace *is* active and the presence of Jesus Christ in a person's life can bring restoration and wholeness. This is the ultimate message of our counseling.

NOTES

All materials quoted are used by permission.

1. F. Philip Rice, **Sexual Problems in Marriage,** (Philadelphia: The Westminster Press), 1978, p. 13.

2. William L. Carrington, M.D., **The Healing of Marriage,** (Channel Press: Great Neck, N.Y.), 1961, pp. 204, 205.

3. Helen Singer Kaplan, **Disorders of Sexual Desire,** (New York: Brunner-Mazel), 1979, pp. 24, 25. A complete discussion of the problem of sexual anxiety is presented in chapter 2, "The Etiology of the Sexual Dysfunctions."

4. Kaplan, p. 57.

5. Dr. Wheat's tapes can be ordered from Christian Marriage Enrichment, 8000 E. Girard, Suite 601, Denver, Colorado 80231.

6. Dr. Niger's tapes can be ordered from Instructional Dynamics—Human Development Institute, 166 East Superior Street, Chicago, Illinois 60611.

7. Morton Hunt, **The Affair,** (New York: New American Library), 1969, p. 29.

8. G. Cummings, **A Study of Marital Conflicts Involving an Affair by One of the Partners,** (unpublished Master's Thesis, University of Southern California, Los Angeles, 1960).

9. Dwight H. Small, **How Should I Love You,** (Harper and Row, New York), 1979, pp. 118-120.

10. Dwight H. Small, **How Should I Love You,** (Harper and Row, New York), 1979, pp. 118-120.

11. G. Cummings, **A Study of Marital Conflicts Involving an Affair by One of the Partners,** (unpublished Master's Thesis, University of Southern California, Los Angeles, 1960).

12. Billie Ables, **Therapy for Couples,** (Jossey-Bass, San Francisco), 1977, pp. 307, 308.

13. John R.W. Scott, **Confess Your Sins,** (Westminster, Philadelphia, PA), 1964, p. 27.

CHAPTER 15

Pitfalls in Counseling

Basic Concerns

Counselors and ministers can slip into numerous potential pitfalls as they counsel people in marital crises. Some pitfalls are unique to ministers; some are not. It is important for each counselor to be aware of the possibilities, but if any of the following problems applies personally or is of concern to the reader, then further study into the area is recommended.

One of the dangers involves *rushing the progress* and growth of the counselee. Because of the many responsibilities of the minister, time availability is limited. A professional marriage counselor does not face this since he/she is committed only to counseling, not speaking, preaching, visiting, administration, etc. Being too busy to listen and give full attention can only bring premature conclusions and limited help. And if the counselee is perceptive and picks up the hurried attitude feelings of rejection, guilt and anger could occur on his part.

Unwillingness or ignorance about *making a referral* is a common error. There can be several reasons for referring a counselee. People with long-term maladjustments, psychotic conditions, severe sexual dysfunctions, or those who require medical or psychiatric assistance or intensive therapy need to be referred. A minister or a professional counselor should never attempt to counsel above his training and ability. There will be other professionals— psychologists, psychiatrists, marriage counselors—who have the expertise which we lack, and for the benefit of the couple we may need to call upon them.

Referring a seriously troubled individual or couple to a professional can also free us to be productive with others. Our time needs to be available to those we can help with our abilities and skills. Many ministers have found that spending eight to ten or twelve months with couples limits availability for crisis counseling or for those with short term difficulties. It may be helpful to set aside ten or fifteen hours per week for your counseling availability and/or let those who come know you will be willing to work with them for X number of sessions or for so many months. At the conclusion of that time you may need to make a referral so they can receive additional help.

Several questions that you can ask yourself may help you decide whether or not to make a referral.

1. Do I have the training and experience necessary to assist this couple?

2. Do I have the time that it may take to work with them?

3. Am I knowledgeable or can I quickly become knowledgeable about this problem?

4. Do I have any negative or even positive feelings which may interfere with their progress?

It is helpful to let counselees know immediately that if you feel that their difficulty could be helped by someone else with more training and ability, you would like to refer them. We need to assure them that we will do whatever we can to help them, and this could include putting them in touch with someone else who could assist them even more than we could.

How To Terminate Counseling

A common problem which is usually reflected in one of three ways involves *terminating counseling*. Counseling can be completed too soon so a relapse occurs, or it continues on too long or the minister is not aware of how to approach the subject.

At some point it may be helpful to raise the question of when the counseling experience will conclude. This, as with other procedures, can be handled gradually and without abruptness. One means is to ask the question, "When would you like counseling to be over and what needs to be accomplished before that occurs? I'd like the two of you to discuss this during the week and then let's talk about it next time." This allows them the opportunity to establish some goals, set priorities and assume responsibility for the continued progress and time involved.

In many cases both couple and counselor alike seem to sense that the time is at hand. Often a question can be raised. "It appears that many of the issues which brought you in have been resolved. What are your feelings at this time concerning future sessions together?" This is open-ended enough to allow the couple to share whatever they would like at this moment.

I prefer to terminate or graduate a couple from counseling in a gradual manner. If we have been meeting every week, then we will go to every other week and then every third week and then perhaps a phone contact. In concluding the sessions with a couple it is important to share with them that if they ever need to call or come in at any time in the future for a similar or totally different situation, they should never hesitate to do so. There is no need for them to feel embarrassed if they ever have to return. There will be no feeling of judgment or shock or disappointment with them on my part, because I am there to help them. In sharing this and anticipating some of the potential conflictual feelings about counseling in the future, anxiety on the part of the couple can be relieved.

Pitfalls

Another problem is that of *excessive silence.* Some pastors or counselors feel that they should remain silent most of the time and not probe or encourage the individual or couple to talk. Counselees who are passive could respond to this silence by feeling anxious. They may see the pastor's silence as a lack of interest or even rejection.

The amount of verbal activity needed by a minister will vary from session to session and couple to couple. This timing of various responses and silence is important. If silence or pauses are too long, this could be an indication of either resistance on the part of the counselee or ineffectiveness on the part of the one doing the counseling.

A counterpart to excessive silence is excessive talking or *dominating the session.* Offering too much advice and moving into action without hearing about the problem meets the minister's needs of control and authority. This problem is characterized by interrupting, changing the subject, lecturing, arguing, showing impatience. There are some dependent individuals who may feel this should be expected from a minister, but this is an erroneous view of what counseling entails. Most couples will reject this style of counseling.

Dominating a session can also be done through *excessive*

questioning. Excessive questioning or interrogating limits the response of the couple. This usually occurs because the minister is not asking open-ended questions but those which can be responded to with a yes or no, or some type of a brief response. Questioning guides the direction of the counseling, but it limits the couple. Questions and statements must be balanced throughout the session. (You will find many sessions, however, when either more comments or questions are used extensively.)

Frequently when interns are asked to listen to tapes of their counseling sessions, they discover that as much as 95% of their input is in the form of questions. By taping and listening to our sessions (with counselee's permission) we can discover the number of questions, learn about the style of questioning we use, and also hear our tone, inflections, pauses and how often we repeat the same word or say "UnHuh". It is often helpful to rewrite each question as a statement.

Another pitfall to avoid is *minimizing problems.* From the minister's perspective the difficulty may seem minor, but it needs to be seen through the eyes of the couple or individual. A small problem often reflects a major one. Discounting it affects the larger problem as well. One subtle way of minimizing concern is the belief that problems are identical from couple to couple. You will sometimes be tempted to think, "I've heard this problem before". You may have, but there will still be unique factors about it.

Similarly, *making abstract statements or generalizations* should be avoided. All communication on the part of the counselor should be concrete and specific. Allowing the couple to make generalizations or abstractions—or making them yourself only furthers confusion.

One common occurrence both ministers and full-time

counselors fall into is *playing God,* or dictating answers and solutions to the couple. Doing this creates a dependency pattern with the couple. Counselors may find their own ego needs are met and inflated when couples become dependent, but helping couples arrive at and discover their own solutions is healthier than telling them exactly what to do. Kenneth Morris described the negative consequences of allowing dependencies to develop:

The inexperienced counselor may enjoy a certain feeling of exhilaration in finding that someone begins to look to him for advice on serious personal and marital problems. It again feeds his latent desire to "play God." It stimulates his will to dominate, which is found in all persons. To be able to direct the lives and set the goals for others and to "solve" their problems gives one a great sense of importance. It inflates the ego and soon gives one a false sense of worth.

Furthermore, to take over the life of another in this manner can lead to very serious consequences. Suppose the mental or emotional state of the counselee deteriorates, resulting in psychiatric treatment and later restoration to normalcy. Then the person may find that the solution given by the minister-counselor to his or her problems were not what were really desirable or best. These are instances in which a lawsuit might well follow.[1]

Numerous questions will be put to the minister by dependent counselees. Throwing the question back to the person or couple can help in not allowing dependency to occur and to break it if it is already occurring. Dependent people also ask for extra counseling time and make numerous phone calls during the week. These should be firmly discouraged with dependent individuals. They may counter your attempts with flattery, which must be ignored.

Another danger to avoid involves *taking sides*. There are times when you will find yourself siding with the husband and occasions when you will side with the wife, but avoid a consistent coalition. Siding should be for a specific beneficial purpose and not because of one's own feeling or bias. That would be destructive. It is helpful at the start of the initial counseling session to explain your position. Explain that there will be ocasions when you will reinforce one or the other, and the couple may even feel that you are being unfair. Tell them that this is a normal response and that you will be attempting to assist them as much as possible. Share with them that your objectivity will enable you to point out or clarify someone's behavior and its effect upon the marriage.

Nonetheless, emotional involvement or *lack of objectivity* is a common difficulty. We are called upon to be emphatic and concerned with the people we counsel, but not to become immobilized by their burdens. We are to be conveyors of the love of God to people who are in need. Our compassion for their ills and hurts is needed, but if we allow our emotional involvement too much freedom, we lose our objectivity. Dr. Maurice Wagner stated:

All counselors are called upon to deal with people who have had extraordinarily dramatic or emotionally charged experiences. It is not easy for the counselor to leave this situation without becoming emotionally involved. The pastor is aware of the love of God and feels compassion for people in distress. The right kind of involvement and rumination is very beneficial.

Through it the counselor may be able to develop a better perspective in coping with the person's immediate needs. But excessive emotional involvement can cause a counselor to lose his objectivity. When this happens his involvement has ceased to be an asset and becomes a liability.

This loss of objectivity is very subtle. Every counselor must consider it an imminent danger. There is an exceedingly fine line between caring and being too emotionally involved to be helpful. On the other hand, there is a fine line between being indifferent and being objective. The effective counselor will be aware of these possibilities and guard himself accordingly. Most counselors become over-involved when a client's problem is strange or bizarre, or when the counselee's problem somewhere touches the counselor's own emotional needs.[2]

Failing to resolve one's own personal difficulties while attempting to counsel others can hurt everyone involved. If a minister or counselor has continuing communication, sexual, financial, or parenting difficulties in his own life, then perhaps when the couple raises some of the same issues he could become judgmental or highly defensive. He may abruptly cut off a person's sharing because of his own anxiety. Ministers have a tendency to resist dealing with their own difficulties by resisting counseling when needed. And yet how can one be helping others when his own problems have been ignored?

A minister may have a deep emotional need to be loved and admired and not be fully aware of its intensity. If the counselee begins to show him love and admiration this could fulfill his deep need. This then leads to pleasure and fulfillment and could lead to unhealthy emotional involvement. If a counselee manifests intense hostility to the minister who needs love and admiration, hostility could be aroused in return. Sidetaking with the less hostile partner could also occur.

Any counselor has an impact upon the life of the couple. It is therefore essential to evaluate one's own feelings about the couple and the process occurring between the counselor and couple. It may be helpful as you listen to a tape recording of your session to evaluate your responses with the following questions:

1. Was the question or statement made to satisfy the counselee's needs, or my own?

2. What was the purpose of the intervention? Did I say it to help the counselee? What was I trying to get across to the couple? Was I personally reacting to something when I made that response?

3. What are my feelings about each person? Do I look forward to seeing them or wish they wouldn't come? Do I become defensive with them? When they are here do I feel resentful, bored, sleepy, excited? Do I think about either one between sessions? Do I fantasize about one of them between sessions?

4. Why do I have the feelings I do? Because of something in my past or something one or the other does?

5. Is there something about their life or marriage I wish I had in my own?

6. If I gave advice, what was the reason? Did they ask me for it, or did I feel compelled to give it?

7. At what point did I feel emotionally involved with them and why?

8. In this session did I talk more than thirty percent of the time, and if so, what was the reason?

9. Do I want the person to think I know all the answers about marriage?

10. Have I so identified with one partner that I reject the other without wanting to get any idea of how the other feels?

11. Why do I ask questions the way in which I do? Am I

curious about the counselee's intimate life or do I want to avoid silences . . . ?[3]

Another problem concerns a *judgmental attitude*. People who come for help need the freedom to be themselves and express themselves in any way necessary. We are not there to judge what they say or the words they select for expression. Dr. Wagner described the problem in this way:

Perhaps it would be helpful to define more specifically what is meant by being judgmental and explain why being judgmental depreciates the effectiveness of counseling. There is a difference between making an objective evaluation and being judgmental. Being judgmental subtly attacks a person's sense of worth. It deals with what a person is, not what a person does. In contrast to this, objective evaluation concerns itself with what has been done and why it was done. A judgmental attitude says the person himself is good or bad instead of evaluating the impact of the deeds.

This is why the judgmental attitude is so devastating to counseling success. When a person is judged he begins to defend himself against his counselor's attitude. He either tries to please him as though he were a parent, or he starts to hide his deepest problems. When a counselee does not feel defensive, he can identify with an island of security from which he can attack his own problem more objectively. When he feels criticized, he tends to be more concerned with persuading his counselor that he has overcome his problem than he is with actually working on his problem. On the other hand, he may give up trying, and take the attitude, "It's no use, I can never do anything about my problem. Even my counselor condemns me."[4]

Being judgmental and freely dispersing decisions is easier than counseling. It is also a way to avoid the struggle of thinking and being insightful. It can serve as a cover up for one's own unresolved marital dysfunctions. There are some who come expecting a minister to be judgmental because of their perception of his position or how he presents himself. There will be numerous situations where our feelings would indicate a spirit of judgment on our part. What will expressing this accomplish for the couple and for us? Perhaps this raises the question of the role of a minister in counseling.

One pastoral counselor shared with us that to keep his attitude in perspective he keeps two objects upon an immaculately clean desk. One is a stone and the other is a large rusty nail. When questioned as to why these are there, his response is simple.

"In my counseling I hear a lot of problems and situations involving sin. I keep the stone there to remind me, Let him who is without sin cast the first stone. Concerning the large rusty nail, about eighty percent of the people who come in ask me what that is for. I tell them, I keep that on my desk to remind me of what a friend of mine did for me many years ago. That is how I introduce them to the person of Jesus Christ."

This approach is one which shows concern. A passage which I have found helpful is Philippians 2:3 (amplified), "Do nothing from factional motives—through contentiousness, strife, selfishness or for unworthy ends—or prompted by conceit and empty arrogance. Instead, in the true spirit of humility (lowliness of mind) let each regard the others as better than and superior to himself—thinking more highly of one another than you do of yourselves". Under this I have penciled in a reminder to myself: "This is the counselor's attitude toward the counselee."

Two other pitfalls to beware of involve *closeness* and

distance. Closeness is a problem unique to ministers. Because of a couple's involvement in the church, a minister may know them intimately. Some couples will not want to come for counseling because of the closeness. With most this will not even become an issue, especially if the minister is open, warm, trustworthy and appears to be understanding, but feelings about this can be explored so each party feels at ease. During this discussion it would be well to clarify with the couple that when you see them outside of the counseling setting in social settings or at church meetings, you will not mention what occurs within the counseling and you would appreciate their not mentioning it either. It is also important that the individual or couple not go to friends or relatives and share what occurs in counseling or ask for additional advice. Too often conflicting information could be shared or others will misunderstand what is occurring in the counseling setting.

A problem which is counter to this potential difficulty is that of *distancing.* Putting distance between ourselves and the couple protects us from emotional involvement in the life of the couple, but distance is a problem because openness, trust and genuine caring are blocked. Distance limits both the counseling and the building up of the body of Christ.

There are several methods of creating distance. One is *denying the expression of emotions.* Such denial is either caused by a counselor's belief that certain emotions (such as anger or depression) are wrong or by discomfort with the outward expression of anger or crying. Such problems may cause one to attempt to limit these expressions in the people he is counseling.

If a crying woman or man upsets the counselor, he may directly or indirectly attempt to control this. Couples need to share and express their feelings, especially within the safety of the counseling. Inexperienced counselors or those who struggle with knowing what to say during the sessions may tend to keep the topics in a safe area, shy away from emotions and conflicts, or channel the discussion to topics such as sports, news, or hobbies.

Sometimes counselees will try to keep the discussion on a theoretical intellectual plane to avoid emotional discussion. This is a defense to avoid their buried emotions and hurt. Reinforcing this through our own intellectualization will not assist a person or couple in changing.[5]

In addition to denying emotions, one might create distance by *avoiding necessary confrontations*. Although the ability to be skillful in confronting is a necessary counseling tool, a minister who has a strong need to be liked may be tempted to skirt confrontations.

Sometimes pitfalls are created by the counselee. One common difficulty is *over-talking* and controlling by one partner. One counselor describes his approach to handling this problem:

One spouse may talk so much and the other so little that this actually represents a communicational problem and also allows the silent one to hide behind the verbiage of the other. Again the therapist may try certain gentle, or even more forceful, manipulations: encouraging the more quiet one, urging them to take turns so that they have more equal time, blocking out the over-talkative one either verbally or nonverbally. Sometimes I suggest to one spouse, "Why don't you and I keep quiet and give John a chance to have something to bubble up from within him that he would like to talk about?" On the other hand, if the therapist knows or strongly suspects the underlying reasons for the defense shown in this over- or under-talkativeness, he may first try the interpretative route. This circumstance may present, on the surface, a communicational vicious circle: The more one spouse talks, the more silent the other becomes; the more silent he is, the more agitated and talkative the other grows. Thus, each pushes the other progressively deeper into silence communicational modes or into excessively talkative ones. This vicious circle must then be spelled out to the couple by the therapist in terms they can grasp.[6]

It is also important to avoid extensive discussions concerning the *past*. As couples bring up situation after situation, debate over the details, who said what and who was right, realize you are getting a biased and distorted picture. If this continues into an extensive quarrel, they may blame you. Past behaviors between the couple do effect the present relationship, but this kind of bickering is useless.

By the same token, *philosophical* and/or *theological* discussions have no place in the marital counseling process. Usually these are brought up as distractors or even resistances. This is the time to guide the couple back to the pertinent issues. If, however, Husband-Wife roles and Ephesians 5 is the issue, this should be discussed. Be cautious, for each will want you to side with his theological position. Even with a so-called "biblical discussion," one could be using this passage as a camouflage to bolster his feelings of insecurity and need for control and domination.

It is, therefore, important to learn to turn questions back to the person or couple, especially when the questions are likely to entrap you. A young wife in a session asks, "Pastor, my husband is just too friendly in his conversation with other women. It just doesn't seem normal for a man to notice all these other women and then talk with them so much. Don't you think that he needs to change his ways?"

The pastor replies, "I believe this is an issue between you and your husband. I'm not sure what is normal, and I'm not sure that's the real issue. I would, however, like you to discuss it with your husband at this time."

In most instances the counselor should *not* serve as an "interpreter" for the couple. As soon as possible the couple needs to talk with one another and answer their own questions and issues.

Otherwise it will be easy to fall into the role the counselee wants us to play. Some people idolize the minister and hang on every word. Others may be angry at him because of seeing him as a parent or authority figure. Some women may be sexually attracted and subtly or openly become seductive. Some would like to monopolize his time and assume a place of special position.

Another difficulty the couple can create is that of *resistance*. There will be occasions when one or both will begin to resist the counseling process. Resistance is manifested in many ways.

With individuals, silence is a common manifestation of resistance, although it can occur with couples as well. The counterpart to silence occurs when one or both engage in a great deal of superficial talk or intellectualization. Even if you try to direct the conversation toward more relevant topics or feeling conversation, they may ignore this and move into safer areas. Over-talking and using a multitude of words to control the session and keep the minister away is another resistance commonly faced.

If fear or anger are involved in the resistance, a pattern of coming late for the appointments may occur. Latecomers usually seem to have a good excuse, but this behavior is part of the resistance. Eventually the meaning and underlying message of their lateness (or even not showing up without canceling) will need to be explored.

There will be some individual or couples who fail to do their homework for one reason or another. Reasons vary from "No time" to "Forgetting" to "The other person wasn't around." A variation of this is to disobey or change the actual assignment, even though the instructions were explicit.

Why does resistance occur? Again, there are many reasons. One or both could be resisting the counselor or minister. This could mean they are having difficulty relating to the counselor personally, or they may have difficulty relating to an authority figure. The resistance could occur because one partner is resisting the other. Since one spouse wants to grow and change, this is a way to express anger toward the other.

In some cases toward the end of counseling you may find the couple resists the final outcome. This could be because of a fear of the process of change or a fear that on their own they might not be able to function. This can prolong the counseling process.

What can be done with resistances? There are several ways to respond. First, recognize the resistance or negative feelings the counselee is having and acknowledge them. This unfearful acknowledgement on the part of the minister as opposed to a defensive stance creates an atmosphere in which the couple or person can deal openly with what is occurring in their life. Encouraging the person to explore this by suggesting this resistance is normal and learning what it means can be beneficial. Showing concern that the person is choosing to call a halt to progress and at the same time expressing a belief in the person's ability to continue to progress may be all that is needed.

Another technique is to join the resistance. This technique means to ally yourself with the person and work with him until he begins to do what you have asked him to do.

Another way of dealing with a resistance is to bypass it. You can change the homework assignment and give alternate suggestions. Or you may ask the couple to describe the homework assignment they would be willing to do during the week. Ask, "What does not completing the homework during the past week mean to each of you and how do each of you feel about it?" In some cases a mild confrontation such as, "If you can't do the homework, I wonder if I can help you."

One of the best ways to help a couple avoid resistance is to face it in advance. It may be helpful to say something like the following: "Often in counseling, even though a couple wants to change and grow, one or even both may be resistant enough to sabotage the counseling or homework assignments. If this were to occur with you, what form of resistance would occur and what do you think would be the reason?" Anticipating difficulties may help to eliminate their future occurrence, or it may make dealing with them easier when they do occur.

Finally, an area of concern to every counselor is the issue of *confidentiality*. The maintenance of a confidential relationship is essential. This can be a touchy issue, for we are all tempted to share our experiences in teaching or from the pulpit. Using fresh illustrations from counseling violates the counseling confidentiality and creates mistrust between a minister and the congregation. Couples need the confidence that what they share will go no further, neither as an illustration in a message nor sharing with one's spouse.

With all of this in mind, how does one relate redemptively to hurting people? In his excellent article, "Jesus' Style of

Relating: The Search for a Biblical View of Counseling,"
David Carlson suggests a model of counseling based on
Jesus' pattern:

> Reviewing Jesus' dealings with people, there appears
> an interesting relationship between the role Jesus chose
> to play and his style of relating. For example, when Jesus
> took the role of "prophet," he preached, taught, con-
> fronted, and called for repentance. When he took the
> role of "priest," he listened, forgave, mediated, and called
> for confession. When he assumed the role of "king," he
> paraded, ruled, and called for the establishment of the
> kingdom. When he chose the role of "lamb," he sacri-
> ficed, accepted ridicule and rejection, and called sinners
> to be healed by his stripes and bruises. When he
> submitted to the role of "servant," he washed feet, served
> food, gave of himself, and called for humility. When he
> played the role of "shepherd," he fed his flock, nurtured,
> protected, and called the lost to be found.

Table 1
Jesus' Role Repertoire

Status	Role
Prophet	Preaching, teaching, confronting, calls for repentance.
Priest	Listening, forgiving, mediating, calls for confession.
King	Parades, rules, calls for establishment of kingdom.
Lamb	Sacrificing, accepts ridicule, rejection, calls for sinners to be healed.
Servant	Serves food, nurtures, washes feet, cares for, gives self, calls for humility.
Shepherd	Nurtures, protects, calls lost to be found.

If we attempt to model our counseling or relating after Jesus' example, then, like Jesus, we should play a variety of interventive roles as we relate redemptively to hurting people.

We can learn from Jesus' style of relating that one can "know" what the problems and solutions are and yet be willing to listen and understand. Because one has knowledge does not preclude a willingness to listen and understand. Nor does it suggest that a counselor must ignore his preconceived ideas of what the client needs. However, it does mean one can be confrontive without excessive explaining, and, he can be confrontive without unnecessarily challenging or raising the person's defenses.

Second, Jesus' style of relating suggests that a counselor can be authoriative without being authoritarian. A danger of prophetic counseling is not the style of counseling as much as the personality needs of the counselor. The prophetic approach lends itself to be used by persons who need their counseling to be evidence of their authority. On the other hand, counselors may be attracted to a priestly style out of needs to avoid using their authority therapeutically.

Jesus' style of relating indicates that one can be right without having to demand that the counselee accept and recognize the counselor's rightness. For example, most of the prophets were not heard, but that is not evidence that their message was incorrect. Often the issue for the counselor is not rightness as much as affirmation of one's worth and dignity. I might add this is often the issue for our clients also. Truth is truth regardless of another's acceptance of it. Most people can be led to the truth more easily than given the truth. While as counselors we may know the truth, our truth for another person cannot change this behavior until it becomes "his truth." That is, the client must hear the truth and understand it for himself before it will effectively change his behavior.

Fifth, Jesus' style of counseling raises the issue of the counselor timing his confrontations and interpretations. Jesus shared ideas, advice, and solutions without demanding his audience hear these before they were ready. The prophetic style counselor is often a person who expects he can change people by saying the right words regardless of their preparation and readiness. As one minister confessed, "When I entered the ministry, I held the rather firm conviction that the Bible possessed all the answers to every human need and problem. I was under the impression that all a counselor had to do was come up with the right Bible verse for the problem, and presto, the problem would be solved. I soon learned in the crucible of everyday ministry that problems are not solved that easily, nor feelings changed that simply." He goes on to claim, "This does not imply that I lost confidence in the authority of the Scriptures to deal with human needs. It does imply that I lost a great deal of confidence in the approach and method I was using. I saw that it was ineffective and too simplistic." (McDill, 1975)

Jesus teaches us also that sin and guilt are concerns equally important to all counseling roles. One can believe in sin and the importance of the consciousness of sin without necessarily playing the role of prophet. Many times clients are painfully aware of their sinfulness and wrongdoing. They are looking for one who can help them deal with their guilt and the negative consequences of their behavior. They come to the counselor craving for the intervention of someone whom they can trust to help them out of seemingly impossible feelings and circumstances. These clients come not because they need to be confronted with their sin but because they need to confront their sin through confession and repentance. This is the very fundamental difference between the prophetic counselor proclaiming truth previously unheard or rejected and the priestly counselor affirming truth the hurting person finds difficult to face. Yet, whenever confrontation is necessary, it is more than speaking the truth. To the Christian counselor confronting is speaking the truth in love (Ephesians 4:15). "Always with grace, seasoned with salt" (Colossians 4:6).

In addition, prophetic counseling will be convicting rather than condemning. The "paraclete," whether Jesus, the Holy Spirit, or a fellow Christian, plays the role of convictor. Therefore, the client will experience acceptance yet reproof and correction. Particularly for our Christian counselees we can proclaim, "There is therefore now no condemnation for those who are in Christ Jesus" (Romans 8:1). It is imperative to remember, however, that while the truth is freeing (John 8:32) at first it often creates considerable discomfort. Also, I have found that when the client experiences condemnation, its source is often self-inflicted, or the work of Satan, or the result of family and friends who are helping the Holy Spirit with his role. The Spirit convicts; people and Satan condemn (see John 16:8). When a person is hurting, whether feeling convicted or condemned, it is at these times the counselor must be able to be a priest more than a prophet.

And last, we learn from Jesus' style of relating that the role of counselor-priest is to mediate between the divine and the human. He is man's representative to God. In counseling this priestly mediatorial function takes on the added dimension of assisting the Christian client to be his own priest, to develop his own priesthood abilities. We do want the client to be decreasingly dependent on the therapist and increasingly dependent on God to work out his own salvation. Hulme argues that the counselor "never violates the priestly prerogatives" of his clients to be their own priest (Hulme, pp. 120-121). While the counselor may mediate for his client, this is not to be the end of the therapeutic exchange. The counseling relationship should be a means to an end, the means to help clients do their own mediating, to develop their own confessional-prayerful relationship with God. "As the priestly function of the counselee becomes blocked, the (counselor's) task is not to jump in and mediate for him, but to (help him) remove the block so that he may resume his own mediatorship" (Hulme, p. 130).[7]

This is our pattern, our model—Counseling is a calling, a ministry, a gift—It is a ministry that is demanding, taxing, sometimes discouraging, yet fulfilling. To be effective one must continue to expand both knowledge and skill—It is essential to remember that we have been called to be faithful—

There will be many couples who refuse to come for help, who give up too soon, who refuse to respond to our counsel or do not relate to us personally. Our task is to be faithful and work to the fullest of our developed ability— Each couple in counseling carries the responsibility for the decision for their growth, change and future choices no matter what to do. There will be numerous couples who in time will see their marriages restored, reconstructed and refined.

This is our goal.

NOTES

All materials quoted are used by permission.

1. J. Kenneth Morris, **Marriage Counseling a Manual for Ministers,** Prentice-Hall, Englewood Cliffs,, N.J., 1965, p. 210.

2. Dr. Maurice Wagner, **Hazards to Effective Counseling, The Journal of Psychology and Theology,** Vol. 1, No. 4, (October, 1973), p. 41.

3. Corydon D. Hammond, Dean H. Hapworth, Veon G. Smith, **Improving Therapeutic Communication,** Jossey-Bass, San Francisco, 1977, p. 239. Adapted.

4. Dr. Maurice Wagner, **Hazards to Effective Counseling, The Journal of Psychology and Theology,** Vol. 1, No. 3, (July, 1973), p. 39.

5. Hammond, Hapworth, Smith, pp. 66-78. Adapted.

6. R.V. Fitzgerald, M.D., **Conjoint Marital Therapy,** Jason Aronson Publishers, 1973, p. 37.

7. David E. Carlson, **Jesus' Style of Relating: The Search for a Biblical View of Counseling.** Presented at a conference on research and mental health and religious behavior, Atlanta, Georgia, January 24-26, 1976. Used by permission of the author.

APPENDIX

The Value of Homework

From **The Bible in Counseling**
by Waylon Ward
Moody Press, 1977
Chicago, pg. 19-20

1. Homework will help to *re-program* the counselee's mind (Rom. 12:1-2). The counselee must come to view life, himself, his problems, and his needs from God's perspective. There is no way this can be done other than by consistent, vital Bible study. This is one great value in using homework; the counselee studies the Bible regularly. He fills his mind with God's thoughts.
2. Homework enables the counselee to *gain new insights* into his life, his problems, and his relationships. The Holy Spirit will guide the counselee into new truth (John 16:13). This insight is basic to most emotional and spiritual healing (Psa. 139:23-24). The Holy Spirit uses the Word of God for this purpose (Isa. 55:11).
3. Homework *reinforces insights and knowledge* the client has gained in the actual counseling session. Through assigned material the counselor can reinforce the areas

on which the counselee needs to concentrate (Phil. 4:8).

4. Homework helps to *establish a God-dependency in the counselee* instead of a counselor-dependence. In certain situations, counselor-dependency is good and is a necessary step for the person. By learning to trust the counselor and to depend on him, the person learns to trust God and depend on Him. It is similar to the parenting process. A counselee, however, can become too dependent on a counselor; but by doing homework, the counselee can learn that God offers help apart from the counselor. When the counselor continually focuses on God's provisions and sufficiency through homework assignments, he or she can keep unhealthy dependency from developing. A good counseling relationship can develop and be maintained while a healthy God-dependency develops.

5. The *comfort and support offered in the counseling session can be spread over the entire time period* between counseling sessions through the homework concept. Counselees often find that the counseling session offers hope, support, comfort, and encouragement, and they find themselves living from one session to the next. With homework assignments, this effect can be spread throughout the time between sessions.

6. Homework assignments make it possible for the counselor to *communicate more information in a shorter amount of time.* This often enables the counseling process to be compressed into a few weeks when otherwise it might take several months.[3] Many counselees need a considerable amount of input in terms of new knowledge. If this input comes only once a week, it means that a large number of sessions will be needed to complete the process. Through homework assign-

ments, this same knowledge can be communicated in less time.

7. Counseling homework helps to enable the client to *establish good habits and reprogram his use of time.* It takes three or four weeks of consistent activity for the homework to become a habit and be useful in re-habilitating a client. (See Adams, **The Christian Counselor's Manual** for more information on this).

8. The counselee's performance on the assignments can often be a *gauge of both his attitude and his progress.* A counselor skilled in the use of homework can tell, from the client's attitude toward assignments and comple-tion of the assignments, exactly how the counseling relationship is developing. Clues to counselee resis-tance, hostility, and repression can be discerned. The person's attitude toward the homework can also show how badly he wants help with his problem. The counselor must be careful not to assume that because the homework is not completed the person does not really want help. There can be other reasons why the homework is not completed, and the counselor must be open to investigate all possibilities.

9. Homework can be used for *evangelism.* With some counselees it has been helpful to use homework assignments to approach the Gospel. By using selected reading material, the counselor can approach the subject of salvation very easily. The material can be assigned in one session and discussed in the next session. In this manner, the counselor can discern the client's attitude and readiness for an evangelistic en-counter.

10. The assignments can be used to *teach the counselee how to study the Bible and have a daily devotional*

time. The study guides in this manual are particularly helpful to teach a person how to approach a passage of Scripture. Once a person knows what to look for and what questions to ask, he can be a more effective student of the Scriptures.

11. Homework can also be used to *establish good relationships and communication in interpersonal conflicts.* Homework has been very helpful to stimulate communication in marriage counseling. When a couple works on a study guide together, they often find real joy in such sharing.

12. Another valuable result of homework is that it gives the *counselee a sense of hope.* He is actively working on the problem all week long. He is doing something he believes will help with his problem. If for no other reason, the activity in and of itself is usually beneficial.

13. Certain types of homework can be used to *gain new information about the counseling problem* as well as to accomplish the other purposes listed above. Many study guides in this manual will help a counselor see some of the conflict in a person's life or marriage relationship. This new information can open doors for healing that would take many sessions to open in other ways.

There are other values to the homework concept, but these seem to be the most prominent and relevant. A counselor skilled in the use and evaluation of homework assignments can often improve his effectiveness. I believe it is a tool that should be used regularly.

TESTS AND INVENTORIES
TO USE IN MARRIAGE COUNSELING

THE COUPLE COMMUNICATION INVENTORY

CCI
Interperson Press
1103 Shore Drive
Twin Lakes, Wisconsin 53181

The Couple Communication Inventory is a diagnostic measuring instrument for use in early-stage counseling of couples with communication problems.

Now in its third revision, the Inventory's reliability and validity have been established in a four-year research program.

Everyone recognizes the importance of good communication in the marriage relationship, but the term "communication" has been used to denote a wide variety of husband-wife interactions. Through a careful research study, the Couple Communication Inventory is able to focus on four specific communication components: communicative sensitivity, communicative openness, negotiation of agreements after conflicts, and communication of appreciation. These four components are shown by the data which follows to be clearly related to degree of marital satisfaction.

By completing the inventory, husbands and wives receive scores assessing each partner's perceived effectiveness — as well as estimates by each spouse of the *mate's* effectiveness — in communicating sensitively, openly and appreciatively. In addition, each partner receives a score indicating how effectively they as a couple can negotiate agreements after conflicts.

Thus, the Inventory gives a couple estimates of their areas of strength and weakness in communicating with each other, as well as some comparisons with other couples. This information should prove useful to them and to the counselor as they begin or continue explorations leading hopefully to improvement and enrichment of their relationship.

A total of 815 persons, 377 couples and 61 divorced spouses, participated in the development of the Couple Communication Inventory (CCI).

Description of the CCI

The Couple Communication Inventory provides scores for these four basic communication components:

1. **Communicative Sensitivity** is defined as listening empathetically, being "tuned in" to the spouse's worries and concerns, and understanding the mate. Cues about feelings come from the mate's communication, verbal and nonverbal. Communicative sensitivity requires active listening-with-concern, imagining what it is like being in the other's place, having his or her feelings and outlook. It means hearing fully and accurately what the other is saying, receiving the messages of the spouse with deep interest and involvement. Communicative sensitivity requires swift recognition of nonverbal cues that the partner is angry, hurt, sad, distressed, tired, discouraged, lonely, impatient, joyful, playful or whatever.

In addition to a communicative sensitivity score for each partner, the CCI provides an estimate by each partner of the *mate's* communicative sensitivity.

2. **Communicative Openness** is defined as leveling with the spouse, willingness to disclose genuine feelings, and absence of avoidance, "chilly" silence and withdrawal. Communicative openness requires candor — telling it "like it is," although openness is not a license for cruelty or "dumping" criticism on the mate at every opportunity. Also, some times and situations are more appropriate than others for open talk and bad news. Communicative openness means being able to admit weaknesses and mistakes, taking risks of being honest, and sharing feelings with the spouse even when it hurts. It means openness to change when there are grounds for change.

In addition to a communicative openness score for each mate, the CCI provides an estimate by each person of the *spouse's* communicative openness.

3. **Negotiation of Agreements After Conflicts** is defined as the ability of the couple to agree on such matters as sex, family finances, in-laws, and effectiveness as a couple in negotiating agreements after clashes. Negotiation requires understanding of sources of conflict, sensitivity to the mate's feelings, leveling as to what each wants, and searching together for an outcome both can accept.

The Inventory provides a score that is an estimate by each partner of their success as a couple in negotiating.

4. **Communicating Appreciation** is defined as the voluntary expression (verbal and nonverbal) of praise, approval, and confirmation, along with avoidance of undeserved criticism. In communicating appreciation, each partner must *take the initiative* to say, "I appreciate you," "I approve of you," and "I love you." These expressions must be sincere as well as enthusiastic,

warm and freely given. If in private, partners never have a good word for each other — never compliment a good meal or express appreciation for bringing home a paycheck, for example — it is likely they also have difficulty resolving conflicts harmoniously, being sensitive, and communicating openly.

In addition to a score on communicating appreciation for each partner, the CCI provides an estimate by each mate of the *spouse's* communication of appreciation.

THE MARITAL COMMUNICATIONS INVENTORY

by Milliard J. Bienvenu, Sr.—Family Life Publications, Inc., P.O. Box 427, Saluda, NC 28773.

This inventory offers the counselor a quick, easily interpreted assessment of communication in a troubled marriage, and numerous opportunities for counseling targeted at identified communications problems.

By completing the MCI, couples can become sensitized to both positive and negative communication patterns. The counselor can capitalize on this increased awareness to provide opportunities for growth and change.

Husband and wife respond to 46 questions by indicating frequency of communication in the vital areas of marriage: Feelings, emotions, economics, communication patterns and behaviors. There are separate forms for male and female. Forms are scored from a key and the totals indicate level of communication in marriage. The 1979 Revision includes an optional socio-economic survey. This form is used not only in marriage counseling but for Marriage Enrichment Seminars and couples' Sunday School classes.

THE MARRIAGE EXPECTATION INVENTORIES FORM II (For Married Couples) by P.J. McDonald (Family Life Publications).

Form II provides the opportunity for a thorough investigation of expectations in nine vital areas of marriage: Love in Marriage, Communication in Marriage, Freedom in Marriage, Sex in Marriage, Money, Selfishness, Religious Expectations, Relatives, and Expectations, related to children.

The MEI's are 8 page questionnaires containing 58 questions in the vital areas listed above. Respondents provide written answers to these thought-provoking questions on separate forms and can either share their answers privately in group programs, later participating in group discussion; or, in counseling, return with their completed forms for help in clarifying issues and changing behaviors.

THE MARRIAGE INVENTORY by David Know

The Marriage Inventory is a systematic investigation of problem areas of marriage through the identification of behaviors. It is easily and quickly administered, and designed as a take-home exercise. Its analysis provides a comprehensive picture of both the individual and the marriage. (Family Life Publications).

A MARRIAGE ANALYSIS by Daniel C. Blazier and Edgar T. Goosman

A Marriage Analysis (BGMA) is a sophisticated instrument for plotting the course of, and increasing the effectiveness of, marriage counseling. The questionnaire consists of 113 multiple choice questions which investigate eight vital areas of marriage: role concepts, self-image, feelings toward spouse, emotional openness, knowledge of spouse, emotional openness, knowledge of spouse, sexual adjustment and security, common traits, and meanings of marriage. (Family Life Publications).

The Marital Pre-Counseling Inventory

The Marital Pre-Counseling Inventory was developed by Richard and Frieda Stuart, and is available for $.50 from Research Press, 2612 N. Mattis Avenue, Champaign, IL 61820. This inventory is given to a couple who is requesting marriage counseling. They complete and return the form prior to their first visit with the counselor or the pastor. Because it is eleven pages long, it will take a person between one and two hours to complete the inventory. The form covers the following: A complete time analysis of a person's day and week; behaviors your spouse does which please you and those you would like them to do more often; family decls; personal strengths; interest; responsibilities and decision-making; communications; decisions concerning children; the sexual relationship and the commitment the person has toward the marriage. By having counselees complete the form prior to the counseling session, several hours of valuable counseling time are eliminated as the counselor is immediately aware of problem areas in the relationship. This is one of the most helpful inventories available.

The Mirages of Marriage

Another counseling evaluation tool that is useful, is a series of questions found in a chapter "How to Check Up on Your Own Marriage" from the book, **The Mirages of Marriage,** by William Lederer and Don Jackson, Norton Publishers. The chapter contains 45 questions with complete instructions for the use of these questions by a married couple. To give you an idea of the type of questions, a few are represented here: "List five instances of your own loving behavior toward your spouse during the last month.

Would your marriage be better if your spouse had some particular skills which you believe he does not now possess? Why does your spouse not have these skills? Can you help him acquire them?" There are many helpful questions for a couple to answer by themselves, for a counselor or pastor to use in counseling and for a teacher or group leader to use with seminars or classes dealing with the martial relationship.

TAYLOR-JOHNSON TEMPERMENT ANALYSIS

The Taylor-Johnson Temperment Analysis (T-JTA) is a 180-question instrument designed to measure nine personality characteristics. It requires approximately thirty to forty-five minutes to complete, and approximately fifteen minutes to score and profile the four answer sheets obtained.

In the January, 1973, issue of the **Family Coordinator**, Dr. Clinton Phillips published an article, "Some Useful Tests for Marriage Counselors." The Taylor-Johnson test was mentioned as one of the five tests. The American Institute of Family Relations in Hollywood has given this test to more than seventy thousand couples over the years, and thousands of other counselors and ministers have used it extensively. It is used for individual, premarital, marital, and family counseling, business and industry placement, placement of Sunday school teachers, evaluation of counselors for Christian camps, and assessment of college and seminary students. This test has been used as the basis for Bible studies in groups, as the traits lend themselves well to biblical teaching.

As stated in the test manual, the T-JTA "is designed

primarily to provide an evaluation in visual form showing a person's feelings about himself at the time when he answered the questions" (Taylor and Morrison 1966-1977). Although the T-JTA is not designed to measure mental abnormalities in psychiatric terms, it does provide measures of temperament and personality patterns with sufficient validity and reliability for emotionally normal couples. The T-JTA measures what is going on within a person and not their actual behavior. It also has the sensitivity to assist in identifying persons who might benefit from more individual or couple therapy.

The T-JTA has scales which are used to assess the personality or temperament of individuals: nervous vs. composed, depressive vs. lighthearted, active/social vs. quiet, expressive/responsive vs. inhibited, sympathetic vs. indifferent, subjective vs. objective, dominant vs. submissive, hostile vs. tolerant, and self-disciplined vs. impulsive. There is also an attitude scale which indicates to the counselor the attitude of the person taking the test and how he or she wishes to be seen. Thus, a high score on the attitude scale suggests that the person taking the test has described himself or herself as wanting to appear more admirable than he or she may actually be, while a low score suggests that the person has been overly critical of himself or herself. The low score reflects a low self-concept.

A unique feature of the T-JTA is the criss-cross testing. In the criss-cross testing, a spouse takes the test to describe him or herself and then, on a separate answer sheet, completes the test again to describe the partner. Very useful information and test profiles are generated when one person's scores are plotted along with the sources showing the partner's view.

The T-JTA manual is thorough and complete. The test is

available in two levels of difficulty, the regular edition, at the eighth-grade reading level, and the secondary edition, at a fifth-grade reading level. It is also available in a Braille edition for blind persons and is currently published in a number of foreign languages (Spanish, German, French) with appropriate norms from those countries where developed.

A strong feature of the T-JTA is the availability of well-validated criss-cross norms. These norms enable the counselor or minister to compare each couple's responses to a well-validated sample of persons representative of the general population. The criss-cross profiles yield interactional information, which allows a couple to look at similarities and differences in perception between themselves.

Since many emotional problems such as uncontrolled anger, depression, worry, lack of empathy, or a low self-image are at the heart of numerous marital problems, it is crucial to take an intensive look at this area for each person. Following are four profiles of a married couple, showing the scores for themselves and then the criss-cross. Look at the profiles, noting the nine traits and their definitions and the four shaded areas (from "excellent" to "improvement urgent"). Study the differences in the scores of this couple to see if you can determine areas in which they both have strengths and weaknesses as well as problem areas between them.

WIFE

TAYLOR-JOHNSON TEMPERAMENT ANALYSIS PROFILE
Profile Revision of 1967

These Answers Describe __BROWN, HELEN_____ Age __40__ Sex __F__ Date __8-1-66__

School __COMPLETED__ Grade __11__ Degree_____ Major_____ Occupation __HOUSEWIFE_____ Counselor __W.S.__

Single____ Years Married __20__ Years Divorced____ Years Widowed____ Children: M __1__ Ages __18__ F __1__ Ages __16__

Answers made by: SELF $\frac{\text{and}}{\text{or}}$ husband, wife, father, mother, son, daughter, brother, sister, or_____of the person described.

Norm(s): 67-68 GEN POP	A	B	C	D	E	F	G	H	I	Attitude (Sten) Score: 5
Mids		2		3	5	4		1	4	Total Mids: 19
Raw score	16	18	36	37	35	20	32	13	18	Raw score
Percentile	66	72	94	87	60	81	96	71	23	Percentile
TRAIT	Nervous	Depressive	Active-Social	Expressive-Responsive	Sympathetic	Subjective	Dominant	Hostile	Self-disciplined	TRAIT

| TRAIT OPPOSITE | Composed | Light-hearted | Quiet | Inhibited | Indifferent | Objective | Submissive | Tolerant | Impulsive | TRAIT OPPOSITE |

■ Excellent   ■ Acceptable   ▭ Improvement desirable   ▭ Improvement urgent

DEFINITIONS

TRAITS
Nervous — Tense, high-strung, apprehensive.
Depressive — Pessimistic, discouraged, dejected.
Active-Social — Energetic, enthusiastic, socially involved.
Expressive-Responsive — Spontaneous, affectionate, demonstrative.
Sympathetic — Kind, understanding, compassionate.
Subjective — Emotional, illogical, self-absorbed.
Dominant — Confident, assertive, competitive.
Hostile — Critical, argumentative, punitive.
Self-disciplined — Controlled, methodical, persevering.

OPPOSITES
Composed — Calm, relaxed, tranquil.
Light-hearted — Happy, cheerful, optimistic.
Quiet — Socially inactive, lethargic, withdrawn.
Inhibited — Restrained, unresponsive, repressed.
Indifferent — Unsympathetic, insensitive, unfeeling.
Objective — Fair-minded, reasonable, logical.
Submissive — Passive, compliant, dependent.
Tolerant — Accepting, patient, humane.
Impulsive — Uncontrolled, disorganized, changeable.

Note: Important decisions should not be made on the basis of this profile without confirmation of these results by other means.

Taylor-Johnson Temperament Analysis (T-JTA), Robert M. Taylor and Lucile Phillips Morrison, by Psychological Publications, Inc., 5300 Hollywood Blvd., Los Angeles, CA 90027. 1966-1977.

Printed by Permission of Psychological Publications, Inc.

HUSBAND

HUSBAND

TAYLOR-JOHNSON TEMPERAMENT ANALYSIS PROFILE
Profile Revision of 1967

These Answers Describe **BROWN, RICHARD**   Age **46**   Sex **M**   Date **8-8-66**

School **U. OF CALIF.** Grade____ Degree **PhD.** Major **CHEM. ENG.** Occupation **CHEM. ENGINEER** Counselor **W.E.**

Single____ Years Married **20** Years Divorced____ Years Widowed____ . Children: M **1** Ages **18**   F **1** Ages **16**

Answers made by: SELF and/or husband, wife, father, mother, son, daughter, brother, sister, or_____of the person described.

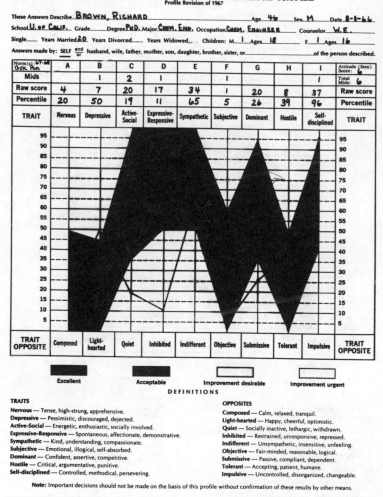

Norm(s):67-68 GEN. POP.	A	B	C	D	E	F	G	H	I	Attitude (Sten) Score:
Mids		1	2	1		1			1	Total Mids: 6
Raw score	4	7	20	17	34	1	20	8	37	Raw score
Percentile	20	50	19	11	65	5	26	39	96	Percentile
TRAIT	Nervous	Depressive	Active-Social	Expressive-Responsive	Sympathetic	Subjective	Dominant	Hostile	Self-disciplined	TRAIT
TRAIT OPPOSITE	Composed	Light-hearted	Quiet	Inhibited	Indifferent	Objective	Submissive	Tolerant	Impulsive	TRAIT OPPOSITE

Excellent   Acceptable   Improvement desirable   Improvement urgent

DEFINITIONS

TRAITS
Nervous — Tense, high-strung, apprehensive.
Depressive — Pessimistic, discouraged, dejected.
Active-Social — Energetic, enthusiastic, socially involved.
Expressive-Responsive — Spontaneous, affectionate, demonstrative.
Sympathetic — Kind, understanding, compassionate.
Subjective — Emotional, illogical, self-absorbed.
Dominant — Confident, assertive, competitive.
Hostile — Critical, argumentative, punitive.
Self-disciplined — Controlled, methodical, persevering.

OPPOSITES
Composed — Calm, relaxed, tranquil.
Light-hearted — Happy, cheerful, optimistic.
Quiet — Socially inactive, lethargic, withdrawn.
Inhibited — Restrained, unresponsive, repressed.
Indifferent — Unsympathetic, insensitive, unfeeling.
Objective — Fair-minded, reasonable, logical.
Submissive — Passive, compliant, dependent.
Tolerant — Accepting, patient, humane.
Impulsive — Uncontrolled, disorganized, changeable.

Note: Important decisions should not be made on the basis of this profile without confirmation of these results by other means.

Taylor-Johnson Temperament Analysis (T-JTA), Robert M. Taylor and Lucile Phillips Morrison, by Psychological Publications, Inc., 5300 Hollywood Blvd., Los Angeles, CA 90027. 1966-1977.

Printed by Permission of Psychological Publications, Inc.

WIFE BY HUSBAND

CRISS - CROSS

TAYLOR-JOHNSON TEMPERAMENT ANALYSIS PROFILE
Profile Revision of 1967

These Answers Describe **BROWN, HELEN** _____ Age **40** Sex **F** Date **8-1-66**

School **COMPLETED** Grade **11** Degree ____ Major ____ Occupation **HOUSEWIFE** ____ Counselor **W.E.**

Single ____ Years Married **20** Years Divorced ____ Years Widowed ____ Children: M **1** Ages **18** F **1** Ages **16**

Answers made by: SELF **(SELF)** or husband, wife, father, mother, son, daughter, brother, sister, or _____ of the person described.

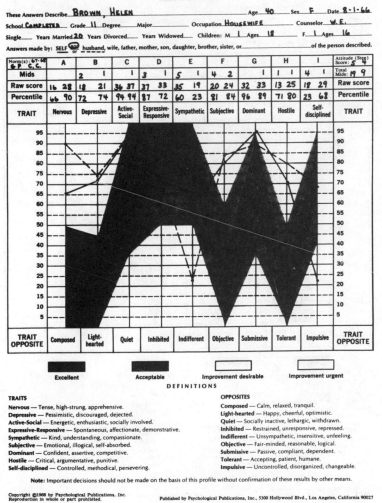

Norm(s): 67-68 G.P. C.C.	A	B	C	D	E	F	G	H	I	Attitude (Step) Score: **5 4**
Mids		2	1	1	3	1	5	1	4	2	1	1	1	4	1	Total Mids: **19 9**
Raw score	16 28	18 21	36 37	37 33	35 19	20 24	32 33	13 25	18 29	Raw score
Percentile	66 90	72 74	94 94	87 72	60 23	81 84	96 89	71 80	23 68	Percentile
TRAIT	Nervous	Depressive	Active-Social	Expressive-Responsive	Sympathetic	Subjective	Dominant	Hostile	Self-disciplined	TRAIT

| TRAIT OPPOSITE | Composed | Light-hearted | Quiet | Inhibited | Indifferent | Objective | Submissive | Tolerant | Impulsive | TRAIT OPPOSITE |

Excellent Acceptable Improvement desirable Improvement urgent

DEFINITIONS

TRAITS
Nervous — Tense, high-strung, apprehensive.
Depressive — Pessimistic, discouraged, dejected.
Active-Social — Energetic, enthusiastic, socially involved.
Expressive-Responsive — Spontaneous, affectionate, demonstrative.
Sympathetic — Kind, understanding, compassionate.
Subjective — Emotional, illogical, self-absorbed.
Dominant — Confident, assertive, competitive.
Hostile — Critical, argumentative, punitive.
Self-disciplined — Controlled, methodical, persevering.

OPPOSITES
Composed — Calm, relaxed, tranquil.
Light-hearted — Happy, cheerful, optimistic.
Quiet — Socially inactive, lethargic, withdrawn.
Inhibited — Restrained, unresponsive, repressed.
Indifferent — Unsympathetic, insensitive, unfeeling.
Objective — Fair-minded, reasonable, logical.
Submissive — Passive, compliant, dependent.
Tolerant — Accepting, patient, humane.
Impulsive — Uncontrolled, disorganized, changeable.

Note: Important decisions should not be made on the basis of this profile without confirmation of these results by other means.

Taylor-Johnson Temperament Analysis (T-JTA), Robert M. Taylor and Lucile Phillips Morrison, by Psychological Publications, Inc., 5300 Hollywood Blvd., Los Angeles, CA 90027. 1966-1977.

Printed by Permission of Psychological Publications, Inc.

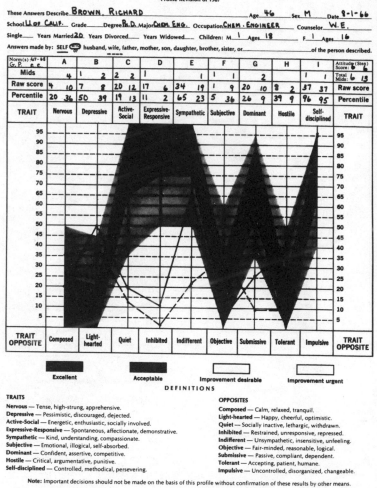

HUSBAND BY WIFE
CRISS-CROSS

TAYLOR-JOHNSON TEMPERAMENT ANALYSIS PROFILE
Profile Revision of 1967

These Answers Describe **BROWN, RICHARD** _____ Age **46** Sex **M** Date **8-1-66**

School **U. OF CALIF.** Grade_____ Degree **Ph.D.** Major **CHEM. ENG.** Occupation **CHEM · ENGINEER** Counselor **W.E.**

Single____ Years Married **20** Years Divorced____ Years Widowed____ Children: M **1** Ages **18** F **1** Ages **16**

Answers made by: SELF ⓦ husband, wife, father, mother, son, daughter, brother, sister, or_____of the person described.

Norm(s) :47-68 G. P. e.e	A	B	C	D	E	F	G	H	I	Attitude (Step) Score: **6 6**
Mids	**4 1**	**2 2**	**2 1**		**1 1**	**1**	**2**		**1 1**	Total Mids: **6 13**
Raw score	**4 10**	**7 8**	**20 12**	**17 6**	**34 19**	**1 9**	**20 10**	**8 2**	**37 37**	Raw score
Percentile	**20 36**	**50 39**	**19 13**	**11 2**	**65 23**	**5 36**	**26 9**	**39 9**	**96 95**	Percentile
TRAIT	Nervous	Depressive	Active-Social	Expressive-Responsive	Sympathetic	Subjective	Dominant	Hostile	Self-disciplined	TRAIT

| 95 |
| 90 |
| 85 |
| 80 |
| 75 |
| 70 |
| 65 |
| 60 |
| 55 |
| 50 |
| 45 |
| 40 |
| 35 |
| 30 |
| 25 |
| 20 |
| 15 |
| 10 |
| 5 |

| TRAIT OPPOSITE | Composed | Light-hearted | Quiet | Inhibited | Indifferent | Objective | Submissive | Tolerant | Impulsive | TRAIT OPPOSITE |

■ Excellent   ■ Acceptable   □ Improvement desirable   □ Improvement urgent

DEFINITIONS

TRAITS

Nervous — Tense, high-strung, apprehensive.
Depressive — Pessimistic, discouraged, dejected.
Active-Social — Energetic, enthusiastic, socially involved.
Expressive-Responsive — Spontaneous, affectionate, demonstrative.
Sympathetic — Kind, understanding, compassionate.
Subjective — Emotional, illogical, self-absorbed.
Dominant — Confident, assertive, competitive.
Hostile — Critical, argumentative, punitive.
Self-disciplined — Controlled, methodical, persevering.

OPPOSITES

Composed — Calm, relaxed, tranquil.
Light-hearted — Happy, cheerful, optimistic.
Quiet — Socially inactive, lethargic, withdrawn.
Inhibited — Restrained, unresponsive, repressed.
Indifferent — Unsympathetic, insensitive, unfeeling.
Objective — Fair-minded, reasonable, logical.
Submissive — Passive, compliant, dependent.
Tolerant — Accepting, patient, humane.
Impulsive — Uncontrolled, disorganized, changeable.

Note: Important decisions should not be made on the basis of this profile without confirmation of these results by other means.

Taylor-Johnson Temperament Analysis (T-JTA), Robert M. Taylor and Lucile Phillips Morrison, by Psychological Publications, Inc., 5300 Hollywood Blvd., Los Angeles, CA 90027. 1966-1977.

Printed by Permission of Psychological Publications, Inc.

Marriage Counseling Report

Institute for Personality and Ability Testing
1602 Coronado Drive
Champaign, Illinois 61820

The **Marriage Counseling Report**, MCR for short, is a computer-analyzed report of paired profiles on the **16 Personality Factor Questionnaire** (16 PF). The program examines individual and joint strengths and weaknesses in the two personalities. Trait patterns and differences that represent potential sources of conflict in the marital relationship are identified to provide leads for in-depth counseling follow-up. Psychologists, counselors, ministers, and other professionals involved in marriage counseling who are otherwise qualified to use 16 PF test materials may use the service. Individuals whose personality testing skills or experience do not currently qualify them to use 16 PF materials may develop the necessary skills by participating in appropriate testing workshops which are periodically held by IPA. Reports are not available to individuals for self-counseling purposes.

A PROGRAM OF READING AND TRAINING TO DEVELOP ADDITIONAL SKILLS IN MARITAL COUNSELING

The following resources have been listed for the minister or counselor who would like to further both their knowledge and ability in marital counseling. The books mentioned will vary in practicality and theory. Having searched through every possible book in order to gain more information in this field those listed are the most practical and helpful. They have been listed in order of importance.

1. **Therapy for Couples,** Billie Ables, Jossey-Bass.
2. **Helping Couples Change,** Richard Stuart, Guilford Press.
3. **Handbook of Marital Therapy,** a positive approach to helping troubled relationships, Robert P. Liberman; Eugene G. Wheeler; Louis A.J.M. de Visser; Julie Kuehnel; Timothy Juehnel, Plenum Press.
4. **Conjoint Family Therapy,** Virginia Satir, Science and Behavior Books.
5. **Marital Therapy: Strategies based on Social Learning and Behavior Exchange Principles,** Neal S. Jacobson and Gayla Margolin, Bruner-Mazel.
6. **Strategies of Psychotherapy,** Jay Haley, Grune & Stratton.
7. **When A Family Needs Therapy** by Gina Odgen and Anne Zevin, Beacon Press.
8. **The Dynamic Family,** Shirley G. Luthman, Science and Behavior Books.
9. **Family Counseling: A Systems Approach,** Laura Sue Dodson, Accelerated Development, Inc.

There are several publishers who continue to publish books in the field of marriage counseling and/or family therapy. The publishers listed seem to be developing the best resources available for this particular field. You may want to write them and ask them to put you on their mailing list for continuing information concerning new publications. Bruner-Mazel Inc., 64 University Plaza, New York, N.Y. 10003; Guilford Press, 200 Park Avenue South, New York, N.Y. 10003; Jossey-Bass Inc., 433 California Street, San Francisco, CA 94104.

TAPE RESOURCES FOR IMPROVING COUNSELING SKILLS

1. **Overcoming Sexual Inadequacy** by Stephen Neiger, Human Development Institute, 166 E. Superior St., Chicago, Illinois 60611.

2. **Sex Problems and Sex Techniques in Marriage** by Dr. Ed Wheat.

Guilford Press produces a number of secular tapes in the counseling field, which have been very helpful.

SPECIFIC RESOURCES TO USE FOR DEPRESSION

TAPE RESOURCES FOR IMPROVING COUNSELING SKILLS

These resources can be used by a minister or counselor in helping a depressed person.

1. **Cognitive Therapy and The Emotional Disorders,** Aaron Beck, Science and Behavior Books.

2. **Cognitive Therapy of Depression,** Aaron Beck, John Rush, Brian Shaw, Gary Emery. Guilford Press.

3. **Finding Hope Again: A Pastors Guide to Counseling Depressed Persons,** Roy Fairchild. Harper and Row.

4. **Control Your Depression,** Peter Lewinshon, Ricardo Munoz, Mary Ann Youngren, Antonette Zeiss. Spectrum Books.

5. **The Secret Strength of Depression,** Frederick Flach. J.B. Lippincott.

HOMEWORK RESOURCES TO USE FOR
THE MARITAL RELATIONSHIP

TAPE SERIES:
1. **Love-Life** by Dr. Ed Wheat.
2. **Overcoming Sexual Inadequacies** by Dr. Stephen Neiger, Human Development Institute.
3. **Communication — Pillar of Marriage** by H. Norman Wright, Vision House.
4. **Sex Problems and Sex Techniques in Marriage** by Dr. Ed and Gaye Wheat, Christian Marriage Enrichment.
5. **What Wives Wish Their Husbands Knew About Women** by Dr. James Dobson, Vision-House.

BOOKS:
1. **Caring Enough to Confront** by David Augsburger, Regal Books.
2. **Celebration in the Bedroom** by Charles and Martha Shedd, Word Publishers.
3. **Communication: Key to Your Marriage** by H. Norman Wright, Regal Books.
4. **40 Ways to Say I Love You** by James Bjorge, Augsburg.
5. **Intended for Pleasure** by Dr. Ed and Gaye Wheat, Revell Publishers.
6. **Making Decisions — A Guide for Couples** by David Leaman, Christian Herald Press.
7. **Men in Mid-Life Crisis** by Jim Conway, David C. Cook Publishers.
8. **Your Husband's Mid-Life Crisis** by Sally Conway, David C. Cook Publishers.
9. **No Fault Marriage** by Marcia Laswell and Norman Lobenz, Ballentine Books.
10. **Pillars of Marriage** by H. Norman Wright, Regal Books.

11. **Straight Talk to Men and Their Wives** by James Dobson, Word Publishers.

12. **The Mirages of Marriage,** William Lederer and Don Jackson, W. W. Norton and Company.

13. **The Measure of a Marriage** and **The Measure of a Marriage Workbook,** Gene Getz, Regal Publishers.

14. **What Wives Wish Their Husbands Knew About Women** by Dr. James Dobson, Vision House.

INDEX